Another Part of the Twenties

Another Part of the Twenties

Paul A. Carter

Columbia University Press
New York

Paul A. Carter is Professor of History,
University of Arizona, Tucson

Library of Congress Cataloging in Publication Data

Carter, Paul Allen, 1926–
   Another part of the twenties.

   Bibliography: p.
   Includes index.
    1. United States—Civilization—1918–1945.
I. Title.
E169.1.C284   973.91   76–27679
ISBN 0-231-04134-9 *(cloth)*
ISBN 0-231-04135-7 *(paperback)*
Fourth cloth and third paperback printing.

New York   Columbia University Press   Guildford, Surrey

In memory of my mother

Contents

Introduction

MY FATHER was attending an Eastern men's liberal arts college when *This Side of Paradise*, F. Scott Fitzgerald's archetypal novel by, for, and about the college student, was first published. Although an avid reader all his life, my father never read it. When he was in college he could not have afforded a raccoon coat, but years later in the bottom of the Depression he bought one in a second-hand store.

My mother went to a coeducational church-related college in the Midwest. Snapshots and a portrait of her from the twenties show a strikingly attractive, high-spirited woman, but she was hardly a "flapper" as that term is ordinarily employed. Her idea of fun was a church social, and for vacations she and my father inexpensively went camping.

In short, they were not the kind of young people the history of the twenties is supposedly all about. I have found that others, like myself born too recently to remember those years, have had the same historical problem as my own: the history of the twenties that we have read about in books cannot be squared with the experience of the twenties about which we have been told.

"Ask your own grandparents. What were they *really* doing then?" I have put such questions to college students with living relatives old enough to remember the twenties, and also to some of the survivors themselves. From the answers, I got the impression that my parents in their day were not alone in having missed a good deal of what we ordinarily characterize as "The Roaring

Twenties." Most of these answers had little to do with flaming youth or stock speculation or jazz, even though the respondents may have been aware that others of their generation during the twenties were behaving quite differently—and that by the thirties some of that behavior (the stock speculation probably more than the jazz) was affecting their own lives as well.

If it is ever proper to generalize from few examples, somewhere between the period's various polar opposites—bond salesman and Bohemian, prude and rebel, snob and sweated worker, all the liberated women and all the sad young men—there seems to have stretched a broad continuum of Americans whose stories have never properly been read into the record. Investigation has confirmed me in this impression. Here, then, in this book is a different perspective on the twenties. It is offered in addition to, not as a replacement of, the more familiar portrait so ably painted by the period's own great journalists and by subsequent memoir-writers and historians. Nor do I claim that my part, fitted together with theirs, adds up to anything like a whole. The whole, like any historical totality, is shrouded in mystery.

Henry F. May pointed out nearly two decades ago, in his perceptive and judicious essay "Shifting Perspectives on the 1920's" (*Mississippi Valley Historical Review*, 43 [December 1956]), that the twenties seem fated even more than most periods to be interpreted anew every few years. Each generation, or fraction thereof, seems to take from—or react against—whatever in that earlier timespan speaks most clearly to its own condition. Some Americans at some moments in the present century have found in the twenties high aspirations by which to measure their own; others have held up that postwar decade as a horrible example of what to avoid. One icon from the Jazz Age gains new adherents even as another loses devotees. Just now for example Ernest Hemingway, who was ruling the roost in American letters not so long ago, is a bit out of fashion, whereas Scott Fitzgerald for the time being enjoys a considerable boom.

"In the still rising prosperity of the Eisenhower period," wrote Professor May in 1956, "far more widespread and soundly based than that under Coolidge but inevitably reminiscent, a reassessment of the earlier period was natural enough." It is natural enough today also, but hardly from the standpoint of our own period's widespread and soundly based prosperity—not, at least, if the condition of the rest of the world be taken into consideration. What the seventies have sought from the twenties is not identical with what the fifties wanted, and the current vogue for Fitzgerald may have its ominous side. The tragic poignancy of "the beautiful and damned" has always lain in the fact that Scott and Zelda really knew, in the midst of all their fantastic partying, that they were doomed. Perhaps today we follow their story—several young people have recently told me this—out of a similar sense that the party's over, even though doom nowadays is conceived in planetary as well as in personal terms.

But what we in the late seventies *need* from the twenties, as distinguished from what we *seek*, may be something more bracing. Herbert Aptheker, in a chapter on "The Black College Student in the 1920s—Years of Preparation and Protest" (in his book *Afro-American History: the Modern Era* [New York: Citadel, 1971]), has shown that the twenties, despite all the wretched poverty and brutal exploitation under which black America lived, were a time of dramatic breakthrough; black Americans were entering colleges and universities in large numbers for the first time—an event of decisive importance for the future, however many obstacles remained, and remain, to be overcome. Another kind of breakthrough is recorded by Anne Morrow Lindbergh, in her diary excerpts *Hour of Gold, Hour of Lead* (New York: Harcourt, 1973): that in the late twenties she serviced, navigated, and co-piloted her husband's aircraft—strenuous, physical, mechanical, "masculine" activities—without causing any eyebrows to be raised. Apparently people were so busy watching the marvel of the airplane itself that they failed to notice that a woman was engaging in "unfeminine" behavior, in sharp contrast to the kind of chauvinism which more recently has prevented any ascent by an American woman astronaut. More subtly in the twenties people like my parents, who did not participate in the stirrings of civil rights but shared in spirit the new excitement about airplanes (though they never could have afforded to fly), expressed in their own way the period's sense of hope: once they got the household budget balanced things were going to be better. The problems were going to be solved.

Their problems weren't solved then, and neither were those of the national economy. But that is not the point. One of the most disquieting features of the mid-seventies, when politics floundered, the dollar drifted, and Africans starved, was a pervasive sense that nothing could be done about it; an "Oriental" fatalism such as the Orient itself has rejected. Times when Americans believed they could cope, even with dire calamities still before them—times like the forties, when they brought forth the nuclear energy that may yet meet a desperate world's needs; like the thirties, when they built the New Deal's schoolhouses and post offices and dams; and, yes, like the twenties, when they invented whole new technologies and wrote great books and flew across the Atlantic and stamped out diseases and planned and dreamed—may still have something urgent to say to us, and through us to the world.

Some readers are bothered by the constant interruption of footnotes. Others are irritated when those footnotes do not appear. I have compromised. This book is noteless, but the essay at the end should enable the persistent inquirer to check out any of my sources. In the course of that essay I have acknowledged a few small personal debts, and I here recognize a far greater one to my wife, Julie Carter, who gave several of these chapters a vigorous critical workout. Mention must also be made of Mrs. Wiladene Stickel, an excellent manuscript typist, through whose hands the entire manuscript passed with numerous stylistic improvements along the way, and of Mr. Leslie Bialler, whose careful copyediting for Columbia University Press has purged the book of various redundancies and barbarisms that somehow had survived all previous readings. Otherwise, however, I shall break with the time-honored custom usually observed at this point in a preface, of listing all who contributed to the study, thereby (despite *pro forma* disclaimers) implicating them in the result. In an inquiry of this kind all the people with whom one's experience has been shared become, to greater or lesser extent, contributors, and the debts literally become innumerable. By default, therefore, the judgment in this case must fall entirely upon the author's own head.

Tucson, Arizona   PAUL A. CARTER

Another Part of the Twenties

CHAPTER I

Just off Main Street:
Towns and Roads,
Three Novelists,
and George McGovern

NINETEEN TWENTY was a good year for government investigators. Some of them swooped down upon suspected "Reds," netting a grand haul of four thousand in a coordinated coast-to-coast raid one wild January night. Others tramped through the mountains sniffing out illicit stills or walked the city streets to knock on the doors of outlaw saloons. Presumably still others scrutinized the taxable incomes of the suddenly affluent, like young Francis Scott Key Fitzgerald, who had just cranked out an instant best-seller, *This Side of Paradise,* after an Alabama belle supposedly declined to marry him until he had proved his earning power. Even the hard-working inquirers who only compiled statistics had a banner year. Those employed by the Bureau of the Census for the decennial ritual of counting the American people discovered that in 1920, for the first time in the Republic's history, more than fifty percent of its population was urban.

Half-truths in history probably outnumber the outright whoppers. This particular statistic has been interpreted ever since as having marked a great watershed in American history—the moment when the long struggle between the country bumpkin and the city slicker entered its final phase. Thomas Jefferson's agrarian faith that those who labor in the earth are the chosen people of God had apparently lost out to Alexander Hamilton's vision of the rich, the well-born, and the able presiding over an industrial America. The "roar" of the Roaring Twenties seemed to be the roar of urban traffic and industry. According to a music critic writing in 1929, even the preindustrial human rhythms of jazz had become "caught up in the incessant movement of the machine, pounding not only in our ears but also continuously in our consciousnesses . . . with its unrelieved tension." Except for a few nostalgic rallyings—the Scopes Trial in Dayton, Tennessee, or the defeat of Al Smith—the rural America of the founding fathers is supposed to have lost its hold on the American imagination after 1920.

Long before 1920, however, one could have found the urban spirit at work in America, for example in the Philadelphia of Benjamin Franklin; and long after 1920 one could have found the spirit of ruralism, for example in the Nashville of Hank Williams. The half-truth in that 1920 statistic lay in the census-takers' definitions of "rural" and "urban" populations as those respectively inhabiting towns of fewer than 2,500 people and those inhabiting towns of more. By an act of mathematical magic resembling Whitehead's "fallacy of misplaced concreteness," a community of only 2,499 souls became a benighted village, while 2,501 residents constituted a cosmopolis. In fact, however, gazing away from Manhattan's Great White Way any night during the decade following 1920, one could have seen wide, dark stretches of the continent where the roar of the twenties was muted indeed; where life was lived by a rhythm in which there was not the faintest echo of jazz.

The novelist, poet, and editor August Derleth—born in 1909, ten years old in 1919, twenty years old as the Jazz Age ended—remembered "hearing the howl of wolves in childhood." His experience of the twenties had been of a world which marked the seasons not by greeting cards displayed in store windows but by the coming and going of plants and birds: a world of farming and gossip and fishing, of men conversing in harness shops, of dam building on rain-freshened brooks, of wild crabapples and wood-chucks and harvest moons—all within shopping distance of Ma-dison, Wisconsin. (Robert Frost, in the twenties and long af-terward, wrote of such a world, but he had entered it from the outside; Frost's readers were forever being surprised to learn that the "Yankee" poet with the northern New England accent had in fact been born in racy San Francisco.) Of course urbanism and its burdens are relative. Even in August Derleth's Sac Prairie, whose population hovered just at the Census Bureau's mystical 2,500, there were those who felt the need of "going into the country for the summer . . . to get away from Sac Prairie"!

Writers, and their most sympathetic protagonists, are com-monly supposed to have fled such places in the twenties as fast as wheels or feet would carry them. But when the denizens of Sac Prairie ventured far into urban America they seem only to have become desperately homesick. In a novella titled *Any Day Now*, published in 1938 but opening in the year 1916, Derleth took one of his characters to Chicago, where she lay awake at night listening to

> the thousand secret sounds of the city, the strange mysterious voices from the great, never-sleeping heart of this alien place, the sullen murmurs of a nocturnal life beyond her knowledge . . . nothing comforting and familiar, like the river's sound at sandbars, or cows lowing in night pastures, or cries of birds and furred crea-tures in the bottoms south of Sac Prairie.

Not that time stops, even in Sac Prairie: "The German popula-tion filtered slowly away, to German cities [Milwaukee, Chicago, St. Louis] from the German villages along the Wisconsin." In the midwinter of 1917 Renna, the heroine of *Any Day Now*, as she reads of professors and students at the University of Wisconsin burning in effigy their own great antiwar Senator Robert LaFol-lette, begins "to be conscious of change, of something different in the air, some psychic thing, intangible and foreign: the hushed madness of the world around her." Presently World War I calls away the sons of Sac Prairie and Chicago and Brooklyn and impersonally blows some of them apart in France. The lover Renna has rejected comes through the war unscathed only to kill himself back home in an automobile "joy ride." Yet all of this is told off-stage. The outer world is a *deus ex machina* and, although it causes people to age before their time and to be hurt and to die, such things had been happening to their forebears in that place for many generations.

II

If the figure of 2,500 divided the rural from the urban in the 1920s, multiplying it by ten should bring us unmistakably over to the city side. In fact it gives us the approximate population during the twenties of Waukegan, Illinois. According to Ray Bradbury, exactly 26,349 people resided there in the summer of 1928, a season he celebrates in his semi-fantastic, semi-autobiographical novel *Dandelion Wine*. (He had actually turned eight years old in Waukegan that summer, but exercising author's license he made his alter ego "Douglas Spaulding" a boy of twelve—the timeless, archetypal boy-age, the age of Booth Tarkington's Penrod.)

Bradbury's present-day readers, if they think of Waukegan at all, remember the racking racial tensions there in the 1960s, complicated by the repressive tactics of the city's avowedly racist mayor; if they are a little older they may remember that in the 1940s Waukegan was always good for a laugh as the home town of the radio comedian Jack Benny. In the 1920s no racial tensions were noticed and Benny was an unknown young man on the vaudeville circuit. But in the 1920s Waukegan had also long since been locked into the structure of Chicago's North Shore suburbia, attached to the lake metropolis by interurban trolley. It was not another Sac Prairie. And yet, that is the way Bradbury remembers it, as "this little town deep far away from everything, kept to itself by a river and a forest and a meadow and a lake." This streetcar subdivision forty miles north of Chicago becomes "Green Town, Illinois."

In the course of that remembered summer Grandfather makes several batches of dandelion wine, but there is never a mention of

Prohibition. Nearby Fort Sheridan, whence Grover Cleveland had summoned troops in 1894 to smash the Pullman strike, is absent, as is the Great Lakes Naval Training Center. So is the city's own harbor on Lake Michigan with its grimy coal docks; one would not know Waukegan was linked to the Chicago–Milwaukee industrial complex in any way. Instead, Bradbury's "Green Town" is an oasis of tree-shaded streets, Victorian frame houses, and ice-cream parlors, surrounded by a green ocean of presumably unpolluted prairie:

> The thin lapping of the great continental sea of grass and flower, starting out in lonely farm country, moved inward with the thrust of seasons. Each night the wilderness, the meadows, the far country flowed down-creek through ravine and welled up in town with a smell of grass and water. . . . It was this, then, the mystery of man seizing from the land and the land seizing back, year after year, that drew Douglas, knowing the towns never really won. . . . Any moment the town would capsize, go down and leave not a stir in the clover and weeds.

A book like *Dandelion Wine* might be read as a tribute to the powerful selectivity of memory and therefore as a caution against the historical or biographical usefulness of any fiction. But Ray Bradbury revisited Waukegan in 1968 and asserted in a letter to me that he "found it absolutely the same, green and deep and jungled by day, and terrifyingly dark at night." He hadn't made anything up; some of the vines he had swung on as a child were still there. It was, of course, an older Ray Bradbury who had written of his boyhood in this way, and between the boyhood and the writing a busy span of history had been compressed; among other things it included the atomic bomb. Since 1945, Bradbury's judgment that one's town might capsize at any moment—victim not so much of untamed nature as of untamed technology—has appeared to many as less a poetic conceit than a rational possibility. In a sense never dreamed of in 1928, it might well turn out to be true that "the towns never really won." But of this foreknowledge the author allowed not a hint overtly to enter the world of 1928 in Green Town, Illinois. And why should he? Bradbury's letter continues: "A boy of 12 lives in a very narrow, intense world. Of course he knows nothing of politics, Grover Cleveland, strikes, real estate deals, etc. He knows his school and the wilderness that awaits him."

Sometimes in *Dandelion Wine* a modern urban consciousness seems on the verge of breaking through. That green ravine, dangerously unlighted at night, is the scene of murder—a familiar-enough urban theme, except that its point is blunted by a suggestion that the killer has come in from the country, not up from Chicago. It is the discovery of his own *personal* mortality, its basic horror unmitigated by any thoughts of its social significance, that shadows Douglas Spaulding's otherwise serene vintage summer. More surprisingly—especially considering that when he did turn twelve years old, Bradbury emigrated to Arizona and two years thereafter to Los Angeles, a town that has erected roads and cars into its state religion—the automobile receives scant mention in *Dandelion Wine*. The only car to figure importantly in the story is a deliberately symbolic "period piece" even for the twenties: a green electric runabout driven by two old maids at a top speed of "fifteen slow and pleasurable miles an hour."

Yet Bradbury's fictional "Green Town" is contemporaneous with Robert and Helen Lynd's real-life "Middletown" (Muncie, Indiana) and is located in the same Midwestern flatland; and the painstaking sociologists who described Middletown in 1929 made it quite clear that the automobile was transforming the inhabitants' entire way of life. It was in the nineties, not the twenties, that Middletonians had sat on porch swings on summer evenings; in the Jazz Age they spent their evenings and their Sunday afternoons in their cars. "Be off with smiles down the nearest road," cried a *Saturday Evening Post* double-spread car ad, "free, loose, and happy—bound for green wonderlands." The Lynds sarcastically pointed out that "the nearest lakes or hills are one hundred miles from Middletown in either direction and . . . an afternoon's motoring brings only mile upon mile of level stretches like Middletown itself." Were Muncie and Waukegan so very different from each other in the twenties? Was "Green Town" immune from the relentless modern pressures so trenchantly described in the Lynds' chapters titled "The Long Arm of the Job" and "Why Do They Work So Hard?"

Ray Bradbury, interviewed on television the day after the first Apollo moon shot—an exploit he still admires—confessed that he had never learned to drive a car. Poverty in youth does not completely explain his confession. That a graduate of a Los Angeles high school could have escaped all his life from the relentlessly conformist automotive pressure of southern California is a tribute either to the staying power of American individualism or to the even stronger molding force of a town in the Midwest. In this instance, at least, a boy growing up in what we usually thought of as a rapidly motorizing America in the twenties remembered his early surroundings as a "Green Town": was he, perhaps, more typical than most urbanized grownups now realize? Indeed, the historian J. W. Smurr reminds us, in a letter to the *Columbia Forum*, a small-town ethos sometimes could and did arise even among those who had been born in very large cities:

> In Booth Tarkington's day (*Magnificent Ambersons*, 1918) a person hungering for vanishing social values . . . simply moved from one neighborhood or section or "addition" to another part of the same city, convincing himself each time that he was escaping from stifling "growth" and somehow recapturing his "hometown." Today's rapidly homogenizing metropolis is not so easy to see in that light. . . . But there was a time when every large American city was just a collection of hometowns. Was there anything more parochial than the urban-born Big City hicks of O. Henry's stories?

"All of us are improbable to one another because we are not present to one another," says an elderly character in *Dandelion Wine*, and generation gaps are nothing new in the American experience. Perhaps a growing boy, perceiving as a trackless desert or jungle—even in a city much larger than Waukegan—the vacant lot his father saw only as a piece of undeveloped property, lived in a mental world altogether foreign to the one adult journalists and historians have set down and dignified as "history." Those elders on their porch swings in the summer of 1928 may in fact have been talking of Al Smith and Al Capone, of war debts and "flaming youth," of Prohibition and the stock market and Henry

Ford. But in Bradbury's remembrance all such formal content of their conversation disappears, leaving only its sensory and ritual qualities. And perhaps such an account is not poetic embroidery so much as it is accurate reporting of how it all sounded to "Douglas Spaulding" at the age of eight, or twelve.

> Douglas sprawled back on the dry porch planks, completely contented and reassured by these voices, which would speak on through eternity, flow in a stream of murmurings over his body, over his closed eyelids, into his drowsy ears, for all time.

Through hindsight we—and he—know it was not to be for all time. The Depression would strike Waukegan as it struck the rest of America, and young Bradbury and his family would find themselves out on the open road in quest not of joy rides but of economic survival, as they rolled southwestward in a beat-up old car and "blew tires and flung fan belts like lost garters down Highway 66."

III

Main Street, the leading fiction bestseller of 1920, has seemed to many of its readers a savage indictment of small-town America. Sinclair Lewis's Gopher Prairie, Minnesota, must certainly be called a less benign microcosm than either August Derleth's Sac Prairie or Ray Bradbury's Green Town. Yet Sinclair Lewis told August Derleth, in November 1937, that if there had ever been a "revolt against the village" by America's regional writers, as the critic Carl Van Doren had asserted and as most literary scholarship since the twenties has agreed, Lewis himself had not been part of it: "The trouble with critics," he declared, "is that they like to create a horse and ride it to death."

"Then you didn't feel you were rebelling against the village?" Derleth asked.

"Nothing of it," said Lewis. "I dislike some things about village life. I disliked some things about city life, too. I got out of Sauk Center [the original of Gopher Prairie] because there weren't any opportunities for me there. Carl [Van Doren] said I couldn't stand the dull people. Well, . . . I loved those people—Carol Kennicott and Sam and Champ and Will Kennicott and Bea. I put into my books what I saw and what I felt. I didn't think it was rebellious then. I don't think it is now, either."

Seventeen years had elapsed since *Main Street* when he said this. The hard historical fact was that Lewis *had* had to leave Sauk Center, Minnesota; and he was to die in far-off Rome. In his interview with Derleth the author of *Main Street* may have been doing as countless others do as they grow older; he may have retroactively romanticized a reality it was too late to change. But it is also possible that in 1937 Lewis remembered his 1920 intentions accurately. Vernon Parrington considered Sinclair Lewis to be that most typical of Americans, the romantic disguised as realist. Certainly, in some of his earlier, pre-twenties writings, Lewis the romantic came unabashedly to the fore.

In 1918 Lewis wrote a serial for the *Saturday Evening Post;* published in hard covers the following year (one year before *Main Street*), it was titled *Free Air*. Its hero hails from the hamlet of Schoenstrom ("Neither the village itself nor the nearby *Strom*," Lewis wrote, "is really *schoen*"), but village life is not what this novel is about. At heart it is a celebration of the automobile, and most of the action takes place on a motor tour from the Twin Cities to the State of Washington. The "free air" of the title refers not only to the signs that used to appear over the air pumps of American gas stations but also to the psychic—and also, Lewis hints, the political or social— liberation to be experienced on the open road.

The story's plot has been dismissed as soap opera: will highborn Claire Boltwood of Brooklyn Heights spurn her fashionable, snobbish friends to marry Milt Daggett, the hard-working garage-owner–mechanic from Schoenstrom, Minnesota? The theme is as ancient as social rank itself. What is unique and touching here is Lewis's notion that the "free air" of the highway his characters travel is the transforming social instrument through which Claire's "adventure into democracy"—and at the same time Milt's growth out of provincialism—can be accomplished. Milt Daggett's road is like Huck Finn's river; its placid natural freedom is contrasted with the corruptions of civilization to be found on its banks. Back of Claire's pilgrimage is East Coast high society, and at its end is the even sillier social pretension of wealthy Seattle-ites who "believed that their West was desirable in proportion as it became like the East; and that they, though Westerners, were as superior to workmen with hard hands as was Brooklyn Heights itself." Rejecting the polar East and West, an eman-cipated Claire tells off her class-conscious relatives and she and Milt elope in his roadworthy but inexpensive car.

The plot aside, this theme of redemption-by-highway is not calculated to speak to the contemporary American's condition. Locked into the urban-suburban commuter stream he is not likely to think of his daily grind as liberation, and if he listens to the smog reports and has read Ralph Nader he is not likely to be enchanted at the thought of free air. If Lewis's heroine discovered "that these Minnesota country roads had no respect for her polite experience on Long Island parkways," the contemporary reader may well reflect that driving on Long Island parkways is now a good deal less polite than on country roads. But we are in 1916. Only a few years earlier Henry B. Joy, president of the Packard Motor Car Company, had asked the Packard distributor in Omaha for directions to the road west and been told "There isn't any."

"Then how do I go?" Joy reportedly asked.

"Follow me and I'll show you." They drove westward to a barbed-wire fence, at which the executive was told: "Just take down the fence and drive on and when you come to the next fence, take that down and go on again." According to Henry Joy, "A little farther and there were no fences, no fields, nothing but two ruts across the prairie." A short distance beyond, however, he found "plenty of ruts, deep, grass-grown ones, marked by rot-ted bits of broken wagons."

In the world of Lewis's early automobilists it was still possible on an American road to pass an occasional prairie schooner. As recently as 1880, five years before Sinclair Lewis was born, exclu-sive responsibility for provision of rural roads had rested with local governments, and the chief means of financing road con-struction had been the medieval *corvée*, which freedom-loving Americans preferred to call "working out the road tax."

In practice these daily stints seem usually to have been lei-surely and sociable affairs. Men gathered with their teams, scrapers, and plows, casually scratched at the road, sat on the fence (according to one observer) "smoking clay pipes and swap-ping stale stories"—and by the next rain, as often as not, their handiwork was again impassable. If an occasional, over-eager local supervisor secured a well-graded and drained stretch of highway, his achievement reached only as far as his political jurisdic-tion—some three or four miles. In 1912, according to one ac-count, America's highway system consisted of "two million miles of unrelated, unconnected roads, broken into thousands of star-like independent groups, each railroad station or market town the center of a star." Less poetically, a staid Brookings Institution study declared: "For more than half a century, the American rural community permitted itself to be mired in the mud."

IV

By the time Sinclair Lewis wrote *Free Air* this system—if that be the right word for it—was undergoing rapid and radical transformation. The Progressive Era saw the rise of a Good Roads Movement—an ill-assorted alliance of bicycle manufacturers, railroad interests, automobilists (the progenitors of the present AAA), professional highway engineers, and the National Grange—which effectively pressured and propagandized for high-way improvement. The presence of the Grange, that onetime rad-ical farmers' organization, in the Good Roads Movement is worth special notice. Rural leaders apparently did not believe that bet-ter highways would accelerate the drain of the farm population away to the cities and so threaten their way of life. "Year after year the human tide flows from the country to the city," de-claimed Senator John Bankhead of Alabama in a rolling burst of Southern oratory:

> Do not let us have great mobs of the unemployed, combining the scum of Europe with the misled boys from our American farms, so long as there are millions of acres of land waiting to be tilled and homes waiting to be built. Good roads will make farm life attrac-tive; they will bring the isolated dweller closer to his neighbor,

and I feel confident they will check the movement of our rural population to the great cities.

But the handwriting on the wall was plain. Nineteen sixteen, the year in which the action in *Free Air* is supposedly taking place, was also the year of passage of the Federal Aid Road Act, providing national funds for highway building in the states on a matching-grants basis—the first such legislation since the time of James Monroe. By 1917 all the states had full-fledged highway departments, and in 1921 an additional Federal Highway Act was passed. Although national management of highways was still extremely limited in scope, here was a powerful new force toward administrative centralization and control.

Matching grants, as we have learned from other examples since then, involve the imposition upon the states of federal standards. Also, compliance with the law required each state to centralize its own primary road system as well. Furthermore, the federal funds were distributed geographically by what Washington deemed to be national requirements, rather than being subsidized to the states proportionately to their area or population (or to their political clout). Coordination, quality control, standardization, and, one might add, mechanization (as that locally conscripted farmer with his horse and grader gave way to construction machinery)— these were terms germane indeed to the temper of modern bureaucratic and scientific industrial society, but they seem hardly in keeping with the spirit of Sinclair Lewis's (or, for that matter, Walt Whitman's) wide-open American road.

Significantly, the Lincoln Highway—an ambitious plan by which auto and tire manufacturers, cement producers, and other entrepreneurs adroitly fused their own interest with that of the public in an effort to create the first real high-grade transcontinental road—was never finished under that emotion-stirring and, at the time, quite natural name. Although hallowed by history—parts of it had been in use between Elizabeth, New Jersey, and Nieuw Amsterdam as early as 1664, and a patch near Bedford, Pennsylvania, had the baptismal origin of George Washington's surveys, not to mention the long, far-western stretches that had been the route of the Pony Express—the Lincoln Highway fell victim to the uniform numbering system which the Federal government began to use on its highways in 1923. Both the Boy Scouts, who had diligently placed and maintained the distinctive Lincoln Highway markers, and American romantics generally were depressed.

But romanticism springs eternally in American hearts. In the end the new, grand continent-wide numbering system, which in the twenties seemed so soulless and impersonal, was to be remembered with nostalgia as it was shouldered aside by yet another nomenclature when the Interstate system got under way.

As with all grand human schemes, the concrete—or blacktop—reality was something less than the prophetic vision. As late as 1930, when the Depression changed highway construction into a means for the maintenance of employment, "only 23 per cent of the total mileage of the country had received any type of surfacing, and only about 3 per cent had been developed to the physical standard of high-type surfacing generally associated with the 'modern highway.' " To the Brookings Institution survey this standard was met by "Portland cement concrete, bituminous concrete, brick, and block." Those who have driven over the bumpy remains of the brick or block streets still to be found in some parts of the Midwest—Ohio has some choice examples—might pardonably conclude that if this was what passed for "high-type surfacing" in the twenties it is a wonder any but the most hardy ventured to drive onto the other 97 per cent. And yet obviously they did.

What Senator Bankhead had expected to pour out along this growing national network were settlers, sharing the moral rejuvenation many Americans believed had invigorated the original pioneers; what came instead was tourism. "A stream of tourists bowls or bumps along all the open trails from Maine to California," wrote Anne O'Hare McCormick in the *New York Times* for August 13, 1922. "Camp fires and tent villages mark its daily course. It draws Main Street across a continent and changes a sparsely-settled countryside into a vast and populous suburbia"—not, perhaps, what the idealists of *Free Air* had in mind. After the Crash came a different wave, for whom camping out was not an adventurous lark but a tragic necessity; it culminated in the "Okies," push-ing their dilapidated cars from the dust bowl toward California's promised land. In fiction, Sinclair Lewis rounded out the twenties by creating the pathetic Sam Dodsworth, who retires from manu-facturing automobiles just in time to see his marriage destroyed.

But of these grim modern futures Claire Boltwood and Milt Daggett are oblivious. When they drive out on the road away from Gopher Prairie, although it gets them eventually to Seattle, in another sense it has not taken them very far: Lewis's native village goes with them. The rural milieu of *Main Street* extends out along that road and is heightened into transcendence by its pas-sage:

> Never a tawny-bleached ocean has the sweetness of the prairie slew. Rippling and blue, with long grass up to its edge, a spot of dancing light set in the miles of rustling wheat, it retains even in July, on an afternoon of glare and brazen locusts, the freshness of a spring morning. . . . For two days of sunshine and drying mud she fol-lowed a road flung straight across flat wheatlands, then curving among low hills. Often there were no fences; she was so intimately in among the grain that the fenders of the car brushed wheat stalks, and she became no stranger, but a part of all this vast-horizoned land. . . . Claire had discovered America, and she felt stronger, and all her days were colored with the sun.

V

"There never was anything to this revolt against the village busi-ness," snapped the aged Edgar Lee Masters when August Derleth put the question to him in 1940. "We didn't do any such thing. Maybe Lewis backed away from something that hurt him, but he wasn't rebelling against the American small town any more than I was, and my guess is he'd have stayed there if the people had ac-cepted him as he was." But of course they had not. Perhaps the ex-perience of such men was not so much a revolt *against* the village as a rejection *by* the village. Not only literary men underwent this experience; George McGovern in the summer of 1972 could testify to a similar home-town reaction. "When I came back to Mitchell after graduate school, I found that my progressive ideas had outpaced the conservative views of my town, of people who had always before dealt with me as a nonpolitical person. That has been a source of unease with me ever since. I feel part of the town doesn't like me anymore."

Sigmund Freud claimed that by the time a person is six years old his character is basically formed. If there be any truth in that claim, then McGovern—incredible as it might have seemed to some of the youths who followed him in the Age of Aquarius—was also a product of the twenties. In 1928, the year Ray Bradbury celebrated as the vintage season for dandelion wine in Waukegan, the six-year-old future senator moved with his parents from Avon, the almost invisible hamlet where he had been born, to Mitchell, South Dakota. Mitchell's population was upwards of eight thousand, well above the abstract line the Census Bureau defined as urban but not far from the five thousand Sinclair Lewis had allotted to Gopher Prairie. And yet, although he confessed in the year he won the Democratic presidential nomination that part of Mitchell didn't like him anymore, quite obviously McGovern's relationship to it was not exactly one of estrangement:

> I still love to go back to Mitchell and wander up and down those streets. It just kind of reassures me again that there is a place that I know thoroughly, where the roots are deep.
>
> There are the big old cottonwood trees, the big American elms, the little roadways in and out of town that have always been there— without much work ever done on them. . . . Everything had a place, a specific definition.
>
> I think that makes it easier to find one's place in the world. When people talk about the small-town sense of community, the role of the family, relationship with neighbors, fellowship of the church, school spirit—I had all those things, and they meant a great deal to me in providing guidelines, a foundation, a personal security.

History as it is made is always more untidy than what gets written down. Were a political analyst to search for the influences of the twenties upon the politics of the seventies, surely he would have looked almost anywhere except in South Dakota. Imagine what H. L. Mencken, with his contempt for the rural "booboisie," might have made of some of McGovern's more corny lines. Imag-

ine the panic of an embattled science professor, testifying in favor
of evolution at the Scopes trial, at the thought of a Fundamentalist
Methodist minister's son as a candidate for the Presidency—one
who, moreover, voiced his political opinions with a preacher's tone
of ethical certainty. Imagine, on the other hand, the views of the
stiff-backed Andrew Mellon, Harding's and Coolidge's millionaire
Secretary of the Treasury, at McGovern's plans for tax reform!

Yet George McGovern clearly did not think of his rural upbringing in the 1920s as something he had had to cast aside in order to
go into the "new politics" of the 1970s; he had never had to be
"radicalized." His mature political radicalism and his severely traditional upbringing seemed to him a coherent whole:

> I do consider myself a radical in the sense that I am willing to go
> beyond the conventional view. I think fundamental change is what's
> needed, so in that sense I don't mind people calling me a radical.
> I've often wondered whether those plains where I grew up don't in-
> vite you to the conclusion that you can move easily in any direction
> you want to go—a mood quieting and yet restive at the same time.

Towns small enough for personal identity to grow out of close
and continuous face-to-face relationships—but at the same time the
possibility, the challenge of testing that identity by going away; the
dialectic is as old as the Republic. Rural America was never quite
peasant America, and much of the urban liberal intellectual's alarm
about "inherent rural conservatism," both in the twenties and afterward, has been wide of the mark. Speaking of large national and
international goals a few days before the 1972 Democratic convention, McGovern concluded: "In a sense, I guess these are small-
town values—neighborliness, responsibility for others—extensions
of what I was always taught to believe."

There is rich historical irony in the fact that a man of such
background developed a charismatic appeal to just those elements
of the population for whom such supportive relationships had become least possible: the floating students, who formed intense but
transient four-year friendships during their college years, and afterward faced vocational choices ranging from the desperate to the
absurd; the migrant workers and ghetto dwellers, deprived by

their lethal environments of normal community or family ties; the liberal professionals, with their primary loyalties not to a place but to a guild, accustomed to forming and coolly breaking personal relationships with each move up the institutional ladder. Whatever moved the insurgent forces that suddenly coalesced behind Mc-Govern's leadership in a few scant months in 1972, surely it was not "identification"—at least, not as Main Street Americans had identified with Harry Truman or as college professors had identified with the elder Adlai Stevenson. The upstart young politicians who ousted the old professionals for one tumultuous season called what they were doing the "new" politics, but somehow in the process they found themselves in step with something very old. Indeed, the truly insurrectionary party in that 1972 election may have been the supposedly stodgy, tradition-ridden G.O.P., whose leader was caught in the act of revolutionizing the structure of the Presidency itself, rather than the colorful Democrats, whose leader preached a sermon in acceptance of his nomination that ended with an altar-call: come home, America, come home.

If, as Henry May has written, there was an "end of American innocence" even before the twenties, some Americans seem never to have gotten the message. But perhaps that perennial innocence is what has really kept the Republic going, even in the dark and blood-guilty years of the twentieth century.

CHAPTER II

"Ancestral Voices,
Prophesying War"

FROM THE AIR you could not smell the mustard gas that lingered in the cellars, but the trenches and entanglements lay like open scars across the land. On a flight from Brussels down to Paris Ray Stannard Baker, press director for the American negotiators at Versailles, saw gangs of German prisoners diligently filling in the shell holes; the craters that remained, "many of them full of water, seen from that height, glistened like eyes full of tears." Meanwhile across the Rhine the American army bands played in the village squares, and the American occupation troops danced with the German girls or sat down to heavy German meals in peasant farmhouses where pictures of the Kaiser and his family still looked down at them from the walls.

In Paris that winter coal was in short supply. But American news correspondents enjoyed the comfort of hot water at any time of the day or night, acutely aware that elsewhere in Europe from the Russian tundra to the back roads of Ireland men still shivered, killed, and starved. There at the Hôtel Vouillemont the reporters tried to interpret the Conference of Versailles as it argued its way toward what one of the newsman later called "the peace that passeth understanding"; and there, on the morning of January 6, 1919, they learned from the *Paris Herald* that back home in America Theodore Roosevelt was dead. Two days later, at 3:00

P.M. Paris time, all the American troops throughout France stood at parade rest for twenty-one minutes while the traditional gun salutes in final honor to a former Commander-in-Chief were fired.

Colonel George S. Patton, Jr., recovering from a wound sustained in the Meuse-Argonne offensive, described that memorial to T. R. in a letter home to his father. In the same letter, having heard that various cities in the United States were to receive as trophies the armored vehicles that had been shot up in the fighting, he suggested that the Chamber of Commerce in the Patton family's home town of Los Angeles ask for one: "I may be claimed as a citizen and I commanded the American Tanks in the first two actions in which they fought. . . . A bronze plate with some such screed on it should be attached to the Tank by my grateful fellow citizens." The younger Patton was not content to rest on such past accomplishments, however; he was busy writing a book of philosophic reflections on war and at the same time working on a tank manual. "I think that in six months we will have to go to Russia for a war," the young officer casually told his father, but even if that happened he expected first to be able to come home for awhile and see the family.

Although American and other Allied forces had intervened in Russia's revolution and were then on Russian soil, the war with Russia that Patton expected did not come. From Archangel, the only place where American and Soviet forces have ever clashed in open combat (if we except the basketball court), and from Vladivostok, where the Yanks had spent most of their time uneasily watching their allies the Japanese, the soldiers were withdrawn. From France also the A.E.F. began to sail for home. Patton, like thousands of others, came home to a hero's welcome, and he used the occasion for missionary work: "Returned Officer Tells of Exploits of Tanks," the *Richmond Times-Dispatch* headlined. "Col George Smith Patton on Foot Led Huge Juggernauts Through Argonne Forest. . . . Believes Steel Machines will Prove as Useful as Airplanes in Future Wars." It was fun, but the euphoria did not last. Within weeks Patton was writing to his old commander, General John J. Pershing: "I went to a War Play last night and the noise of the shells and the machine guns made me feel very homesick. War is the only place where a man really lives."

In more realistic moments George Patton knew that in all probability he would soon have to adjust to the ways of a shrunken peacetime army. The typescript he had worked on in France between November 1918 and March 1919, on the subject "War As She Is," had contained a vigorous argument for universal military training in peacetime, partly on the ground that it was a force for social leveling: "The boy who has served his time as a soldier . . . has seen rich and poor doing just what he is doing. He is considerate for the democracy of the squad room." Universal service was also a character-builder, the Tank Corps veteran believed; "at the end of his year of service the boy emerges a man, courteous, considerate, healthy, and moral," Patton wrote also in 1919.

But in the twenties this was to plead for a lost cause. The United States, which after the Civil War had reduced its formidable legions to a small Indian-fighting force, was about to repeat its historic tradition of rapid demobilization. By the outbreak of the Second World War, the Regular Army would have dwindled to an establishment smaller than Denmark's. Patton blamed the politicians: "The illusory security of our isolation and the short term of office of our law-makers make them unwilling to burden their constituents and prejudice their own chances of re-election by imposing present financial burdens to fend off future national catastrophes," he fumed in 1928. "Under their benevolent despotism our voteless army is bound to pine in a coma of incipient dissolution." Future wars, therefore, would begin as in the past with the hasty improvisation of untrained armies. "Since, then, our next war will be fought on the quantity rather than the quality basis," Patton sarcastically concluded, "it behooves us to determine the best methods of warring with the amateur masses our destiny has foredoomed us to control."

But what should a career officer do in the meantime? He could go back to school; in the American army after the Great War, as Barbara Tuchman has pointed out, "there was not much else to do." Such was the choice of Patton's fellow St.-Mihiel veteran, Captain Joseph Stilwell, who in 1919 enrolled at Berkeley to study Chinese—a choice that would one day make possible Stilwell's nominal command of Chiang Kai-Shek's ill-fated armies. The postwar career decision of George S. Patton was equally rich with historical irony. For a man who had led huge juggernauts (light two-man Renault tanks, actually) through the forest and who believed that the steel machines would prove useful as airplanes in future wars, Patton's choice might seem surprising: he went back to where he had served before the war, in the horse cavalry. The next war was not likely to be fought along the rail lines and paved roads of western Europe, Patton reasoned; it was far more likely to take place in back country on dirt roads, or on none. Tanks were, as yet, relatively delicate and fragile mechanisms; when most needed they sometimes embarrassingly ran out of gas. Horses, of course, could forage off the country and go anywhere.

Mexico, where George Patton had served with Pershing in pursuit of Pancho Villa in 1916, was a prime prospect for such a theater of conflict. Before the end of 1919 Patton proposed that letters be written to his old comrades urging reenlistment for a new Mexican War, and as late as the Munich crisis of 1938 he still was expecting hostilities with Mexico. (Here we must avoid the cheap wisdom of hindsight; given the acrimony of U.S.–Mexican relations during the twenties and thirties, Patton's was not an altogether unreasonable forecast.) And thus, in the post-Armistice years, the man who was to become the great tankmaster of World War II reverted to his peacetime rank as captain, played polo, rode in horse shows, and lectured with true Theodore Rooseveltian vigor to the officers under his command:

> The successful cavalryman must educate himself to say "CHARGE." I say educate himself, for the man is not born who can say it out of hand. . . .
>
> Civilization has affected us; we abhor personal encounter. Many a man will risk his life, with an easy mind, in a burning house who recoils from having his face punched. We have been taught to restrain our emotions, to look upon anger as low, until many of us have never experienced the God sent ecstasy of unbridled wrath. . . .

Therefore, you must school yourself to savagery. You must imagine how it will feel when your sword hilt crashes into the breast bone of your enemy. You must picture the wild exaltation of the mounted charge.

II

Not all who for four long and murderous years had seen the ecstasy of unbridled wrath, and its results, believed it had been sent from God. Shortly after Warren Harding took office in 1921, for example, the Army staged a military show to attract the new President's interest. But according to one contemporary's account, "after an afternoon spent in watching big guns theoretically eliminating tanks, tanks hypothetically cleaning out trenches, trenches spouting machine-gun fire from blank cartridges and airplanes bombing imaginary cities," the President "returned to the White House filled not with militant patriotism but with horror and pity." Small wonder, after an event as shockingly abnormal as the Great War, that when Warren Harding called the nation back to Normalcy there was a profound popular response. Thoughtful military men like George Patton raised the logically proper objection: war will not turn its face away from us merely because it is frightful. To publicize its own conception of America's future needs, the Army in 1919 ran an impressive motorized convoy over the still uncompleted Lincoln Highway, and between 1920 and 1924 the Air Corps hero General William Lendrum ("Billy") Mitchell demonstrated the vulnerability of American arms to air attack by sinking surplus battleships with aerial bombs.

Harding's cautious successor, Calvin Coolidge, in 1924 endorsed a national observance of Defense Day with one of that President's typical epigrams: "I wish war might be made impossible, but I would not leave my country unprotected meanwhile." Provided, of course, that the protection did not cost much money. The cost-conscious Yankee in the White House noted that the American defense establishment was "now, in proportion to our national power and interests, one of the smallest in the world," and he pledged himself to "the purpose of keeping down to its lowest possible point the professional military organization of the United States"—doctrine that has a quaint and far-off sound from our standpoint today as we contemplate the colossus of the Pentagon. In the year that followed this prudent Presidential statement Billy Mitchell, whose zeal for adequate defense had led him to accuse the military high command of "incompetency, criminal negligence, and almost treasonable administration of national defense," was court-martialed. President Coolidge confirmed the sentence, but relented enough that he gave the airman back half his pay.

"No doubt this country could, if it wished to spend more money, make a better military force," Coolidge told the American Legion at its national convention in Omaha on October 6, 1925, "but that is only part of the problem which confronts our Government." In this area, at least, the thrifty Vermonter was not merely trying to reduce government expenses; he was also challenging the Republic to make more constructive use of its income. "Our country has not wished to maintain huge military forces. It has been convinced that it could better serve itself and better serve humanity by using its resources for other purposes," Coolidge declared. "Our people have had all the war, all the taxation, and all the military service that they want." To the Legionnaires, publicly committed as they were to the support of military training in colleges and schools, the President's remarks must have sounded like downright heresy:

> The real question is whether spending more money to make a better military force would really make a better country. I would be the last to disparage the military art. It is an honorable and patriotic calling of the highest rank. But I can see no merit in any unnecessary expenditure of money to hire men to build fleets and carry muskets when international relations and agreements permit the turning of such resources into the making of good roads, the building of better homes, the promotion of education, and all the other arts of peace which minister to the advancement of human welfare.

Calvin Coolidge's optimistic belief that "international relations and agreements" would enable his generation of Americans to beat their swords into plowshares seemed fairly reasonable, given the atmosphere generated in 1922 by the Washington Conference on Naval Disarmament—a conference which, surprisingly for any such undertaking in any era, actually accomplished its goals. But Coolidge's optimism was not universally shared, and in many quarters the expectation of another European conflict remained strong. The opening pages of the *Saturday Evening Post* for January 17, 1925, for example, were given over to a short story by F. Britten Austin titled "When the War God Walks Again." Illustrated with a photograph (courtesy of the Ordnance Department) showing in profile one of the new intermediate-weight tanks climbing out of a trench, the story described a future war in which horse transport and horse-drawn artillery are things of the past, and the troops move in caterpillar-tread buses. "All your ideas are of the last war," one officer in the story chides his fellows. "They've stuck fast in your heads for these ten years since it ended"—a timetable which would have made the prophesied new war begin perhaps as early as 1928. The tale ends with all the defending infantry and artillery wiped out, so that the decision is entirely the result of tank-to-tank fighting. The infantry has become as extinct as the dinosaur, and "speaking as an ex-infantryman, sir," remarks the chief of staff of the victorious army, "I say, 'Thank God'!"

The warfare of the future might not be exclusively a battle of land ironclads, speculated former war correspondent Will Irwin. The tanks might be followed by infantrymen firing gas-grenades, and preceded by waves of bombers, whose attacks upon civilian populations would "make even the slaughter of Verdun seem by comparison like bow-and-arrow warfare." Irwin did not infer from his prophecy that Americans should forthwith provide themselves with such weapons. Instead, at white heat he wrote *The Next War: An Appeal to Common Sense*—"an attempt," as he later explained, "to portray the lethal nature of future wars and a plea to eliminate warfare from the scheme of civilized society." Where Calvin Coolidge appealed to his hearers' hopes for a better world, Will Irwin appealed to their dread of a worse one; for the alternative to abolishing war, Irwin felt sure, was nothing less than "the downfall of civilization."

George S. Patton told the officers under his command at Schofield Barracks in 1925 that a man must school himself in order to fight: "Like a cold bath the first plunge is the hardest. Later, if he live, custom, fatigue, fatalism and pride will make him master of his emotions, for devoid of fear no normal man can ever become." On the contrary, Will Irwin argued in *The Next War*, men must school themselves *not* to fight. They must "quarrel in their thoughts with the institution of war," because Patton's kind of virtues had been made obsolete by a rampaging technology.

III

Unlike some antiwar activists, who contemplated the horrors of war from afar, Will Irwin had fully earned his Cassandra credentials. In the general rush of American correspondents to Europe in 1914 he had asked for an assignment from George Horace Lorimer of the *Saturday Evening Post*. Lorimer turned him down on the ground that the war was, from a journalist's point of view, a passing fad. "I'm going to play this war hard for six months—in case it lasts as long as that—and then drop it," the *Post*'s editor told Irwin over the phone. But the reporter persisted. Other editors signed him on, and Irwin sailed. He arrived in Louvain just as the Germans were marching in—black-plumed Uhlan lancers on splendid bay horses George Patton would have admired, and then the endless ranks of infantry, singing.

Before the next four years were done the reporter had experienced a great deal more, from such homely details as "the smell of half a million unbathed men" that hung in the air for days in the Belgian towns through which the invading army had passed, to such remembered horrors as "the gray-green streak down Douaumont Ravine where lay tens of thousands of German dead, the rib-bones sticking everywhere out of Vimy Ridge, the wave of moaning from the three thousand wounded and dying in the Casino Hospital at Boulogne":

> Memory is a confusion of trains loading and unloading the wounded, shell-cases and gas-cases together, of new cots filling the halls and vestibules of the Casino, of nurses working until they staggered. . . . Remembered pictures: a slim little girl of a nurse renewing a bandage with delirious men on cots to right and left

clutching and babbling at her, and the patient squirming. Her quiet voice saying, "There, there my man! *Be* a man. You're not badly hurt!" . . . an officer of the Medical Corps showing me two jars. One contained healthy lung tissue, looking like thin, crinkled paper, the other tissue from the lungs of a man dead of poison gas. It looked like old leather on a town dump.

We have all seen the pictures, at least, of the effects of napalm and of nuclear radiation, and we may have become hardened to accounts such as this. But for Will Irwin's generation of Americans such sights were raw and new. Even the remaining handful of old Indian-fighters and Philippines veterans had not known the ugliness of slaughter on so colossal a scale. Most poignantly among Irwin's recollections, in the midst of violence and chaos there was always some remnant of the pastoral:

> Verdun itself utterly deserted, every house hit, all the untended lawns and gardens flaming with wild red poppies. . . . Among the wreckage of broken mortar and blasted trees a pond remained unpolluted, and on it swam majestically two white swans. They were nervous wrecks. Approach them, and they stretched their necks and squalled.

That battlefield experience improves people's character—one traditional justification of war—Will Irwin angrily denied. "Anyone who says that the average man is a better man because of the war of 1914–1918, is lying—consciously or unconsciously to himself," he testified from a lecture platform in 1924:

> If war were what old-fashioned theology used to call a "means of grace," if it sent its victims to death and its survivors back to civil life better men, it would be your [the churches'] business to support it, no matter how great its physical agonies. But I, who saw the late war from its first battle to its last, who saw it in six nations, who saw it at front and rear, am here to tell you that it is not. . . . From first to last during the great war, a thousand soldiers of all nations, if one, asked me what it was all about, anyhow? And this, mind, was not a straight inquiry of one who wants to know, but a rhetorical question, plainly put by way of eliciting the answer, "Nothing!"

His fellow veteran Ernest Hemingway, once he got out of the transiently antiwar mood expressed in *A Farewell to Arms,* would attest that it is possible to believe in *nada* and still be convinced one has to go on fighting regardless. Even "that old, unquestioning valor to which death in battle for one's country seemed a sacrament, an act of supreme consecration," was not quite so dead as Irwin assumed it was when he wrote *The Next War*. The Second World War would show thousands of heroic examples, civilian as well as military, among imperturbable Londoners, worldly-wise Berliners, emperor-worshiping Japanese—even among the supposedly more modern-minded Russians and Americans. But in 1921, with the conspicuous failures of Versailles weighing freshly on all the participants' minds, Irwin struck a responsive chord. Published in April of 1921, *The Next War* promptly became a best-seller; by August—seven years after the invasion of Belgium—it had run through twelve printings.

Irwin's judgment was not, in the formal sense, pacifist. In ancient eras of rudimentary transport and communication, he conceded, war might even have been "a positive if costly benefit" to mankind, as the only practicable means of diffusing culture. However, "modern invention has changed all that. We no longer need a process so essentially wasteful to transmit the results of progress." In short, civilization had outgrown war—or perhaps it was the other way around. Illustrating his point with juxtaposed photographs of the damage remaining from artillery fire in the Waterloo campaign of 1815 and of the wreckage created by the greater guns of 1915, Irwin warned of the even higher destructive potential of a conscripted science and technology. April 22, 1915, when the first greenish clouds of chlorine rolled across the French and Canadian lines at Ypres, was for Will Irwin "a sinister date in the history of warfare," not only because of the specific physical and psychological ravages of poison gas but also because it symbolized what science was capable of spawning in the service of Mars. In that sense, the gas attack at Ypres was the Hiroshima of the First World War.

The war reporter's dread was shared to some extent in the scientific community. At the 1924 centennial of the Franklin Institute in Philadelphia, Leo Hendrik Baekeland, President of the American Chemical Society, stated that the science of chemistry had reached the point where it could wreck the world: "The complete destruction of entire cities [is] merely a matter of somebody giving the order with such authority that the chemists would have to obey."

But the point could be made with less solemnity. That same year Will Irwin contributed a "Heroic Ballad, 1976" to the "Conning Tower" column of the *New York World*. It began:

> All hail the sturdy vats and tanks
> That brewed the gas of victory,
> All hail, all hail thy patriot ranks—
> Industrial Chemistry!

The narrator describes how his dirigible squadron "slipped our mooring-mast" and proceeded toward the enemy's homeland:

> We sought his city's wide expanse
> Whence all his railroad lines were laid,
> And where ten million perjured hands
> Maintained his export trade.

In the ensuing gas raid many civilians perished, to be sure, but

> They were not Nordics; let them die!
> A lesser folk, decadent, frail;
> Scarce reached they six-point-forty on
> The anthropometric scale!

Although Irwin's personal politics were Republican, his poem concluded with an almost Marxist bite:

> And ere the fiscal year was done
> Our trade had won its guerdon due.
> Our balance rose from three per cent
> To nine point forty-two.

IV

Caught in the middle of the argument between people like Will Irwin and people like George Patton was the generation that had not yet reached military age on Armistice Day. "For four years, more or less," wrote Oliver LaFarge in 1925, "those of us especially in the East made little plan for a career, little choice of a pro-

fession, except this, that when we were old enough we should go
to fight." Then the war ended, and some of them went instead to
college. The Armistice instantly created a "generation gap." Absent
from Armageddon, how in retrospect did these still younger men
judge the Great War? According to LaFarge the college generation of his day was, by and large, not pacifist. But it equally rejected the wartime Establishment's morality-play interpretation of
the war: "Our elders' talk of Crusades and Galahads was untrue."
Instead, it had come to conceive of World War I as "an abominable
necessity."

LaFarge noted however that there were pacifists on the scene
also, who could not be dismissed as radicals (as they could, he
thought, in France). Pacifism in America came out of the church,
"and the church to-day votes rousingly Republican." But LaFarge
doubted that the campus pacifists had any idea how hard a task
they had taken on. If they were really serious they should abandon
all else they were doing, and "devote themselves day and night to
rolling their snowball. You cannot save the world in the intervals of
selling bonds or attending classes." Their immediate foe was not so
much militarism as apathy. "The great and inert majority of boys at
college to-day" were neither pacifist nor militarist. "The truth is,
that between the horror of the next war and our disgust with the
last, most of us have come not to think about war at all."

Those who did think about it, and who took a formal pacifist
stand, were in many instances reacting against the bellicose wartime behavior of the church itself, whose basic teachings they interpreted as antiwar. "I send you out not to die, but to kill Germans!" one visiting preacher had told an audience of college men
on a Sunday evening in 1918; one begins to understand why col-
legians in the twenties were starting to reject the institution of
compulsory chapel. Another warlike clergyman had mounted a
machine gun on the pulpit in his own parish church for the duration of hostilities. During the disenchanted mood that followed the
Armistice, however, the bloody God of Battles whose wrath some
churchmen had lately been calling down upon the enemy faded
from the skies, and the Christmas angels resumed their annual

caroling of peace on earth. A bad conscience about the churches'
conduct during the late war triggered in some quarters a willing
response to antiwar and even pacifist appeals.

"If the churches should say today, with one voice, 'Thou shalt
not!' there would never be another war," Will Irwin declared in
1924. But during the twenties the American churches were rarely
able to speak with one voice; both the Fundamentalist–Modernist
split, symbolized in the Scopes "Monkey Trial," and the Catholic–Protestant split over Al Smith made that inability painfully clear.
Furthermore, it was an unfortunate time for the churches to attempt to make any high claim of authority, either moral or political. The nation was entering what Robert T. Handy has named
"the American religious depression," an era marked by declining
church membership and a generally unfavorable public image for
organized religion. Nonetheless, antiwar partisans made the most
of the forum religious organizations afforded them, hoping against
hope. After all, had not the united voice of at least the Protestant
churches enacted Prohibition (a measure, incidentally, which old
newspaperman Will Irwin opposed as ardently as he opposed war)?

For draftable young people in the churches the war question was
not one for abstract assent or dissent. Should there be another
outbreak, the choice of what to do or not to do must devolve upon
them personally. The stereotypes of the Roaring Twenties must not
mislead us here. Alongside the flaming youths celebrated by
F. Scott Fitzgerald, and the other young folk who adopted as their
own the sardonic anticlericalism of H. L. Mencken, there was also
the phenomenon of organized and socially concerned church
youth. Thus, 7400 students from a thousand American colleges and
universities converged upon the 1924 international convention of
the Student Volunteer Movement, still committed to its prewar
slogan: "The Evangelization of the World in This Generation."
Rejecting both nationalistic "preparedness," which on a show of
hands drew about three hundred votes, and absolute pacifism,
which won five hundred, the vast majority of the delegates em-
braced a principle of international order: "We believe that war is
un-Christian, and that the League of Nations is the best means of

preventing it, but we would resort to war in case an unavoidable dispute had been referred to the League or World Court without successful settlement."

In an age of lightning-swift military technology this perhaps sounds like a cumbersome and legalistic answer. But that may not have been the most important consideration. To these young college men "war has lost its former glamor," the *Christian Science Monitor* editorialized, and then drew a highly optimistic conclusion: "When the youth of the world decide that there shall be no more wars, there will be none." Such statements of course must be read in historical perspective. Idealistic youths grow up and make "realistic" compromises. Eventually they become the command generation, in charge of wars to be fought in turn by the next crop of youths. Their elders can also be caught up in the same historic cycle. When he wrote his personal memoir *The Making of a Reporter*, in the grim and difficult war year 1942, Will Irwin dedicated it "to my son, William Hyde Irwin, Engineer Corps, U. S. Army."

Antiwar activists during the twenties could not know, however much they might subconsciously suspect, that their protest was going to fail. They were prone to man's—especially the young man's—perennial faith that he holds his future (and the world's) in his own hands. Antiwar liberals, and many humanitarian conservatives, believed that a militarist society could be transformed through persuasion; radicals affirmed that if worst came to worst it could be overthrown. Logically, the view that war was a profit-seeking enterprise involved some overlap between pacifism and socialism, which had its own optimistic affirmations about the future; even in religious circles, some youthful opponents of war stood considerably to the Left of the SVM.

In Milwaukee in 1927 the National Student Conference, an ad hoc convocation sponsored by the YMCA, not only declared against war but went on record as "opposed to the general imperialistic policy of the United States Government." The resolution prompted Colonel Stephen Park, head of the National Reserve Officers' Association, to charge that the speakers who addressed the conference were "getting their salaries straight from Moscow," and Chaplain Alva J. Brasted of the Second Army Division to cry that "such action savors of treason":

> What have these young saints to say of the Covenanters of Scotland, of the iron legions of Cromwell, of the tattered patriots of Valley Forge, of the men who cursed and shot with Jackson at New Orleans, of the millions who heard the call of Lincoln . . . ; of the splendid American boys who went down to the fields of battle in Europe during the World War! Their [the students'] puling proclamation should brand them for what they are: fanatics who would preserve the Eighteenth Amendment, regardless of cost or effort, but traitors to their flag in any hour of their country's need.

But Susumu Kobe, a Japanese student at the University of Washington who attended that Christian conference, found the experience encouraging. Despite America's new and stringent immigration laws, in particular the act of 1924 singling out Japanese nationals as aliens ineligible for U.S. citizenship—a measure which had caused July 1, 1924, to be observed in Tokyo as "Humiliation Day"—he was going back to Japan to tell his countrymen "that America is not as bad as they think she is"; that "under the surface of things there is a love for peace and friendship." As for his own nation, Kobe assured his peace-minded hosts, "Japan is not preparing for war. It may have done so in the past, but I give you my word of honor that Japan is, perhaps, the most peaceful nation in the world to-day."

Immediately after the First World War the Kobe *Japan Chronicle,* back in that student's homeland, had not been so optimistic: "At present Japan is definitely preparing for war with either Britain or America, and America and Britain are preparing for war with Japan." But then the Washington Disarmament Conference took place, limiting the Japanese Imperial Fleet to a fixed (and inferior) ratio to those of Britain and America; and it became possible for a prominent U.S. Senator, Thomas J. Walsh (best known for his relentless investigation of Teapot Dome), to tell one of his Montana constituents that "a war with Japan is about as likely as a war with Mars."

Not all Americans agreed with Walsh. The California-based Hearst newspapers continued to warn of the "yellow peril," and Billy Mitchell, in his campaign for increased military air strength, made dramatic headlines with statements that war with Japan was inevitable. Confronted with such headlines the Japanese naval attaché in Washington, Isoroku Yamamoto, replied that he did not look upon U.S.–Japanese relations "from the same angle as General Mitchell." He had never thought of America as a potential enemy, he added, "and the naval plans of Japan have never included the possibility of an American–Japanese war." Yamamoto was popular with his American hosts, from whom he had learned to play highly competent bridge and poker, and he seems to have enjoyed his American tours. Still, it is an admiral's job to be professionally prepared. Yamamoto returned to Japan in 1927 to push the development of naval aviation—including the dreaded Zero fighter plane—and to denounce the naval limitation agreement by which the American, British, and Japanese navies were pegged at the ratio of 5:5:3. In 1940, though personally opposing war with the United States, he would conceive and doggedly see through to success the daring sea–air strike at Pearl Harbor.

In the meantime, among some Americans and Japanese, the hopes for peace remained high. At a dinner in New York on April 25, 1925, tendered by the Commission on International Justice and Goodwill of the Federal Council of Churches, the new Japanese Ambassador to the United States, Tsuneo Matsudaira, asserted: "There are no issues between the United States and Japan awaiting settlement by force of arms." Japan was making no secret deals; she had withdrawn her garrisons from the former German sphere of influence in China, a sore point at Versailles; she had amended her laws dealing with nationality, whereby overseas Japanese had formerly been considered subjects of the Emperor even if they became legal citizens of another country. "As far as can be seen into the future no situation will arise which cannot be adjusted by ordinary and friendly diplomacy," Matsudaira concluded. "War between our two countries is a matter of physical impossibility, and we are destined to live in peace for all time."

V

"Deep and profound is the hold that warfare has on the world, on its governments, its institutions, its history, its literature, in the plans of the old, and in the imagination of the young." But it is not instinctive, declared the enormously influential American educator William H. Kilpatrick, in an address at a Quaker school in Philadelphia in 1921 on the subject "Our Schools and War." "During our late war learning to kill was judged by our competent military authorities to require careful teaching," a point also being made at about that same time by cavalryman George S. Patton. Logically, then, if war was a form of learned behavior, it could also be unlearned, as dueling—individual warfare—had been unlearned. Therefore, the Columbia Teachers College professor reasoned, a large part of the burden of achieving peace must rest upon the public schools.

First, the teachers trained in America's normal colleges must themselves be taught the new catechism: that war is not inevitable; that the "social integration" of mankind *is* inevitable; that competitive armament is folly. They must thoroughly understand the Great War that had just ended. Then in turn they must teach the children under their charge (1) that modern war is horrible ("taking care not to overstress this especially with the very young"); (2) that war is unnecessary (a fact to be learned by "both boys and girls"); (3) that world integration is the shape of the future ("This will, of course, be suitable only for the advanced"); and (4) that unlimited national sovereignty is anachronism. Teachers should downplay in their classrooms the German atrocity stories that had been a staple of the Allied press for four years: "We have too many children of German parentage in our midst." Finally, perhaps with a politic nod toward local pressures of the sort encountered in the P.T.A., Kilpatrick suggested that educationists should cautiously endorse the League of Nations. "When finally we have settled our partisan disputes . . . about the League, then the teachers must do their utmost to make it work."

To the present-day reader this program may sound insufferably didactic, especially coming as it did from a leading exponent of the new and, in theory, spontaneous and undogmatic "progressive" education. But this belief that the schools had a primary responsibility toward peace was widely and sincerely shared by members of the educational establishment, who thus carried to its zenith the familiar American gospel that there is no goal, from universal affluence to racial justice, that a well-financed public school system cannot accomplish. "The world war was the result of an education," wrote University of Wisconsin professor H. C. Wegner in the *Educational Review* that same year; the German General Staff's detailed plan for the invasion of Belgium had been of less decisive importance than the indoctrination in Kaiserism young citizens of the Reich had received, year in and year out, in Germany's highly efficient schools. Conversely, world peace must also be the result of an education, of a different kind. To limit armaments by treaty, helpful though it might be in relieving surface tensions, was to go at the war problem from the wrong end; first it would be necessary to limit the forces that raised the armies and set them in motion. By the time the young had reached voting and fighting age, it was already too late.

Discussing the topic "Teachers and World Peace" for the *NEA Journal,* Major General John F. O'Ryan, Officers' Reserve Corps, U.S.A., confessed in 1923 that he could trace the genesis of his own military career to "one particularly inspiring picture of Phil Sheridan waving his hat and yelling: 'Turn, boys, turn! We're going back!' " in a textbook of American history. O'Ryan therefore proposed, as a first—and admittedly small—step, the substitution of "peace heroes" for "war heroes" in the schoolbooks American children used. Indeed, in the twenties the schoolbook theme generated a fair amount of muckracking. In 1924 three university professors studied twenty-four standard public school American history texts and twenty-four popular supplementary readers. Both in the proportionate space allotted to military exploit as against civilian history, and in the way the former was described, they concluded, the books' overwhelming tendency was to glamorize and glorify war. Commenting on these findings, the editor of *The Nation* echoed Dr. Kilpatrick's faith in the well-nigh limitless possibilities of education, either to regenerate or to damn: "War is not innate. It is produced by our concepts and what we teach our children. . . . The time to teach the truth about it has come." Then, in prescriptive language implying that war propaganda should in effect be supplanted by peace propaganda (for a generation which had become suspicious of *all* propaganda!), the liberal weekly explained:

> The future demands a type of history that will not exaggerate the place of war, which will show its true nature, and which will develop in children the will to peace. Parents should demand such histories, school boards should instal them, publishers should issue them, and historians should prepare them.

But what if parents and school boards and publishers—or historians, for that matter—did not want them? Schools are not wholly autonomous; they reflect the dominant values of the societies that create and pay for them, and they rationalize those societies' unconscious psychic needs. The trouble with handing the war problem over to the schoolteachers, contended popular psychologist Havelock Ellis in 1919, was that "war is bound up with the passions, and can only be treated like the passions"; it could not be abolished by reducing it to a unit in the social studies curriculum, even if every student who took that unit received an "A." "In reality," as Sigmund Freud grimly wrote from war-torn Vienna in 1915, "there is no such thing as 'eradicating' evil tendencies."

From a hardboiled Freudian standpoint, if organized reason could not accomplish the end of war, as Kilpatrick hoped, neither could organized religion, as Will Irwin believed. "Love" and "hate" are opposite sides of the same ambivalent coin, Havelock Ellis continued; "We cannot have one without the other." Inevitably, therefore, throughout history "the great human lovers, prepared to love even their enemies, are a neglible minority." Even Christianity had been able to keep its adherents out of the army only for its first three hundred years. When it captured the state after the conversion of Constantine it was in turn captured by the state, with all the state's time-honored and inalienable right to make war. The peaceful first-century Christian, who believed literally that the meek would inherit the earth, was transmuted into the Christian crusader, who rode under the banner *In hoc signo vinces*. In the godless twentieth century the soldier of the Cross may have become more rare, but he was still riding. Those same church young people who had learned the Biblical injunction to love your enemies, bless them that curse you, and do good to them that hate you, had also sung many a rousing chorus of "Onward, Christian Soldiers."

Henry Mencken had nothing but contempt for pacifism, religious or otherwise; "a man who has never stood in battle," he wrote in 1918, "has missed the most colossal experience of [his] sex." But Mencken disliked civilian bloodthirstiness also. In 1930 the Sage of Baltimore penned a characteristically savage *American Mercury* editorial titled "The Charm of War." "Human beings are not naturally humane," Mencken argued, " . . . they take a keen delight in cruelty whenever it seems to be safe." And, he asserted, America's own social pattern for the suppression of spontaneous individual behavior—what Mencken (and others) mistakenly termed "Puritanism"—probably exaggerated this natural human tendency:

> It explains . . . why such a people as the Americans, who labor under extraordinary inhibitions in normal times, surpass all other peoples in frenzy when the band begins to play. They must crowd into a few war years all the barbaric lusts of a generation. No wonder they always carry on in a frantic and obscene manner, and are sneakingly ashamed of it afterward, and try to deny and forget the fact. If they had more freedom on every day they would be decenter on their moral holidays.

H. L. Mencken's formulation, of an outwardly peaceable people who at long intervals went off on war-drunks, comparatively considered was unfair to the Americans. Could the savage conflict then raging in China among the forces of Chiang, Mao, and a host of individual warlords, or the murderous Chaco War just getting under way in South America, or the bloody communal riots in India *all* be blamed on Puritanism? Moreover the *American Mercury*'s editor, an amateur Freudian like so many other intellectuals of the twenties, may have been unduly pessimistic even from the standpoint of his Viennese mentor. So it would seem from some of Freud's own words.

In 1932, under League of Nations auspices, Sigmund Freud engaged in an exchange of open letters with the physicist and humanitarian Albert Einstein on the topic "why war" (*Warum Krieg?*). Reiterating his well-known belief that "there is no use in trying to get rid of men's aggressive inclinations," Freud nevertheless told Professor Einstein he thought it possible to combat the war spirit by indirect means: "If willingness to engage in war is an effect of the destructive instinct, the most obvious plan will be to bring Eros, its antagonist, into play against it. . . . Anything that encourages the growth of emotional ties between men must operate against war." To combine Mencken's perspective with Freud's: might not humankind, "if they had more freedom on every day" to "encourage the growth of emotional ties," be enabled one day to overcome war?

Sadly, in Germany at that moment the power of the state was being captured by a mass movement whose leaders had learned the secret of encouraging the growth of emotional ties—for the movement's members only—in exchange for their renunciation of more freedom on every day. Sigmund Freud and Albert Einstein both had to flee for their lives from that horror, and in due course George Patton with his tank battalions and Einstein with his atomic equations set about the task of stemming the Nazi tide. Billy Mitchell's military honors were posthumously restored, and the question *Warum Krieg?* was adjourned for another generation. Indeed, except among historians the fact that there had been a peace movement in the twenties was all but forgotten. There is a civil rights tradition in America, going back at least to the Emancipation Proclamation, but outside of the Quaker and other small historically pacifist churches there is not much of a peace tradition. Lacking such a continuous heritage, demonstrators in the sixties against the war in Vietnam sometimes acted as if the idea of antiwar protest had never occurred to any generation prior to their own. To themselves, as well as to their prowar opponents, could have been applied the words of Pete Seeger's protest song: "When will they ever learn?"

The tragic irony is that George S. Patton in his day, on the basis of the long and bloody record of man's history, would have felt entitled to ask—from exactly the opposite point of view—the same question.

CHAPTER III

In God Some
of Us Trusted

"TEN OR FIFTEEN years ago," said a distinguished Divinity School dean in 1929, "we had dared to hope that we might be on the verge of some general revival of religion. That hope was probably based on ignorance of what wars do to the souls of men." Knowing that in the American Civil War religious revivals had regularly swept through the camps of both Northern and Southern armies, and hoping for a similar result in the war of 1917–18, church and YMCA workers carried their evangel to the A.E.F. along the Western Front—only to encounter some unexpected snags. One evening in France, for example, after a religious service in which several soldiers made public confession of their faith, a young man came up to "Y" secretary Allyn K. Foster to explain why he had not.

"I am mightily interested in what these men did tonight, and I wanted to do it, too, but I cannot believe everything the church people believe."

The evangelist surprised the inquirer with his reply: "I cannot either, and I do not wish to." Then Foster asked the soldier for a bill of particulars. "What is it you do not believe?"

"I don't believe the world was made in six days."

"Well, I wasn't there, but I don't think so either," the YMCA secretary replied. "What else?" There followed a colloquy on such subjects as Jonah and the whale, after which Foster asked the prospective convert, "Cannot a man follow Christ without settling such matters as these?"

That line should have been the clincher, but the soldier had the last word: "The church people back home would not receive me if I expressed doubt about these things."

Some church people back home, Allyn Foster had to admit, expressed no doubts whatever about such things. Questioned sharply by Clarence Darrow at the Scopes monkey trial in 1925, former presidential candidate William Jennings Bryan took his stand on Jonah and the whale: "I believe in a God who can make a whale and can make a man and make both do what He pleases." The Fundamentalist–Modernist controversy erupted in the American churches during the postwar decade, and liberals who fondly imagined that religion in America had made its peace with Darwinism around 1880 were suddenly realizing that the battle had now to be fought all over again. ("In one college a new professor happened in his first lecture casually to use the terrifying word 'Evolution,' " reported the president of Brown University in 1923. "Whereupon the whole class hissed him.") "Christianity, if we may judge by some of its leaders, has been trying to live up to its past, when the precise thing it needs is to outlive a great deal of it," Allyn Foster concluded in 1929, after a decade spent visiting colleges in every state of the Union as Student Secretary of the Northern Baptist Convention's Board of Education, and tangling with the Fundamentalists at every step along the way.

Conservative churchmen as well as liberals had engaged in war work, and they had had their own explanation of why the troops were "over there": the American Expeditionary Force was locked in a death-grip with a foe who had taken the Godless theory of evolution seriously, and who followed it to its logical conclusion. "Darwinism had saturated the war-lords with all the catchwords essential to the prosecution of their designs," wrote Alfred W. McCann in *God—or Gorilla?* (1922), "and the people . . . were prepared to follow to the end, little dreaming of the carnage, starvation and disease toward which their 'progressive' evolution was now thundering its flight." To James M. Gray, Dean of the Moody Bible Institute in Chicago, World War I was no crusade to make the world safe for democracy; rather, Gray asserted in 1917 (after the United States had declared war), it was a divine judgment upon the world's sins:

> Belgium, whose sorrows we deplore, is reaping what she sowed in the atrocities of the Congo. . . . Russia is receiving of the Lord's hand for the persecution of the Jew, and Turkey for her treatment of the Armenian. . . . And the United States? Is there any nation on the earth today, more proud, more worldly-minded, more self-contained, more needing a humbling at the hand of God in the experiences of a distressing war?

But to the consternation of such prophets, the humbling did not take place. After the war the United States, as it established Normalcy, assumed Britain's former imperial credit role, and rejected the League of Nations, seemed if anything even more proud, worldly-minded, and self-contained than before. Fundamentalists might console themselves with the thought "we told you so": "Sometimes the disease [of sin] is hidden, and there are those who think that it is cured," wrote one such conservative, J. Gresham Machen, in *Christianity and Liberalism* (1923). "But then it bursts forth in some new way, as in 1914, and startles the world." (In one well-thumbed university-library copy of that book someone later penciled in the margin the further notation "and 1939.") If the world was startled, however, it was not converted. In Jazz-Age America, while some college students hissed evolution, others hissed religion; Joseph Wood Krutch, lecturing at Caltech, was told beforehand that he would be well received "if, one, you stop by twelve-fifty so that they can get their lunches and, two, are very careful not to say anything in favor of either religion or morality." "Modernists" in religion, steering a course so to speak between H. L. Mencken and William Jennings Bryan, were caught in a furious verbal crossfire. And Rabbi Abba Hillel Silver, also a veteran of the college lecture circuit in the twenties, hinted in his book *Religion in a Changing World* (1931) that American Judaism was beset by a similar kind of polarization.

"To be modern in thought and religious in spirit is a rare com-

bination," Allyn K. Foster conceded in 1929. So also Joseph
Wood Krutch in that year wrote somberly of *The Modern
Temper*, and Harry Elmer Barnes forecast *The Twilight
of Christianity* (and of all other theistic faiths). "The old supernatural criteria . . . should be discredited and abolished as
rapidly as possible and supplanted by strictly secular and mun-
dane considerations," Barnes intoned, and a chorus of *American Mercury* readers said "Amen." But the Rev. Mr. Foster
continued to hope against hope; after a decade of frustration and
rebuff, he could still entitle his own tract for the times *The
Coming Revival of Religion*. "To rationalize away all the mystery of religion is not to be soundly modern," Foster insisted. "At
the heart of science and at the heart of religion is ever the inscrutable mystery which always eludes accurate measurement and yet
which unfolds both in nature and in the lives of men."

II

Neither Clarence Darrow nor William Jennings Bryan, facing
each other in 1925 in a hot and crowded courtroom in Dayton,
Tennessee, seemed very much interested in pondering inscrutable mysteries. "We have the purpose of preventing bigots and ig-
noramuses from controlling the education of the United States
and you know it," Darrow cried; "I am simply trying to protect
the Word of God against the greatest atheist or agnostic in the
United States," Bryan retorted. But elsewhere in the America of
the twenties, well-intentioned negotiators worked at securing a
cease-fire.

The warfare between science and theology had gone on quite
long enough, the Scottish scientist J. Arthur Thomson told an audience at New York's Union Theological Seminary in 1924.
"Science is essentially impersonal, while religion is essentially
personal. Religion has to do with an aspect of reality that is
beyond science." So conservative an American cleric as Bishop
William T. Manning, a dogmatic High Churchman, along with
more liberal religious leaders like Henry Van Dyke, Francis J.
McConnell, and Henry Churchill King, signed a "Joint Statement
upon the Relations of Science and Religion" prepared in 1923 by

Caltech's Nobel Prizewinning physicist Robert A. Millikan. Signers of this manifesto from the science side included the presidents of the Smithsonian Institution, of the American Museum of Natural History, and of the American Association for the Advancement of Science, as well as William James Mayo of the renowned clinic, and William Wallace Campbell, Director of the Lick Observatory.

"The names do not matter—religion, science, call them what you will," Dean Willard Sperry of the Harvard Divinity School loftily declared in 1929. "What matters is the profoundest and the most characteristic of man's endeavors, his endeavor to know the nature of his universe. So long as that endeavor goes on the prospect of religion lives." Riverside Church, the Gothic skyscraper John D. Rockefeller, Jr., was then building near Grant's Tomb, expressed that common endeavor concretely and physically: the carved figures adorning its west portal included those of Charles Darwin and Albert Einstein.

But not everyone who lived through the twenties was prepared to let the ministers (or architects!) of reconciliation get away with it. "Slowly but surely science and historical criticism are driving the half-way liberals to make a decision," argued the militant secularist Harry Elmer Barnes, and on this point the equally militant Fundamentalist J. Gresham Machen agreed with the author of *The Twilight of Christianity*. "It is highly misleading to say that religion and science are separate," Machen concurred. "On principle, it cannot be denied that the Bible does teach certain things about which science has a right to speak," and events in ancient Palestine were just as much a proper subject for scientific study as any other kind. To escape this confrontation by deliberately splitting off an "essentially personal" religion from an "essentially impersonal" science, as Professor Thomson advised, was to cast loose upon a chartless sea of subjectivism where no reliable distinction was possible between reality and hallucination. "It is a poor religion," Machen argued, "that can abandon to science the whole realm of objective truth in order to preserve for itself merely a realm of ideals."

Not all Fundamentalists were so confident in their faith as Dr.

Machen; the legislative enactment of anti-evolution laws by a half-dozen states during the twenties seemed to imply that science did *not* have a right to speak about certain things taught in the Bible—or at least not to speak about them to schoolchildren. But many shared Machen's impatience with Barnes's "half-way liberal." Once you have opened this particular door, the radical freethinker and the fervent Biblicist agreed, there is no closing it. For all his devotion to inscrutable mystery, the Northern Baptist half-way liberal A. K. Foster had to concur:

> It is sometimes said that religion and science are two games played on the same board. But the mere board possesses no magic competent to unify two wholly different games. You cannot play checkers by the rules of chess.

Therefore, it must all be one game. "Science and religion are one in process," Foster concluded. Even if they eventually run into mysteries which elude accurate measurement, "both work the same way."

But if both worked the same way—if "the Church is a clinical laboratory dedicated to working out a cure" for the ills that afflict mankind, as another young minister put it in 1923—then the training of religious workers might have to be drastically changed. "We take nothing for granted. Not even God," said Dr. Shailer Mathews, the portly and enthusiastic Dean of the Divinity School at the University of Chicago, in an interview for a popular magazine. "Many individuals have lived religion experimentally in the past, but in more or less haphazard ways. What we aim at is a technique that will always yield results and that anyone of intelligence can learn." Forty years before, Mathews reminisced, his own generation in theological seminary had "studied a limited number of subjects in a hard-and-fast way"; now (1930), "beyond formal courses in religion, an almost unlimited range of subjects is open to students"—and they no longer had to master Greek or Hebrew for graduation. Instead, they "touch most of the sciences enough to learn their technique":

> For instance, they get a working knowledge of mental hygiene. Any religious leader meets people obsessed by fears, worries, split

personalities, inhibitions, complexes. It's his duty to help them if he can.

We study sociology as scientists. Some students are always making community surveys. Sunlight, housing, divorce, gangs, many other social factors have much to do with whether people are "good" or "bad." We train men to observe such factors, so that later they may use them. [The doctrine of Original Sin, Mathews explained, was a theory of human behavior adequate to the scientific knowledge of Saint Augustine's time, but overthrown by more recent research.]

In every direction, the approach is experimental. First, we ask, what are the facts? Second, what can religion do about them? Third, what technique does scientific knowledge suggest? . . . We're living in a world overrun with new problems; religious experimentation can help in all. There is a move toward new moral standards in business, as in the home, growing out of a growing recognition of human equality. New ways of coöperation and coördination are being found, with vast room for experimentation——

"But," the interviewer interjected, "do you call that religion?"

"It's living, isn't it?"

"One side of living."

"Exactly; you don't think, do you, that religion is something apart from life, locked up?"

"I suppose not——"

"Certainly it is not. Religion is the technique of applying God's force of love to whatever one has to do."

But what about that inscrutable mystery at the heart of religion (and of science) which always eluded accurate measurement? For example, the reporter asked, "What about prayer?"

"There," Dean Mathews said earnestly, "you touch vast possibilities for religious experiment":

We have powers, hitherto unexplored, by which we can extend our wills and influence outward events. Does this sound preposterous? I'm not saying we have such powers, only that it's possible; and if we have them, it would seem no more wonderful to me than, say, radio. . . .

The sun is "good medicine," as people have always known. The knowledge was of limited value until scientists discovered how and why sunlight heals, and began "manufacturing" it.

People of all faiths have always believed that prayer, too, is "good medicine." We want to know how and why.

"This is tremendously interesting, Dean Mathews," the magazine writer interrupted, "and suggests—well, I wish you'd tell *what it means for me*—I mean, for the average person who isn't going into the ministry." For example, "Could a man make more money if now and then he prayed about his business?"

"I think so—if he is honest and serious."

"Could he get a better job?"

"I haven't much doubt of it."

"Improve his personality?—make people like him?—be more popular?"

"Certainly."

"Get just about anything he wants?"

"At least, anything he might want intelligently and morally."

"Then God, you'd say, is still on the job, here and now?"

The Dean tamped the ash in his pipe. "It's a common notion," he explained, smiling, "that God is *emeritus*, like an elderly professor. . . . But I think it's provable that He hasn't quit. . . . Remember this: We're at the beginning of something new, and big."

By the time Shailer Mathews gave out this affirmative pipe-puffing interview, something new and big was transpiring outside the walls of his religious laboratory. Elsewhere in Chicago in 1930 men were making less money, whether or not they prayed about their business; nor were they getting just about anything they wanted, even if they wanted it intelligently and morally. As an actual institutional program, this experimental variant on Modernism had unfolded in the prosperous sunshine of the twenties, and—despite the Dean's optimism—it withered in the Depression's autumnal chill. Nevertheless, Shailer Mathews articulated the religious hunger of a great many Americans. In Lloyd Douglas's 1929 novel, *Magnificent Obsession*, the central character—a brain surgeon—reads the Bible for the first time in his life and finds in it "secrets of a tremendous energy to be tapped by any man with sense enough to accept the fact of it as he would any other scientific hypothesis, and accord it the same dignity, the same practical tests he might pursue in a chemical or physical laboratory." It is worth noting that *Magnificent Obsession* sold a quarter of a million copies in its first ten years.

III

Whether the young minister in the twenties had been trained in evangelism or in experimentation, when he graduated and got out into a parish he soon discovered that neither kind of religious preparation had much to do with what he typically was hired for: to "make contact." "Sometimes there would be four or five activities in the same evening," the assistant pastor of one busy urban church recalled, "and I 'contacted' them all." In a local congregation with seventeen separate official departments, divided into endless subdivisions and committees, this could be quite a scramble: "Christmas wasn't too bad, but imagine a dozen Hallowe'en parties in succession, with grapes for dead men's eyes and wet gloved ghostly hands." The most demanding event was the Men's Club meeting: "The gymnasium would fill up with men who wrangled over routine like twelve year olds, watched second-rate entertainment from an agency, had refreshments and went home—except those of the inner circle who stayed to tell stories." (The imagery is WASP, but Catholic and Jewish equivalents may well be imagined.) In the busy building where this sort of thing went on, the hurrying clergyman summed up, "there were Scout troops, community boys' athletics, church school athletics, social service clubs, mothers' clubs,—almost every activity imaginable, and incidentally a church."

"I was too busy in that church to think or to enjoy life," its former junior minister confessed. But church laymen also, in the recreation-oriented twenties, sometimes privately acknowledged that "religious" activities of this kind were not really much fun. At an Episcopal church in upstate New York, after one noisily cheerful evening meeting, a young member of the vestry cornered the rector in his study and told him a few of the facts of parish life:

Did you notice the crowd tonight? There must have been a hundred and fifty men present, and I'll wager half of them were there under compulsion. . . . Why should we drag ourselves away from home, on one of our few free evenings, to eat a poor dinner, try to talk to men we don't know, listen to an amateur quartet, sing our own songs off key, and be afflicted with the punk tenor we were obliged to applaud to-night? . . . What good does it all accomplish?

The pastor tried to remonstrate with him, arguing that this was not just another effort "to save souls through church suppers"; for some of the people at the church that evening, lonely newcomers to the city, the dinner had been "a real event." In a time of geographically dispersed membership and loosening parochial ties, such activities were an attempt to create *esprit de corps*, to make the parish a social entity. Moreover, the pastor told his protesting lay leader, these dinners and smokers, and all that went with them, were signs of a change in religious ideas; they were "a reaction from the stiffness and starchiness which characterized church people of the past."

But the young vestryman couldn't see it. "Perhaps it started in some such way," he conceded, "but a decade or two of that sort of thing has destroyed its usefulness. . . . Did you ever hear of any one attending a church supper or a parish bazaar voluntarily, in a spirit of exuberant or expectant gladness?" What had all these social gatherings really done for the parish? "Aren't we simply spending our time refining enough oil to make the wheels go round? What does all the machinery *make?*" he pointedly asked.

Indeed, the rector mused after the young layman had left his study, the church's forced joyless busyness might only be a mask for its declining vitality. Youth especially seemed turned off by all the wheel-spinning: "It is no unusual thing to hear the frank acknowledgment among church leaders that we must recognize the loss of one generation and prepare now [1928] to win the next." Such pessimistic notes were frequently sounded by religious leaders during the Jazz Age. Harvard's Willard Sperry, hopeful though he was of a détente between science and religion, was not so hopeful of *institutional* religious regeneration: "The truth is that in America we spend altogether too much time and effort in simply keeping churches alive."

The exception tests any rule, and not all churchmen in the twenties would have mourned the decline of the church or written off the rising generation as beyond salvage. In particular, the Fundamentalists commonly argued that it was their opponents' churches, not their own, that were in this kind of trouble. "Organization is one of the curses of the liberals," Hillyer Hawthorne Straton—son of a prominent Fundamentalist pastor in New York, and himself a ministerial student in Philadelphia—told Granville Hicks in a 1927 interview.

> They don't have anything else to do. Of course Fundamentalists have the vice, too, but not to the same extent. They are too busy saving souls to bother with organization. . . . We're told that we ought to be liberal and give dances, but I've seen too many churches die that way. All I do is to preach the word of God, and it holds the young people as well as of old.

Young people? Unchurched liberals, in the twenties and afterward, often jumped to the conclusion that "the old-time religion" was by definition a brand of religion practiced primarily by senior citizens. Not so, this young Fundamentalist declared; his father, John Roach Straton, had "a fine class of young people" in the New York City parish church from whose pulpit the elder Straton thunderingly denounced evolution, Al Smith, and Sunday baseball. As for Hillyer Straton's own congregation in West Philadelphia, "Half my crowd Sunday evenings are under twenty-five."

"Do you think the modern generation is bound for the dogs?" Hicks asked him.

The young minister smiled. "That's where Father and I disagree."

Quizzing this "son of a Fundamentalist prophet" on science, on anti-evolution laws, and on the dogma of the Virgin Birth, Granville Hicks got from him exactly the conservative answers which youths just out of college in the twenties were *not* expected to give. Finally, Hicks remarked: "The colleges are filled with Modernists. What are you going to do about it?"

"Convert them," Straton shot back. "Give them the truth! The average young person is a Fundamentalist till he goes to college and gets his faith knocked out of him. Get hold of him and give him the gospel message. That's the way to save our generation."

Hicks rose to go, and Straton accompanied him to the door, smiling. But his face was stern as he shook the interviewer's hand. "Good-bye, brother," the serious young churchman said. "God be with you. I hope you may some day come to see the light."

IV

To other young clergymen starting out in the twenties, the light was not all that clear. "The problem for us who are preparing to be prophets," one of them declared in 1923, "is that we are overwhelmed with too many situations: the situation in the Ruhr, the situation in Russia, the situation in the oil fields abroad and the coal fields at home, the situation in the divorce courts." It was not that they were wandering with Matthew Arnold "between two worlds, one dead, the other powerless to be born. It is rather that our world is born; and it is too big for us." Envying both the "seminoles," the Fundamentalist seminary students who were "learning to thunder the urgency of baptism and brimstone," and the secular radicals, who propounded attractive but unconvincingly simple Utopias, many of these perplexed young seekers fell into a diffident silence.

The minister who broke that silence quite often only made a fool of himself. He "becomes a smatterer in political economy and sociology, [and] preaches earnestly (and inaccurately) about many isms," Bishop Charles Fiske charged in 1928. "Unfortunately it takes a long time to become an expert, and the lifetime of any particular ism is usually short." By the time such a bandwagon chaser might learn enough to speak with authority on any one issue, "he finds that something else has taken its place." On the other hand, if he neglected to keep himself informed about political economy and sociology—and much else—he would find himself out of touch with a public many of whom knew more about such matters than he did.

In the words of a black Topeka schoolteacher, speaking to an African M. E. Church national meeting in 1929, "The average minister is woefully unqualified to properly present the gospel message in keeping with the advancing intelligence of the present generation." The scientific revolution in particular, despite the determined efforts of mentors like Shailer Mathews, seemed to have passed him by. Such, at least, was the harsh judgment of the Director of Science Service, Edwin E. Slosson:

> The Einstein theory of relativity, the Planck theory of quanta, the chromosome theory of heredity, the hormone theory of temperament . . . will influence the philosophy, theology, religion and morals of the future as much as did the Copernican theory in the sixteenth century and the Darwinian theory in the nineteenth. . . . A student in engineering or biology will sit up half the night discussing these theories, but your modern theological graduate is bored by them.

Slosson (who will reappear in the next chapter) did not distinguish among Fundamentalists, Modernists, and "half-way liberals" in this assessment. When a liberal did undertake to wrestle with the new knowledge—as when one young minister delivered a sermon on the topic "Can a Gland Sin?"—it commonly threw him for a fall, and members of his congregation might be upset that the subject had even been mentioned.

But the problem of communication between pulpit and pew—or between pulpit and street corner—was more than simply intellectual, and it long antedated the twenties. Despite robust evidence to the contrary (examples: Peter Cartwright, Dwight L. Moody, and in a different way Henry Ward Beecher), American folklore had long held that the "man of God" was by definition out of touch with "real life." Typically, a non-churchgoing layman severely wounded one ministerial candidate's ego by telling him: "Life is a football game, with the men fighting it out on the gridiron, while the minister is up in the grandstand, explaining the game to the ladies." Or as Stanley Walker expressed it in 1929 in the *New York Herald Tribune:* "Before stepping into a New York pulpit, a minister should have had a year on a metropolitan daily as a cub reporter, assigned to the police blotter and the night courts."

"There are times when one is a little ashamed to be known as a clergyman," Bishop Fiske had to confess. "I like to take off my clerical collar and travel in mufti, sitting in the smoking compartment and taking part in the spontaneous conversation of a group of men who do not feel that they are under restraint because of the censorious and accusatory presence of a parson." (What minister, priest, or rabbi, however dedicated, has not indulged at times in fantasies of being incognito?) On the other hand, the bishop was uncomfortably aware that an effort to break out of this stereotype of the clergyman as bigot and prude might entrap a man in an equally obnoxious stereotype of the clergyman as Babbitt, however much his traveling companions in that smoking compartment might praise him as a good mixer, go-getter, and regular guy.

Even more galling than the roles of the killjoy and the Kiwanian, for many clergymen of that period, was the role of the panhandler. Whether a church was Fundamentalist, Modernist, or "half-way liberal," in order to meet its bills—even in the prosperous twenties—it typically had to beg. "Are the processes of mendicancy, sycophancy, servility, and general self-abasement, as prevailingly practiced by our churches, building up the church in the esteem of the public?" Lloyd C. Douglas asked in 1926. To some degree, he granted, this situation was the logical outcome of America's traditional religious voluntarism; once the church lost its ability to command, it perforce had to coax. Yet there were other voluntary associations in America during the twenties which did not function that way; Douglas acidly compared the typical suburban parish church's "every-member-canvass," and its attendant indignities, with the typical suburban country club's "assessment" of its members, a levy enforced by quick expulsion of those who did not pay their dues. Although Douglas himself was and remained a successful parish minister (until earnings from his books became great enough to live on, at which point he retired to write full time), his discontent with the ministerial beggar's role may subtly have influenced his initial decision to become a novelist. Perhaps it is significant that in his best-selling religious novel *Magnificent Obsession* the church and the clergy, as such, play only a marginal role. Rather than lecture and catechize people, or mix with and glad-hand them, this churchman seems to have found the storyteller's role more dignified—and more effective.

The damage that can be done to anyone's psyche by the enforcement of stereotyped role-playing has been brought home to us in recent years by the black and women's revolutions. For the American clergy, as much as for blacks and women, this is an old, old story. "I wish my congregation wouldn't think I am like an undertaker's folding chair, useful for weddings and funerals alike, and with just as much feeling," one sensitive cleric protested—anonymously—in 1927 in the pages of the mass-circulation *American Magazine.* "I often long to call out to my flock, and say, 'Look! I am not stuffed with sawdust. I can feel those pins you stick in me. I am alive. I am a man.'"

Years before, Emerson had said it all to a graduating class in divinity: "Let their doubts know that you have doubted and their wonder feel that you have wondered." Similarly, the anonymous clergyman of 1927 admitted, "life puzzles me, as it puzzles everyone, and I have nights when I am sure of nothing at all." Then why didn't he say so? Because, this minister insisted, if he confessed that he had doubts just like those of his parishioners, "they would lose confidence in him." But that's not the point, Ralph Waldo Emerson might have replied, and here may be the real measure of the distance American religion—and much else—had traveled between Emerson's time and the 1920s.

It may also explain something of the dynamics of 1920s-style religious conservatism. Liberal and radical interpreters have often too simply understood Fundamentalism as the work of a "priest-craft" tyrannizing over a people who would be enlightened if given a chance—for example, if given an education in science. But quite often it seems to have been the other way around: the *layman* insisted that the *minister* express dogmatic certainty. This may have happened sometimes even when the layman's own faith had waned; he still might want his pastor to express the eternal verities

for him, just as he might want a President who would express for
him certain homely old values he did not actually live by himself.
In this connection it is worth noting that Calvin Coolidge, to the
mild discomfort of some of the worldly-wise journalists who covered his comings and goings, when he went to church made it
manifest that he was at ease in the "old-time religion." As Myron
Stearns—himself a minister's son—wrote, after observing Coolidge
at worship in Washington, D.C.'s severely plain First Congrega-
tional Church,

> It is impossible for me to avoid running over, in my mind, the cir-
> cumstances that have allowed me, gradually, in a different part of
> the country, to drift away from this particular form of worship, and
> in the end question even many details of the creed itself. Obviously,
> the President has never chanced into such circumstances. He sits
> with an arm extended along the back of the pew, thoroughly at
> home.

V

"The less we talk about religion, probably, the nearer we come
to the heart of it." Thus, in 1924, the genial essayist Christopher
Morley to his own satisfaction refuted *all* the religious controver-
sialists of the day—H. L. Mencken as much as William Jennings
Bryan, Rabbi Silver along with Cardinal O'Connell, Science Service director Edwin Slosson as well as Imperial Wizard Hiram
Wesley Evans of the Ku Klux Klan. We should talk less about
religion, Morley implied, because talk distracts from an ultimate
reality that cannot be put into words. This is the mystic's classic
stand, and the lives and thought of the Quaker Rufus Jones and the
black pastor Howard Thurman (who first became acquainted with
each other during the twenties), and of others like them, "remind
us that the mystic is also indigenous to twentieth-century
America." In this uncontemplative republic the mystical mode of
religion may be a minor theme, but, as Hal Bridges noted in his
study *American Mysticism from William James to Zen*, it
is a persistent one. And for every mystic who expressed what he
had found by writing a book, Rufus Jones contended in 1930, there
were hundreds who remained "mute and unnamed."

Zane Grey, the Western novelist, who turned out his tales at an average rate of two or three each year and whose sales can be reckoned in the tens of millions, hardly qualifies as one of the mute and unnamed. But he does qualify, in certain of his moods, as a religious writer—of a kind who would have agreed with Christopher Morley's axiom that "God is known, if at all, in solitude." Morley, however, as a seasoned city-dweller, did not believe that solitude need be sought by riding out over the purple sage. "I don't think that any man who has worked in downtown New York can be much of an atheist," the urbane journalist affirmed. "In that great jungle of violent life, under the glittering spires of such steep cathedrals, he must inevitably be a trifle mad."

But Zane Grey—a confirmed New York-hater—preferred to find his solitude, and his madness, more directly. On the trail or in the saddle, at places like the Grand Canyon, Monument Valley, or (for an Eastern example) the shoreline of Long Key, it was possible to experience "the fleeting trance-like transformation back to the savage," Grey asserted in a magazine essay "What the Desert Means to Me" (1924). And as the protagonist of Grey's novel *Wanderer of the Wasteland* (1923) discovered, that trance-like condition in which one "really did not know he was there," if it represented a throwback to the primitive, also "could be the last lesson to a thinking man—the last development of a man into savage or god":

> Adam realized that during these lonely hours he was one instant a primitive man and the next a thinking, or civilized, man. The thinking man he understood; all difficulty of the problem lay in this other side of him. He could watch, he could feel without thinking. That seemed to be the state of mind of an animal. Only it was a higher state—a state of intense, feeling, waiting, watching suspension!

Furthermore, by a discipline as arduous as any imposed by a Zen master—in the story it included deliberately enduring the ravages of summer in Death Valley, with its midnight furnace winds—this "state of apparent unconsciousness" could be brought under willed control:

> It had grown until he gained a strange and fleeting power to exercise it voluntarily. . . . After many futile efforts he at last, for a

lightning flash of an instant, seemed to capture the state of mind again. He recognized it because of an equally swift, vague joy that followed. . . . That emotion, then, was the secret of the idle hours—the secret of the doing nothing. If he could only grasp the secret of the nothing! Looked at with profound thought, this nothing resolved itself into exactly what it had [first] seemed . . . merely listening, watching, smelling, feeling the desert. That was all. But now the sense of it began to assume tremendous importance. Adam believed himself to be not only on the track of the secret of the desert's influence, but also of life itself.

The secret of the doing nothing. There is language like this in the writings of Plotinus, in the teachings of Suzuki, in the *Tao Teh Ching.* The warm, menacing wind rises to a gale and then moans away into silence, and Grey's Adam can no longer sleep: "This silence belied the blinking of the stars. It disproved the solidarity of the universe. Nothing lived, except his soul." One more step, and this seeker might achieve illumination; beatitude; *satori*—or the condition sought by young American Indian braves on their purgative vision-quests. But this is a Western novel, not a book of meditation. So the hero's reverie must be interrupted, as he hears the roll of rocks signaling that the villain is out doing his dastardly deeds; or he (accidentally and innocently) glimpses the virginal heroine standing naked in a sunlighted natural pool. The moment of transcendence passes, and the story plot moves on.

In addition to its mystical element, *Wanderer of the Wasteland* is also overlaid with a more orthodox, if confusing, Judaeo-Christian symbolism. In a Southwest whose geographical details are mythically hazy and inaccurate, a choice which may well have been deliberate (Grey had traveled enough in that region to know better), a man named "Adam" flees, is expelled from, man's civilized Eden to wander in the wilderness, in expiation for a brother's murder—a punishment specifically likened in the story to the curse of Cain (Gen. 4:11–14). In the desert a regenerated Adam meets a woman named Magdalene who likewise has been acting out the consequences of past sin. Caught in a rockslide released by her crazed and jealous husband—in effect, the Biblical punishment

for adultery (Deut. 22:24; John 8:7)—this Magdalene faces her destruction in a posture that is cruciform, "arms spread aloft, every
line of her body instinct with the magnificent spirit which had been
her doom." And so it goes. Yet when Grey's protagonist directly
confronts the moral theology of the "old-time religion," he angrily
rejects it. Watching another woman dying, in this case with tuber-
culosis—she is the mother of the young girl-sprite he has surprised
at the pool—Adam rebels, and we realize that if this is a mystic, he
is a mystic who has also read Darwin:

> To be devoured by millions of infinitesimal and rapacious animals
> feasting on blood and tissue—how insupportably horrible! . . .
> When Adam considered life in nature, he could understand this
> disease. It was merely a matter of animals fighting to survive. Let
> the fittest win! That was how nature worked toward higher and
> stronger life. But when he tried to consider the God this stricken
> woman worshiped, Adam could not reconcile himself to her agony.
> Why? The eternal Why was flung at him. She was a good woman.
> She had lived a life of sacrifice. She had always been a Christian.
> Yet she was not spared this horrible torture. Why?

Refusing answers such as J. Gresham Machen or Shailer Mathews
or Lloyd C. Douglas—or Job—gave to that ultimate question, this
Zane Grey hero pushes toward a more radical conclusion:

> He hated this mystery of disease, this cruelty of nature. . . . Was
> life only nature? Nature was indeed cruel. But if life was an endless
> progress toward unattainable perfection, toward greater heights of
> mind and soul, then was life God, and in eternal conflict with na-
> ture?

Onward and upward progress, however, was no longer so fully
satisfactory a resolution of the Problem of Evil as it had seemed to
some of the earnest Victorians who had pondered this same theme.
Rather than "let the ape and tiger die," as Tennyson advised, Grey
insisted that "something of the wild and primitive must forever
remain" in man. Indeed, "if the primitive were eliminated from
men there would be no more progress. All the gladness of the
senses lived in this law. The sweetness of the ages came back in
thoughtless watching." Yet this thoughtless watching must always

be in dialectical tension with an ever-advancing intellect that strove to overcome and master all of humanity's "primal instincts"—even while it remained healthily in touch with these impulses from "the dim, mystic dreamland of the primal day, from the childhood of the race" when "nature was every man's mother." Sigmund Freud could not have put the battle between Ego and Id more acutely, even though Zane Grey's resolution of this struggle was not exactly the same as Freud's.

In this instance, rather than call upon the ghost of Sigmund Freud (a ploy which has tempted many interpreters of the popular culture of the twenties), it may be more helpful to invoke the spirit of Arnold Toynbee. America has always been hospitable to religious experimentation. Some of the religious concerns of the twenties—the struggle of young clergy for a ministry that would be both meaningful and up-to-date; the conflict of science and religion, with its desperate gropings for détentes and cease-fires; the vague or confused popular mysticisms, which could be practiced without ever becoming institutionalized in a church—might be regarded merely as the latest chapters in an old story that also included Swedenborgianism and spiritualism, Emerson and Brigham Young. But they might also be read as early symptoms of far more radical transformations yet to come.

So had it been in ancient Rome when an ancestral faith began to wane. Some of its adherents simply dropped away, or, if they were members of the governing elite, kept up the appearances of the national civic cult while privately turning to the consolations of philosophy. Other Romans militantly reaffirmed "that old-time religion" as they understood it; still others borrowed, combined, and improvised. Decorous established ways of worship gave way to strange experimental cults, and the vital faiths of other lands, other civilizations, other social classes flowed in and displaced what had been that people's own.

Our own civilization, on Toynbee's hypothesis, apparently has yet quite some distance to go. America's twentieth-century magistrates, our Calvin Coolidges and Jerry Fords, have remained religious traditionalists; few if any have manifested much interest in philosophy. Even this century's more innovative Presidents, such as FDR and JFK, in their personal practice of religion have been safely conventional—and American political mores at present would not sanction anything else. In Rome, moreover, when the ruler changed his religion it made a real difference; in America, the republican-capitalist values brought to power in the revolution of 1776 may have made forever irrelevant the profession by a chief magistrate of any sectarian faith, whether orthodox or unorthodox. In any event we have not yet reached the point at which the Syrian Sun-god and Isis and Mithras have begun seriously to challenge Mars and Quirinus and the Capitoline Jupiter, and it is probably just as well.

CHAPTER IV

Science, Democracy, and Mystery

"A MAN in a faded gray raincoat and a flopping black felt hat that nearly concealed the gray hair that straggled over his ears stood on the boat deck of the steamship *Rotterdam* yesterday, timidly facing a battery of camera men. In one hand he clutched a shiny brier pipe and the other clung to a priceless violin." Thus on a spring day in 1921, with the Harding Administration not yet a month old, America was introduced to Albert Einstein. Reportedly not fluent in English, the shy, shaggy-locked visitor shook hands all round but gave no verbal interview. Newspaper reporters had to content themselves with physical description: "Under a high, broad forehead are large and luminous eyes, almost childlike in their simplicity and unworldliness." After he got ashore, correspondents competent in German took down his remarks, and a story duly appeared in next morning's *New York Times*:

EINSTEIN SEES END OF TIME AND SPACE

Destruction of Material Universe
Would Be Followed By Nothing,
Says Creator of Relativity

THEORY "LOGICALLY SIMPLE"

The destruction of the material universe had no great journalistic urgency, and even in the *Times* this account was relegated to page 5. The front page was devoted to more immediate matters: "Talk in Ireland of Peace and War"; "Harding Summons Rail Men's Leaders"; "Illinois Legion Protests Against Release of Debs"; and—familiar-enough reading for a Manhattan resident, then or today—"Two strangely shot in Madison Square Park; one of five bullets hits choir singer on way home from church . . . police unable to discover who fired the shots and why." Car dealers in Greater New York reported good spring sales, and baseball fans looked forward to the new season. Yet, strangely, the gentle visiting scientist was not lost in the shuffle. Thousands of New Yorkers turned out to greet the Einstein party at the pier, and some of them crowded into City Hall afterward for Mayor Hylan's reception.

Einstein himself seemed puzzled at the public interest shown in him and in his theories. Relativity did have some bearing on ultimate philosophy, the savant acknowledged, puffing on his pipe, but "the practical man does not need to worry about it." For some Americans, interest in his scientific theories merged into enthusiasm for the political cause he championed. Traveling in company with Chaim Weizmann and other Zionist leaders, Einstein was in this country to enlist American support for the yet-unborn State of Israel, and more specifically for the establishment of the Hebrew University on the Mount of Olives in Jerusalem. The *Chicago Tribune* picked up a cable from Germany that gave the Zionists' mission an ugly urgency: Rudolph Leibus, a fanatical nationalist, had recently urged the murder of Einstein, and paid the equivalent in marks of a $16 fine in a Berlin court for saying so. On New York's own City Council, alderman Bruce Falconer refused to vote the scientist the freedom of the city—the usual formality—and his vote prompted a shouting and fist-waving session on the Council floor. But Falconer denied being moved by "racial or religious prejudice"; his private physician was a Jew and many of his friends were Jews, the lawmaker asserted. Three days later he found fresh justification for his vote on the ground that Einstein had been born in Germany, with which the

United States—more than two years after the Armistice—was still technically at war. Therefore, pacifist and internationalist though he was, the physicist "might be regarded as an enemy alien," the councilman explained.

If Einstein was ruffled by this teapot tempest, he showed no sign. A German-speaking *Times* man sought out the Einsteins in their New York hotel and found the physicist bubbling with enthusiasm for America: "I like the way you light up the windows with the signs. I like the cheerful way you arrange the electricity up and down the streets. . . . And the movies? I am enthusiastic about them. . . . In general, the pictures shown now are not so artistic, but they will get better, very much better all the time."

Midway through the conversation Mrs. Einstein, whom the reporter described as "a charming little gray-haired lady," slipped in and sat down in a chair beside her husband. Perhaps the interviewer would like a copy of Einstein's book on relativity in an English translation, she suggested.

"No," said the professor. "Why that? He doesn't come here for relativity. He comes here to see me."

Other New Yorkers, some of them having even less knowledge of relativity than the *Times* man, came in droves to see Einstein. They jammed the Metropolitan Opera House to the doors for him and Weizmann; they rode up on the subway to Columbia and City College to hear Einstein lecture on relativity, in German and in halting textbook English. He journeyed to Princeton (later destined to afford him refuge from Hitler's tyranny) to receive an honorary D.Sc. He went to Washington for a meeting of the National Academy of Sciences; again speaking in German—a language, we must remember, that had been banned throughout much of America only three years earlier—Einstein voiced his hope "that the field of activity of scientific men may be reunited and that the whole world will soon again be bound together by common work."

While in Washington, he visited President Harding at the White House, prompting a headline: "Einstein Idea Puzzles Harding, He Admits as Scientist Calls." The puzzlement was bipartisan. Into a windy Senate debate on April 18 the flowery-tongued, white-mustached Democratic Senator John Sharp Williams of Mississippi interpolated a comment on the theory of relativity: "I frankly confess that I do not understand Einstein; I frankly confess that I do not believe the Senator from Pennsylvania understands Einstein; . . . and I do not believe that even the Senator from Massachusetts [Henry Cabot Lodge, with his Harvard Ph.D.!] would make a very positive pretense in that direction." But such expressions of bafflement were curiously mingled with affection. The *New York World* was struck by the fact that of all the recent distinguished visitors from abroad, including the Prince of Wales and Queen Marie of Romania, the one inspiring the most spontaneous popular demonstration had not been "a great general or statesman but a plain man of science. . . . It is something when New York turns out to honor a stranger bringing gifts of this recondite character." Nor was it all vulgar curiosity toward a celebrity, the *World* believed; the public was engaging in "a sincere tribute of admiration to the physicist who, amid the turmoil of war and the distraction of material interests, has kept his mind fixt on the star of pure science."

Albert Einstein's name over the next two decades became a kind of talisman. "Einstein" in the American vernacular became a synonym for "genius," particularly of the impractical or absent-minded variety. Certainly this European physicist's personal style was different from that of his American colleagues, as portrayed four years later by the *Independent* under the caption "Must Scientists Wear Whiskers?": "The fact is that in America . . . a convention of scientists, such as the American Association for the Advancement of Science annually brings together, is as clean-shaven, as youthful, and as jazzy as a foregathering of Rotarians." The author of the Special and General Theories of Relativity hardly fitted that stereotype of the scientist, "fully as much a man of the world as his brother, the business man." Indeed, Einstein's unworldliness may have been part of his charismatic appeal— especially considering that few then had any inkling where the harmless-looking equation $e = mc^2$ was going to lead.

"I have only two rules which I regard as principles of conduct," Einstein told an American journalist, M. K. Wisehart, who traveled to Berlin in 1930 to write him up for a U.S. popular magazine. "The first is: *have no rules.* The second is: *be independent of the opinion of others.*" For many Americans with no idea what he was talking about, Einstein's stubborn insistence upon going his own way had a familiar ring; in sixteen words he had summed up the self-reliance theme of Ralph Waldo Emerson. Ignoring his socialism and his mathematical rigor, the American businessman and the American bohemian could unite in admiring the man as a rugged individualist who was doing his own thing.

Perhaps also in the decade of the twenties Albert Einstein, with his disarming simplicity and his concentration on goals far transcending the corruptions of his times, filled a psychic need for some Americans in much the same way as did two other seemingly simple men, Charles Lindbergh and Calvin Coolidge: the Swiss-German-Jewish seer may have been another kind of Puritan in Babylon. Einstein's own obvious enjoyment of America was surely not unwelcome news for Americans, and his Zionism itself may have had an intrinsic appeal beyond the ethnic boundaries of New York, through its kinship with Puritan and pioneer traditions in the American past—however much America's own intellectuals in the twenties condemned both Puritanism and the frontier.

II

Not everyone loved Albert Einstein. One year after that triumphant first visit, even while American astronomers were making their way toward a desolate spot on Australia's northwest coast to observe a solar eclipse—and, they hoped, confirm or refute Einstein's most recent theory—that theory's author was forced temporarily to flee for his life from his homeland. Members of the same extremist group that had recently murdered Walter Rathenau, Germany's foreign minister, were threatening the same fate for Einstein and other prominent German Jews, including Theodor Wolff, editor of the *Berliner Tageblatt,* and the Hamburg banker Max Warburg. Passing over the fact that the cruel ideology then surging upward in Germany rarely excused its chosen enemies for their mild behavior, the *New York Times* expressed surprise that anybody should want to assassinate Dr.

Einstein: "He is gentleness personified, and it is incredible that he ever gave anybody any of the ordinary forms of offence." But perhaps the form of offense Einstein gave was not ordinary. That he was Jewish may have been less important than that he was incomprehensible.

According to another *Times* editorial, "The Declaration of Independence itself is outraged by the assertion that there is anything on earth, or in interstellar space, that can be understood only by the chosen few." *Self-evident* truth was what the Declaration had proclaimed, and some apparently felt that this must be the case not only in politics but also in science. "Newton's law of gravitation can be stated in a few simple sentences, and its essentials can be made clear to the average reader," complained Charles Lane Poor (himself a professor of celestial mechanics) in 1924. "The theory of Einstein . . . is, on the contrary, complicated in the extreme; it cannot be expressed in words. It is impossible to read the works of Einstein and his followers and from their words and phrases to know what they really mean." The implication was obvious: if a theory cannot be made clear to the general reader, it is probably invalid. In a democratic age, common sense was felt to be the property of common men.

Also, from the time of Francis Bacon to the time of Thomas Huxley, scientists themselves, whether aristocrats or democrats, had drummed it into the mind of Western man that science is "organized common sense." As a weapon against doctrines judged to be contrary to common sense—such as those of the Church— that slogan had at times been highly effective, and advocates of science were understandably reluctant to give it up. Therefore, to some conventional minds, the abstruse higher mathematics in which the new physics was phrased became the modern equivalent of religious mumbo-jumbo. One *Times* reader in 1922 expected a "battle royal to be waged between men of science, of which one class will fight with the brilliant and dazzling arms of mathematical formulae and the other with the dull yet solid weapon of applied common sense." In 1923 Captain T. J. J. See, an astronomer in the employ of the United States Navy, cried: "The Einstein doctrine that the ether does not exist, and that gravity is not a force, but a property of space, can only be described as a crazy vagary, a disgrace to our age!" It did not matter that the notion of an "ether"—an impalpable medium pervading all space, which transmitted light, electricity, and gravitation, but whose own existence was absolutely incapable of measurement— is on the face of it as wildly improbable an idea as anything dreamed up by Einstein. The wild idea of yesterday becomes the entrenched dogma of today. For the scientist as for any other man, Einstein himself once observed, common sense can be defined as a deposit of prejudices laid down in the mind prior to the age of eighteen.

But Einstein, as a physicist, also believed that even the wildest mathematical idea must have *some* verifiable relationship, however shadowy, with the world of "common sense." "For our purpose it is necessary to associate the fundamental concepts of geometry with natural objects," he told his Princeton hosts in 1921. One such natural object was the planet Mercury, whose eccentric orbit was predictable from Einstein's assumptions but unaccountable from Newton's. Another was the image of a star whose emitted rays had passed near the sun en route to Earth, photographed during a solar eclipse. According to Einstein the light would be displaced from its normal apparent position in the sky, bent by the sun's mass. In September 1922, to check out this strange idea, Americans from the Lick Observatory in California tramped through prickly desert scrub near Wallal Downs, a telegraph station in far western Australia, to put up their tents and temporary observatory in preparation for a total eclipse of the sun. On September 21 the appointed moment of darkness came; behind the black circle of the moon the sun's corona or halo appeared, displaying one streamer two and a quarter million miles long; the flickering bonfires of the solar prominences sprang into view. Five photographic plates were exposed before the moon passed by. A similar British venture in 1919, netting only seven star images, had been judged inconclusive; but when the Americans developed their plates after the 1922 eclipse they found they had bagged more than threescore stars. Measured by other astronomers who could not know the results beforehand, the pinpoint images averaged out to a mean displacement of 1.74 seconds of arc, almost exactly as the Einstein equations predicted.

Lick Observatory director W. W. Campbell, the expedition's leader, declared he was satisfied; the Lick Observatory would make no further efforts to verify Einstein. But that did not end the argument. Two months after those observations in Australia— and a few days after Einstein had been awarded the Nobel Prize—a special meeting of the Communist Party of the Soviet Union condemned Einstein's theory as "the product of the bourgeois class in decomposition . . . reactionary of nature, furnishing support for counter-revolutionary ideas." Some Americans, bourgeois or otherwise, concurred in this condemnation, if not in its Marxist rationale.

The theory of relativity became a staple item in collegiate and other public debates during the twenties. "Is Einstein Wrong?" asked the editors of the *Forum* in one typical symposium in 1924. Yes, argued Charles Poor; those "transformations" by which Einstein proposed to account for the slight kink in Mercury's orbit are what we used to call "approximations," no more. No, replied Archibald Henderson, "there are no errors of Einstein." It was not necessary that the hypotheses upon which relativity rested be "in accord with 'common sense' so-called, but simply that they fit the facts—that the relativistic calculations accord with observation and experiment." But they don't, Professor Poor insisted; the alleged refractions of starlight measured by the Lick Observatory expedition could be accounted for by distortions in the sun's corona or the earth's atmosphere. Mystified by this disagreement, Professor Irving Fisher of Yale—whose own discipline was economics, in those pre-Crash years a field hardly less arcane—concluded with resignation: "Astronomers and physicists must fight it out and the rest of us must wait."

Among the many who could not follow the mathematical pros and cons, some were not willing to wait. Far from resting contented with the conclusions of "common sense," imaginative listeners to such debates may have found in the strangeness of Einstein's theory precisely its appeal. "In place of gravitation, in place of the attraction of one body for another," wrote Professor Poor in what he intended as a rebuttal,

> Einstein substitutes a transcendental conception of warped space and of geodesic lines along which a body freely rolls. The sun does not attract the earth, it crumples up space, twists and warps space in some mystic fourth and even fifth dimension, and the earth, carried by its own inertia, wends its way along the easiest path amid the bumps and hollows of crushed and crumpled space. And in this four-dimensional space the ordinary laws of geometry do not apply.

None of this had much to do with stocks and bonds, or with any of the other supposed preoccupations of the twenties. And yet, pragmatic America from time to time throughout its history has been hospitable to transcendental conceptions. The descendants of those who yielded to the "Divine and Supernatural Light" with Edwards, or who affirmed with Emerson "the identity of the law of gravitation with purity of heart," may have found in Einstein their guide to the new century's *mysterium tremendum*.

III

Albert Einstein was not the only bearer of strange new tidings about the universe. Max Planck's quantum theory, wrote Edwin Slosson in 1922, was "quite as important and even more disconcerting to ordinary ideas than the relativity theory, but the public has not yet heard so much about it—perhaps because Planck is not so picturesque as Einstein." True, the prestige of science in some quarters might be at an all-time high—too high, in the opinion of some. A disapproving *Nation* editorial in 1928 lamented that "A sentence which begins with 'Science says' will generally be found to settle any argument in a social gathering, or sell any article from tooth-paste to refrigerator." But in these higher reaches it was by no means clear *what* "science says." In the previous century literary men had responded to what "science said" by writing Darwinist stories, poems, and essays; but (as Frederick Hoffman noted in his study *The Twenties*) despite a modish adoption of "relativity" as a catch-phrase by the literary *avant-garde*, nobody attempted to write an "Einsteinian" novel. Both the opponents and the defenders of Darwin assumed, not always correctly, that they understood him. In contrast, as *Harper's* said in 1929 of the Einstein theory, "We see an extraordinarily animated public interest in an alleged discovery which hardly anyone understands."

But events like the Scopes monkey trial showed that even the more "common-sense" variety of scientific endeavor in the twenties was imperfectly reported, and still more imperfectly understood. "Science, of late, has been good news," H. L. Mencken remarked in 1927. The newspapers, he went on, "discuss it copiously, and with a fine enthusiasm. But . . . they seldom discuss it with any intelligence." Anti-democratic conclusions could be drawn from such a judgment, and the Sage of Baltimore often drew them. But it is noteworthy that Albert Einstein, remote though he seemed from the common man, never did. "It is of great importance that the general public be given an opportunity to experience—consciously and intelligently—the efforts and results of scientific research," the physicist would write in 1948, after the atomic bomb had made the importance of that effort more painfully obvious. But who was to give the public that opportunity? The scientist—again, Einstein himself is an honorable exception—hardly qualified. "In the scientific world," Sir Richard Gregory told the British Association for the Advancement of Science in 1921, "the way to distinction is discovery, and not exposition, and rarely are the two faculties combined."

"How is scientific knowledge to be democratized?" the American historian James Harvey Robinson asked in a little book published in 1923, *The Humanizing of Knowledge:*

> Scholars and men of science almost always write more or less unconsciously for one another. This is a natural outcome of their training. They must prove their preparation to deal with the subject in hand. . . . The specter haunts them, not of a puzzled and frustrated reader, but of a tart reviewer, likely to accuse them of superficiality or inaccuracy. There is a heavy prejudice in learned circles against the popularizer.

As a result, Robinson argued, "Scientifically and philosophically trained writers apparently have no idea how hard their books and articles are for the general reader," and he proceeded to quote some horrible examples. Much of the difficulty was sheer pedantry, Robinson contended: "A considerable and beneficent revolution" could be wrought if only the college instructor and textbook writer would "confine himself, at least in addressing beginners or laymen, to telling only such facts as play so important a part in his own everyday thinking that he could recall them without looking them up!" Robinson was also aware of the infectiousness of enthusiasm: "It is a good rule for a writer to assume that nothing in his favorite subject that fails to interest *him* vividly and persistently is likely to interest the outsider who reads his book."

This is not an instance of the humanistic scholar condemning the scientist as a cultural barbarian; we are not listening in on the feud between Sir Charles Snow's "Two Cultures." Quite the contrary, Robinson's polemic grew out of a session at the 1922 meeting of the American Association for the Advancement of Science. By that time, in part moved politically by the popular anti-science sentiment manifest in the statutes that outlawed the teaching of evolution, America's scientific establishment had taken steps to put its own house in more comprehensible order. In 1921 "Science Service" was founded in Washington, D.C., as a scientific news syndicate on the model of the Associated Press. A circular of instructions to writers of articles for Science Service made it clear that advice like Robinson's had fallen on receptive ears:

> The first consideration . . . is to tell or interpret a scientific event. But the news stories must be so well written that large national newspapers will use them without rewriting or revision, either in form or language. Write your story so that those who know nothing about science will understand and want to read it. Weave in the scientific background that the man in the street does not have. Use simple words. Make your story as graphic as if you were talking about it.

Yet the writer must not achieve his simplification by distortion: " 'By Science Service' must stand for accuracy of content and implication." It was an exacting assignment the science news bureau set for its writers, and, in the case of news made by the likes of Einstein and Niels Bohr, a staggering one. But the first director of Science Service tackled his job with relish. Blond, broad-featured Edwin Emery Slosson, a native of Kansas, had long had a foot firmly planted in each of Lord Snow's "Two Cultures." A Ph.D. *magna* from the University of Chicago in its exciting early days, he had taught chemistry at the universities of Kansas and Wyoming; but he had also served as literary editor for *The Independent,* an esteemed journal of general opinion, for which he wrote vigorous and provocative editorials between 1903 and 1921. He had conducted a course in "physical science for journalists" at Columbia University's School of Journalism, and in 1920 he had undertaken to write on the scarcely easy theme *Easy Lessons in Einstein.* "He was able to interest anyone," asserts the *Dictionary of American Biography,* "not only in the accomplishments of science, but in science itself, without offending the purest of the scientists." Tirelessly he poured out articles, lectures, and publicity until his death in Washington on October 15, 1929, just nine days before the Great Crash. Standard accounts of the twenties never mention him, but of all the host of journalist-intellectuals who committed their thoughts to print during that decade he may ultimately have been one of the most influential.

Science Service evidently met a felt need; fifty newspapers in the United States and several in Canada promptly subscribed. By 1927 the agency had ventured also into radio broadcasting, with a "Science News of the Week" program carried over seventeen stations. At the end of that year the annual meeting of the A.A.A.S. held a symposium on "Science and the Newspapers." Such a session would not have been possible twenty years earlier, said David Dietz, science editor of the Scripps-Howard chain. The scientists would not have considered the subject dignified or proper or even ethical, and the newspapermen would have been uninterested. "Those were the days when science was synonymous with ten-syllable inunderstandable words, to be treated appropriately by the staff humorist and the cartoonist." H. L. Mencken's gibes, accordingly, had become out of date and unjustified. Indeed, two researchers studying "biology in the public press" concluded from their statistical analysis of 4,000 articles (some 26,000 column-inches) in fourteen prominent dailies that "newspapers appear to be more up-to-date in things biological than are college and high-school texts in the subject." They recommended, therefore, that teachers make use of newspaper articles in preference to those ponderously assembled textbooks whose ink was hardly dry before they were obsolete.

Books as well as newspapers carried the popular scientific message. By 1927 an "Outline of Science" had sold 100,000 copies; George A. Dorsey's *Why We Behave Like Human Beings* had been a best-seller for three years; and the titles in a Library of Modern Sciences—such as *Stories in Stone, Animals of Land and Sea, The Earth and the Stars*—were reportedly doing well. And the next generation's attention was being engaged; thousands of children were writing entries for a national prize essay contest in chemistry. The commercial potential here was great, and so was the temptation to pad sales by sensational or overly simple writing at the expense of accuracy. One book publisher's secretary-treasurer, Robert S. Gill of Williams & Wilkins, warned against the latter tendency: "If the gospel is really to be spread, it must have a multitude of patrons, not a multitude of the patronized."

IV

But how was the gospel to be spread to the kind of busy citizens who felt, in those booming twenties, that they literally could not afford to take time out to read anything in the newspaper beyond the financial page, let alone a whole book? Harrison E. Howe, editor of *Industrial and Engineering Chemistry,* told the A.A.A.S.'s symposium on science and the press that it was futile to begin with fundamental research if one were to arouse interest among such Americans. "The businessman, indeed the professional man, prefers to have you begin with something with which he is familiar—the milk bottle, a cake of soap, a mirror, his automobile." But was this assertion really true? To take so prosy an approach was to overlook the perennial lure of whatever is different and far-off—a lure to which educators were (and are) largely immune. But Edwin Slosson told the American Association for Adult Education in 1928 "that archeology and astronomy—essentially remote and unpractical—head the list of the sciences in order of popular interest, and that the essentially practical sciences are low on the list." Slosson ascribed this preference "to the same cause as that operating in the selection of, say, 'futuristic art' as a subject of study in a women's club rather than 'domestic economy.' " Well might a liberated woman who had had quite enough of domestic economy, thank you, have cried "Right on!" And perhaps her spouse also might have craved more from science than counsel for managing his investments.

To insist relentlessly upon the practical was also to overlook one of science's appeals to its own practitioners. The man in the street conceivably might admire the scientist's self-sacrificing dedication or appreciate the contributions of science to human welfare; he rarely suspected that the scientist was also enjoying himself. "Enthusiasm and fun charge the atmosphere at Leiden, Cambridge, Cornell, and Johns Hopkins," wrote one contributor to the A.A.A.S.'s austere *Scientific Monthly* in 1928. The scientist might express his own enthusiasm and joy "on a Saturday afternoon working in a laboratory, perhaps malodorous and dark," while others were displaying theirs "standing in the rain and getting sore throats yelling 'Block that kick!' " But if the latter saw "no fun in looking through a microscope or scrutinizing test tubes or listening to radio signals coming from half way round the world, nothing is proved. It all depends on what kind of fun one likes best." If the problem was one of "humanizing" the scientist for the layman, this might have been one of the most effective solutions; the twenties, an era of Babbitt busyness, were also a time of energetic hedonism.

Moreover, to dwell upon the milk bottle, the cake of soap, the mirror, the automobile was to leave the job of science education half-done. It was in effect to substitute technology for science. "The scientists have gone off all by themselves and made a magic that even they didn't foresee," wrote Robert L. Duffus in *Collier's* for January 12, 1924. "This magic is transportation and great cities and wars and Ford factories and much else. . . . [But] these are the mere by-products of science, the symbol and pro-phecy of its coming power for good or evil." The common man had taken these gifts of science but otherwise gone on in his accus-tomed unscientific way, "thinking with his spinal column, his liver, his adrenal glands—with anything but his brain." And the common man, in his capacity as a citizen, could not afford thus to let others do all the thinking about science for him. "Science, represented not by a few specialists in laboratories, but by all of us, must make possible a planned civilization. The present one is haphazard rather than planned, and—well, take a good look at it yourself."

George Horace Lorimer, the doggedly reactionary editor of the *Saturday Evening Post,* who later became an ardent foe of the New Deal, would have bristled at the idea of a "planned civili-zation." But he shared in this worry that basic, theoretical science was being hustled offstage by its more glamorous sibling. "The Science sisters, Pure and Applied, are a strange pair," Lorimer wrote in a 1926 *Post* editorial:

> Applied in the starry-eyed goddess, the wonder worker, who gets on the first page of newspapers and captivates the imagination of men. She speaks the language of the people, gives them what they want, and every year perfects new gifts to make life easier or longer or more amusing. . . . She is her own press agent and the sun never sets on the advertising she gets. . . .
>
> Pure Science is the wallflower, the elder sister who lives secluded and remote, unknown and unpraised. She does not advertise her as-tounding feats, and could not if she would, for the only language she knows is a jumble of Latin, Greek, calculus, and mathematical for-mulas. Only a few professors can understand what she is driving at.

The past thirty years, for basic theoretical science, had been the most fruitful in the world's history. In due course, the *Post* editor predicted, technology would harvest those findings and get the credit, while Pure Science continued to starve in her usual ob-scurity.

Charles E. Wilson, President of General Motors in the late for-ties and afterward Dwight Eisenhower's Secretary of Defense, once said he opposed spending good hard money on basic research, explaining that he didn't care what made potatoes turn brown when they were fried. Some of his Establishment forebears in the twenties seem, on this point at least, to have been more enlightened. In the belief that "the funds now available for the support of research in pure science in the United States are far below what our population, education and material resources demand," leaders in science, business, and politics created a National Research Endowment to support fundamental scientific investigation. Among them were A. A. Michelson, the measurer of the speed of light; Robert Millikan, the first American physicist to have won a Nobel Prize; George Ellery Hale, director of the mighty Mount Wilson Observatory; John J. Carty, vice-president of American Tel & Tel; Owen Young, board chairman of General Electric; Treasury Secretary and financial entrepreneur Andrew Mellon; former Presidential candidates Charles Evans Hughes and John W. Davis; and elder statesmen Elihu Root and Colonel E. M. House.

"It is true that money cannot buy genius, but many a genius in science has defaulted because he has had to eat," declared Herbert Hoover, who logically and inevitably became chairman of the National Research Endowment's board. America did not lack competent scientific researchers, he affirmed, but "with the comfort of their families at heart, such men reluctantly accept well-paid industrial positions instead of poorly paid academic posts." National Research Endowment support would, Hoover hoped, give able investigators the "comfort in life, freedom of action and opportunity for constructive thought that industrial and administrative officers in this country, certainly of no larger calibre, habitually enjoy."

The profit angle was of course present; the pure science of today nourishes the technology of tomorrow, which produces the dividends of the day after. Even the rarefied field of astrophysics, A.T.&T.'s John Carty testified, had "useful" applications. Still, it is interesting that Herbert Hoover—so often typecast as the "Great Engineer," with an engineer's limited intellectual and social vision—should have considered "the discovery of a law of nature" to be "a far greater advance" than a study in an industrial laboratory leading to the improvement of some process or machine. "We must add to knowledge," Hoover concluded, "both for the intellectual and spiritual satisfaction that comes from widening the range of human understanding, and for the direct practical utilization of these fundamental discoveries." "The pure scientists," Carty cried, "are the advance guard of civilization."

V

"A new idea comes first in the mind of one man. That means that the new idea starts out in the world with a majority of 1,600,000,000 against it," wrote Edwin Slosson in 1926. "This instinctive mass reaction against new ideas . . . is essentially the same as the common aversion to a foreigner: 'E's a stranger. 'Eave 'arf a brick at 'im." Although the director of Science Service was careful to point out that scientists themselves were no more immune to this tendency to "neophobia" than other kinds of men, to some extent such an argument nonetheless smacks of elitism. In the country of the blind the one-eyed man is king, and at least the scientist has the one eye. "Newton's law would never have passed if it depended upon a popular vote," and even today, in a plebiscite of the entire planet, Slosson believed, "the Copernican theory would be repealed by an immense majority." Copernican and Newtonian, not to mention Einsteinian, theories are not something the masses will discover if left to themselves.

With this leader-follower point of view pervading the writings of the science publicists, it is small wonder that their outpourings were taken in some quarters not as enlightening instruction but as arrogant propaganda. This backlash was especially apparent in the evolution controversy, as the transcript of the Darrow-Bryan clash at Dayton, Tennessee, in 1925 made painfully clear:

MR. BRYAN: Your Honor, it isn't proper to bring experts in here to try to defeat the purpose of the people of this state. . . .
MR. DARROW: You insult every man of science and learning in the world because he does not believe in your fool religion!

It should be remembered that the trial judge made both men apologize.

Despite the attempts at a cease-fire between science and religion (noted in our previous chapter), the need to combat what they considered to be "fool religion" was implicit in many of the science publicists' writings. At that 1927 A.A.A.S. symposium on "Science and the Newspapers," for example, William E. Ritter spoke of "the necessity of displacing the legendary, mythical and merely authoritarian knowledge which has constituted [man's] theology by his verified and verifiable experiential knowledge of himself and the world." But perhaps all that this showed was that the science educator himself was as much in need of updating his world view as were those whom he hoped to educate. Terms like *verified* and *verifiable* had become a good deal more slippery than they had seemed to Thomas Huxley, and some (but by no means all) scientists who breathed the new relativistic atmosphere were deciding that science was after all reconcilable with theism. In a sense, science was suffering through a generation gap. In 1928 James Truslow Adams argued that the scientific assumption of a previous generation, namely mechanistic materialism, had hardened into a present popular dogma, whose blind advocates were as bigoted as anybody living in Dayton, Tennessee: "Were the citizens of our cities and graduates of our high schools really so much more intelligent than the shirt-sleeve mountaineers? Do they really know so much more about the universe?"

Politically troublesome questions were being raised by the new explainers of science also. When a writer for Science Service's *Science News Letter* in 1927 described the mulattoes of North America as combining "something of a white man's intelligence and ambition with an insufficient intelligence to realize that ambition," such a statement could be taken merely as a reflection of the incompleteness of scientific knowledge itself; in the twenties, scientists' opinions on race were very much in a state of flux. But specific changes in scientific knowledge could not abate a certain conservative, even anti-political, streak that ran through the popularizers' writings, Edwin Slosson's in particular. "It is an old saying in political history that 'revolutions never go backward,'" Slosson wrote in 1922 to introduce a series of articles for the news monthly *World's Work* on "Science Remaking the World." "Perhaps they never do, but sometimes it seems that they don't go forward either. . . . The political revolution is too much like the

automobile motor when the gear is disengaged. It makes a lot of
noise and some explosions and throws out a lot of hot air, but it
does not move the car of progress." What, then, did move that car?
Slosson's answer was explicit:

> The extension of democracy which the politician promises is being
> widely accomplished by the scientist who, by placing the exclusive
> luxuries of former ages within the lives of all, raises the humblest to
> a higher plane. The democracy of science is a leveling-up process
> while the democracy of the communist is a leveling-down process.

Warren Harding himself might have said "Amen." This was the
same social conservatism that had been argued years earlier by
William Graham Sumner, the laissez-faire champion, in his essay
"The Absurd Effort to Make the World Over." Later in that series
on "Science Remaking the World," Slosson illustrated his point in a
way that cried down not only revolution but even ordinary political
persuasion. When Roentgen discovered the X-ray, according to
Slosson, he had not had to found an "International Society for the
Conversion of the World to the Idea of the X-Rays":

> He did not have to raise an endowment fund and hire a salaried
> staff, organize a corps of local organizers, and publish a weekly
> organ. No, he simply announced his discovery in a modest paper
> that you can read in ten minutes . . . but in a few months every
> laboratory in the world was taking X-ray photographs. Yet the X-ray
> has really accomplished more in the world than many a reform
> movement that makes a great noise and requires tremendous effort.

Slosson did concede in this article that "science provides the motive power, but not the motive for the use of power." Yet that is a
most important hedge. To motivate such use, noise and effort and
conceivably even revolution—and organization for those purposes—might after all have a place in the scientific scheme of
things.

Edwin Slosson might have done better had he taken a hint from
one of the men he so successfully popularized. Albert Einstein's
civic passions—Zionism, pacifism, socialism, world government—were as much a part of the man as the equations with which
he attempted to unlock the riddle of the universe, even though the

social concerns were not expressed with the same logical clarity as
the equations. Nor were these political commitments something
Einstein indulged in merely as a private or nonscientific person
after he had closed the door of his laboratory. Many Americans
know by now that Albert Einstein in 1939 signed a letter to Franklin Roosevelt, as a result of which that obscure formula $e = mc^2$
was translated into the most terrifying kind of everyday reality.
(Einstein apparently did not *write* that letter; his associates in
science and politics had to use his universally familiar name, as
"Mr. Scientist," in order to capture FDR's sometimes maddeningly
short attention span.) Not so many Americans are aware that Albert
Einstein was afterward instrumental in founding the Federation of
Atomic Scientists, a group of savants who responsibly labored in
the arena of public and political persuasion for the purpose of
bringing the jinn they had let out of the bottle back under control.

At the 1927 meeting of the British Association for the Advancement of Science the Bishop of Ripon suggested that the scientists
take a ten-year holiday, during which their laboratories would all
be closed "and the patient and resourceful energy displayed in
them transferred to recovering the lost art of getting together."
"Science has been leading us rather a giddy chase for the last two
or three decades," said the *Chicago Evening Post*, and as a
result the good bishop's feeling was shared by multitudes. But such
a proposal was quixotic. "It is not possible to call a halt," Sir Oliver
Lodge replied. "If we stopt, the world would go to pieces." To
hold the pieces in place it would indeed be necessary to recover—
or discover—the art of getting together. But closing the laboratory
doors was not the way to achieve it. One of the ways people had to
get together was precisely in their respective capacities as scientist
and citizen.

Fifty years later, both the bishop's proposal and the physicist's
reply have their ardent partisans. To have contended that science
should remake the world without check or interference from the
politicians (or the people) may have been irresponsible, a surren-
der on Edwin Slosson's part to the self-satisfied complacency that
was also part of the spirit of the twenties. But to have anticipated
Sir Charles Snow's "Two Cultures" argument, and interpreted it to

mean that the layman must abandon *any* attempt to understand and socially apply the insights of science because the scientist and the non-scientist can not now speak to each other at all, would have been more irresponsible still. Neither politically nor intellectually have we worked our way out of this problem.

CHAPTER V

Prohibition and the Democratic Faith

"ARE YOU a bit disappointed not to find some beer in our dining rooms?"

The question was one any foreign visitor to the United States in 1921 had to expect. Albert Einstein fielded it gracefully. "I cannot say alcohol is as bad as people think it is," he mildly replied. But nevertheless: "Prohibition shows the strength of your democratic Government against private interests. In a corrupt State this could not be done."

"Do you consider it against personal liberty to take liquor away?" the persistent interviewer asked.

"How could that be in America?" the scientist innocently replied. "You have a republic. You have no dictator who makes slaves of people. Nothing that is done by a democratic Government could be done against freedom."

That statement may tell us less about American life in the twenties than it does about the democratic idealism of Albert Einstein. Rarely today do we consider Prohibition as having been an affirmation of democratic principles; in the twenties it was regularly attacked as a denial of them. And yet, the European visitor to these shores could have found many Americans who justified the Noble Experiment as a natural extension of their national ideals.

In the words of James H. Timberlake, Middle America had enacted Prohibition in the first place "out of an earnest desire to revitalize and preserve American democracy." Like other efforts to revitalize and preserve democracy at about the same time, such as Woodrow Wilson's declaration of war against Germany, that crusade was destined for repudiation. Taking effect at midnight on January 16, 1920, the Eighteenth Amendment marked the opening of a decade when Americans realized that any formerly existing democratic common front had been shattered. The dilemma Prohibition presented for democrats was poignantly expressed in Ring Lardner's humorous novel, *The Big Town* (1925):

> "What makes we New Yorkers sore is to think they should try and wish a law like that on Us. Isn't this supposed to be a government of the people, for the people and by the people?"
> "People!" I said. "Who and the hell voted for Prohibition if it wasn't the people?"
> "The people of where?" he says.

Some in the twenties affirmed their belief in a revitalized democracy, but insisted that for the accomplishment of that goal Prohibition would have to go. Others, equally opposed to Prohibition, denied that democracy's preservation was desirable, arguing that the anti-liquor law was a dreadful example of the consequences to which unsupervised democracy could lead. Herbert Agar, for example, saw in the enactment of Prohibition a striking demonstration that the majority is incompetent to decide a question in its own best interest, and concluded that the right to vote should be sharply restricted; in short, democracy can be saved only by its partial denial. Similarly, H. L. Mencken fulminated against the "democratic pestilence," which had reached its fullest development in America and resulted in "such obscenities as Comstockery, Prohibition, and the laws against the teaching of evolution."

Disillusion was a factor in the powerful and eventually successful drive for Prohibition's repeal, and by the logic of hindsight we have tended to apply that disillusion retroactively, as a historical judgment of our own upon the Noble Experiment. Nevertheless, alongside the democratic "wet" liberals like Clarence Darrow and the anti-democratic wet cynics like H. L. Mencken, throughout the twenties there were some "dry" Americans who maintained that by their efforts American democracy had not only been revitalized and preserved but also given a great push forward. Harry S. Warner, for example, writing in 1928 under the imprint of the World League Against Alcoholism, answered the "personal liberty" question in the same way Albert Einstein had answered the interviewer: he titled his book *Prohibition, An Adventure in Freedom.* The Volstead Law, Warner contended, had not been imposed upon an uncomprehending electorate by a well-organized fanatic minority in a brief period of war hysteria, as wet folklore so often claimed. Quite the contrary; it was the climax of "one hundred years of trial and error," during which the temperance forces had tried every other possible approach to liquor control and found them all ineffective. Prohibition met all the tests of proper democratic action: the test of time, the test of full discussion, the test of decisive majority expression (forty-six of the forty-eight states had, after all, ratified the constitutional change).

By the time this dry rationale was written Walter Lippmann had already published his cautionary essay *The Phantom Public,* and today, wiser in the ways of public relations, we may be more skeptical than Harry Warner was about the import of electoral majorities, however decisive. And yet the sociological categories suggested in Joseph Gusfield's *Symbolic Crusade,* of "assimilative" as against "coercive" social reformers—the one perceiving the drinker as a deviant who must be persuaded to accept the reformer's values, and the other judging the drinker as an enemy who must be prevented from flouting those values—are altogether too simplistic in that they obscure the reformer's own self-image as an underdog. As Warner saw the matter, the wets, by playing Goliath to the drys' David, had inadvertently helped the temperance cause. The year-in, year-out hostility of the Eastern metropolitan press and of the organized liquor interests, "with millions of dollars invested yearly in wet news, publicity material, speakers and in the influencing of public officials, legitimately and illegitimately," had successfully "retarded prohibition," and thereby "helped to insure the democratic process against hasty action."

Harry Warner was not alone in this judgment that Prohibition had been a political triumph of the popular over the powerful. In radical language jarringly out of phase with its usual dowager tones—then or today!—the *Ladies' Home Journal* for March 1923 declared: "The prohibition embroilment is shaping its course as an inevitable class issue. The fashionable rich demand their rum as an inalienable class privilege," crying " 'To hell with the benefits to the poor there may be in prohibition!' " In similar vein Roy A. Haynes in his book *Prohibition Inside Out*, also published in 1923, expressed scorn for "the remnant of the old organization of manufacturers and dealers of liquor in pre-prohibition days, learning nothing by experience, forgetting nothing, wearing in its heart a Bourbon hope of its return to the throne of debauchery from which it was hurled by the wrath of the American people." Endorsed in a "Foreword by the late President Harding," an irony many Americans would not have perceived at the time, Haynes's book concluded: "It is the beverage liquor interests, the criminals, the vice-capitalists who *fear* we shall succeed. It is the leaders of the world who *wonder* if we shall succeed. It is the 'little people' of the world who *hope* we shall succeed."

II

From a post-Depression perspective, we know that a great many of the "little people" who voted for Franklin Roosevelt in 1932 voted also for Repeal the following year. The theme song of the 1932 Democratic national convention, "Happy Days Are Here Again," has often been described as prophetic of a forthcoming new deal for the American people. But to some in that joyous hall it may have meant primarily the prospect of legal beer. Here, however, the wisdom of hindsight may be a positive handicap. Four years earlier, when the doggedly dry Herbert Hoover defeated the pro-Repeal candidate Al Smith, it was not so clear which was the more genuinely popular side. In effect, Harry Warner told his wet opponents in 1928, we have both played in the same game of marshalling public opinion for a democratic decision, and our side won. As Lord Bryce had put it long before in his *Modern Democracies*, "The prohibition movement has not proceeded from any one class or section of the community"; it grew "mainly because it appealed to the moral and religious sentiments of the plain people." As such, Warner concluded, its victory called for democratic acquiescence by the wet minority.

Who were the members of this wet minority? Warner divided them into the "missed"—those whom the drys had not yet reached to educate or persuade—and the "opposition." In the latter category he grouped the "social drink users," whose position he dismissed as elitist and undemocratic; "the group with an alcoholic appetite," whose problem he saw as transitory ("Most of these men are well along in life; they will pass on"); those with "adventure or bravado motives," which he also saw as transitory ("Being prompted by adventure, it tends to be temporary . . . young men and women do grow older"); the "self-privileged," who chose for themselves which laws they would obey, a position Warner also saw as fundamentally undemocratic; and finally "the trade, formerly legal, now illegal." For all the newfound affluence of entrepreneurs like Al Capone, Warner affirmed that drinking in America was doomed; the Noble Experiment was here to stay. Its remaining wet opponents, he conceded, were free to use the same methods of persuasion the drys had had to adopt before gaining the sanction of constitution and law, but they must not engage in undemocratic shortcuts such as nullification.

But there remained the nagging question of personal liberty, even against decisions democratically made on behalf of decisive majorities. The Prohibition controversy illustrated the old dilemma so painfully recognized by Abraham Lincoln during the Civil War: "Must a government, of necessity, be too *strong* for the liberties of its own people, or too *weak* to maintain its own existence?" Prohibitionist Harry Warner tried to turn the argument in a different direction: "Is 'personal liberty,' not in the abstract but definitely in the lives of men, women and children, greater where drink goes out, even with the aid of the heavy hand of the law, than it is where drink remains?" To support his own answer to that question he cited a writer as far from the usual godly, church-going, uptight stereotype of the dry as could well have been imagined, namely Bernard Shaw:

> If a natural choice between drunkenness and sobriety were possible, I should leave the people free to choose. But when I see enormous capitalist organizations pushing drink under people's noses at every corner and pocketing the price, whilst leaving me and others to pay the colossal damages, then I am prepared to smash that organization and make it as easy for a poor man to be sober if he wants to as it is for his dog.

But what if a poor man considered that option and then, of his own free choice, rejected it? Even then, Warner contended, temperance could be construed as an affirmation of personal liberty rather than as its negation. Far from being a suppression of individual freedom, Prohibition was "the liberation of the individual from the illusion of freedom that is conveyed by alcohol." In this respect, the drys' argument against liquor resembled the Marxists' argument against religion; they saw the alcohol "high" as a surrogate for effective action, which prevented the exercise of any real freedom of decision. Further on in his polemic Warner quoted a former United Mine Workers president, Tom L. Lewis (not to be confused with John), as having said that "there is no easier way possible to make the unfortunate man, or the oppressed worker, content with his misfortune than a couple of glasses of beer." If the workingman in America of that period had largely left the church, as the statistics indicate he had, then perhaps religion had been displaced by a more powerful—or at least more congenial—opiate for the people!

Historically, Warner pointed out, the question of personal choice had been raised in the first place not by the wets but by their dry opponents. Paradoxically, prohibitionism had grown up in the first place among that sector of the population—the old-stock WASPs—which traditionally had been regarded as the most individualistic. Within the temperance movement itself, the debate over "personal liberty" had been intense ever since the time of Lyman Beecher, who for all the vehemence of his temperance views had opted for moral suasion and had opposed legal coercion. But times had changed: "No one now would care to have such forms of personal liberty as freedom to duel, to keep slaves, to sell narcotics to all who call, exist again freely. . . . They are out of date, and for the same reason that auto speeding is restricted in a crowded city." (On this last point the Flivver King himself concurred: "Booze," said Henry Ford, "had to go out when modern industry and the motor car came in.") Far from being nostalgic or reactionary, therefore, from the standpoint of dry apologists like Harry Warner the Prohibition movement contemplated "a new order of civilization."

The modern view, Warner argued—for all the world like an academic sociologist—is that the claims of the individual must be balanced against those of family and society. Man is not an autonomous atom; "he is also a member of a community, a citizen, a father, a taxpayer, a fellow worker. . . . Or he is an auto-driver . . . whose freedom and happiness are limited by the sobriety of other drivers." The trouble with the "personal liberty" argument was that the consequences of the excesses of drink could "not be confined to the drinker; that the worst burdens fall, not upon him who becomes intoxicated, but upon those who suffer because of the toxic habits of others." In short, this dry advocate put down the rugged individualism of the drinker in much the same fashion that the New Deal's advocates would later put down the rugged individualism of that conscientious dry, Herbert Hoover! If the drys in general did not realize that an effort to be one's brother's political keeper had sinister statist implications, neither did most of the New Dealers.

III

To be sure, this particular experiment in social control—or, if one prefers, social liberation—ultimately failed; and the drys themselves conceded that an important component in that failure was "the disintegration of popular support." But they tended to

attribute that loss of support to public misunderstanding abetted
by well-financed wet propaganda. Here again our post-Repeal
perspective can be an interpretive pitfall. Three-point-two beer
was indeed one of the earliest fruits of Franklin Roosevelt's
Hundred Days, and Jim Farley did make ratification of the
Twenty-First Amendment a matter of party regularity in the
Democratic state organizations. But some dry observers at the time
were inclined to see Repeal as the handiwork not of insurgent popular democracy but of the economic royalists. In addition to the vote of the common man, Roosevelt in 1932 also received the vote of Pierre S. du Pont, primarily because of the
liquor question—a choice the industrial baron of Wilmington,
Delaware, speedily regretted.

"If the American people had had respect for all laws, good or
bad, there would have been no Boston Tea Party." Sympathy
with some of the crusades and confrontations of more recent years
may have inclined us to sympathize with such a statement from
the 1920s. But a quotation must also be carefully identified by its
source. In this case it was the elder William Randolph Hearst,
who was then at the height of his Red-baiting and Oriental-hating
career; he has not ordinarily been identified in political folklore as
a tribune of the people.

Hearst said those provocative words on April 26, 1929, as he
launched a temperance essay contest in the *New York
American*. (The first prize of $25,000 was won by Franklin
Chase Hoyt, presiding judge of a children's court in New York
City, who advocated leaving the Eighteenth Amendment intact
but amending the Volstead Act to define "intoxicating liquors" as
"all alcohol products of distillation" (e.g., gin, brandy, whisky)—
in effect a return to the old "ardent spirits" definition of Lyman
Beecher and Benjamin Rush.) It is a truism that social action in
America requires organization, and organization costs money. For
that purpose $25,000 prizes even in 1929 were, comparatively
speaking, trifles. More to the point, as Methodist Board of Temperance spokesman Deets Pickett later argued, was that of the
total contributions received in 1929 by the Association Against the

Prohibition Amendment, 75 percent was given by only fifty-two men.

Fletcher Dobyns in a book entitled *The Amazing Story of Repeal*, published in 1940, dug a little further into the historic antecedents of the AAPA. The Association's first president, William H. Stayton, had been executive secretary of the old Navy League, an industrial elite group whose doings have been probed many times by progressive and Left journalists and historians. In 1926, according to Dobyns, a new group took over the leadership of the Association Against the Prohibition Amendment, while retaining Stayton as president. Prominent in this group were Pierre, Irénée, and Lammot du Pont; John J. Raskob of General Motors (in dissent, as usual, from Ford!); and Charles H. Sabin, director of sixteen large corporations and chairman of Guaranty Trust of New York, a Morgan bank. (Other, more obviously self-interested contributors included Fred Pabst, the Schaefer Brewing Company, Colonel Jacob Ruppert, W. Fred Anheuser, and August A. Busch.)

With telling effect, Dobyns quoted a letter dated March 24, 1928, from Wilmington, Delaware, by Pierre du Pont; it was addressed to William P. Smith, Director of the AAPA:

> Dear Bill:
> I shall be glad if you will make known to the officials of the *Saturday Evening Post* my personal interest in the affairs of the Association Against the Prohibition Amendment, also the interest of my brothers Irénée and Lammot. I feel that the *Saturday Evening Post* is intimately related to both the General Motors Corporation and the du Pont Company and that the aim of this paper is to promote the welfare of the people of the United States. As I feel that the prohibition movement has failed in its original aim and has become both a nuisance and a menace, I hope that the officials of the *Saturday Evening Post* will join in a move toward better things.

Dobyns also neatly reversed the wets' old argument that Prohibition had been foisted upon the masses by minority pressures during an abnormal wartime situation. It was rather the wets, he contended, who had pushed Repeal through to ratification in 1933 while the Depression was still at its peak and the people desperate, ready to listen to any promise—before they had had a chance for (so to speak) sober second thoughts. And they had been duped, Dobyns intimated, by the men of the AAPA, for whom Repeal was not a struggle for popular liberty but rather a "struggle to save themselves hundreds of millions of dollars by substituting for the income tax a liquor tax to be paid by the masses." Battling in 1930 against the rising tide of Repeal, the assistant pastor of one busy urban parish emphatically concurred: "The power of the church really unleashed can overcome any 40 billion dollar clique of business men who want to get revenue for the government and dodge their corporation taxes." Conceding that "good people who want prohibition have been fooled into voting against their own convictions," this clergyman argued that in the long run the popular will would prevail, and that, in spite of apparent evidence to the contrary, that will was dry.

The artlessly Marxist implications in this type of reasoning were soon obscured, however, because the crusading radical bitterness against those "vested interests" which supported Repeal merged unexpectedly into Old Guard Republican bitterness against the Roosevelt Administration which actually accomplished Repeal. Fletcher Dobyns's case was argued with restraint and backed by substantial documentation, but for perspective it must be set alongside a similar book by Ernest Gordon published in 1943, *The Wrecking of the Eighteenth Amendment*, the tone of which is almost hysterically anti-FDR. Yet even that less savory tract for the times contained a lengthy chapter on "Wall Street and Repeal," followed by a chapter on "The Press and Prohibition"; the latter takes on added significance now that we have learned more about mass-media manipulation.

Gordon thought the anti-clerical image of the ministry that one finds so strikingly in the media of the twenties was specifically and consciously the work of wet interests: "The Protestant ministers have for years been the ones to clean up after the distillers and brewers. They have helped the alcohol-sick at their own doors and in little missions," and for this they have suffered "an

attack . . . unparalleled in American history, in movie and theatre, in novel and magazine and newspaper." This charge strikingly resembles the "conspiracy" thesis that had been so dear to
the hearts of the Populists, and it is subject to the same criticisms
that have been made of that thesis. (On the other hand, we
should not therefore assume without further examination that the
charge is entirely unfounded.) A cartoon by a liberal Methodist
minister of the pre-Repeal period vividly captured this aspect of
the controversy: it depicted a roly-poly figure labeled "the real
'Repealer' " hiding behind a cadaverous dummy attired in "Puritan" costume complete with high-crowned hat and buckled shoes.
The scarecrow was labeled "Caricature of the Dry Cause."

In short, the victory for personal liberty contained in the
Twenty-First Amendment was more ambiguous than it seemed.
Not all the right-wing elitism was on one side, nor was all the left-
wing democratic liberalism on the other. In other words, the fight
over Repeal was a more *normal* kind of American political controversy than we have usually assumed.

In addition to the Association Against the Prohibition Amendment, its organizational heir the American Liberty League,
founded in August of 1934, must share in this ambiguity. The
name "Liberty League" might have had a "liberal" connotation
when those tycoons' energies were being directed toward the
overthrow of Prohibition; but scant months later it carried quite
another, as they were directed into a last-ditch defense of unham-
pered private enterprise against the assaults of the New Deal. In
particular we should remember that Al Smith—so symbolically
important a political figure in the America of the twenties—was
active both in the AAPA and in the Liberty League. Sometimes
his activity in the latter has been charged off to personal pique at
Roosevelt over the outcome of the 1932 nominating convention;
in any case it is questionable whether the traditional clear-cut
"liberal" image of the pre-1932 Al Smith can hold. But there is a
chicken-and-egg problem here. Was Smith's activity in the American Liberty League merely a sign that his latent conservatism—sensed by Walter Lippmann as early as 1925—had at last
come to the fore? Or did it show, rather, an urban liberal's intu-

itive concern that illiberalism might lurk behind the New Deal's liberal façade?

IV

None of these ambiguities are resolved by the fact that the wets and the drys both contrived to make their case sound underdog. "We are working against a highly-organized, well-financed body of Drys," declared Mrs. John B. Casserly on April 14, 1931, "who have made it their business to obtain control of the key positions in our whole system of government." But this is of course a standard gambit of the "outs" against the "ins," of whatever stripe; Mrs. Casserly was speaking before a highly organized, well-financed body of wets, the Women's Organization for National Prohibition Reform. Its founder and president was Mrs. Charles H. Sabin, and her husband, as we have seen, was a leading figure both in the equivalent association for men and in the national business establishment. Other founders of the WONPR included Mrs. Pierre du Pont, Mrs. August Belmont, Mrs. J. Roland Harrison, Mrs. Coffin Van Rensselaer, and Mrs. R. Stuyvesant Pierrepont—hardly the representatives an American democrat in the Jackson-Bryan tradition would have chosen to typify "the little people of the world."

To dry apologist Fletcher Dobyns, it was inconceivable "that the women of America had transferred their intellectual and spiritual allegiance from women like Frances E. Willard, Jane Addams, Evangeline Booth, Carrie Chapman Catt and Ella Boole"—dry champions all—"to such women as Mrs. Sabin, Mrs. du Pont, Mrs. Belmont and Mrs. Harriman." It was, rather, a public relations triumph engineered by fashionable society. "If . . . the members of this set have something they want to put over, they have only to issue invitations to teas and meetings at their houses, or request people to serve on committees with them, and the social climbers will fall all over themselves in the enthusiasm of their response." Once more the struggle of wets and drys was seen as a struggle of the classes and the masses, at least from the standpoint of the drys.

In fact, one of the most effective weapons a WONPR spokeswoman could use was an elitist put-down of their opponents. "If the WCTU and the Anti-Saloon League had ever had opportunity to observe the power of an intelligent woman of the world," wrote Grace Root in 1934, ". . . they must . . . have seen the Repeal handwriting on the wall as soon as Mrs. Sabin took leadership in the field against them." Driving the point home, Mrs. Root's book *Women and Repeal* contained a pair of photographs showing the presidents of the rival women's organizations. Mrs. Sabin of the Women's Organization for National Prohibition Reform, her well-groomed socialite good looks enhanced by the lighting and printing techniques used at that time also in portraits of motion-picture stars, contrasted most cruelly with Mrs. Boole of the Woman's Christian Temperance Union, whose robust countenance—split by a wide and toothy grin—branded her as the stereotype of the Eternal Frump. The contrast was evident out in the field also; in the State of Washington, for example, writes Norman H. Clark, "Mrs. Sabin's lieutenant was Miss Agusta Ware Webb Trimble, recently returned from London where, in a twenty thousand dollar gown, she had met the Queen."

But had not the Woman's Christian Temperance Union drawn from elite leadership also, though perhaps from a less glamorous elite? Biographers of Frances Willard, for example, who headed the WCTU from 1879 until her death in 1898, have made much of her New England Puritan lineage, and critics of Prohibition have considered it a bourgeois attempt to impose WASP values upon the recalcitrant American masses. And yet, on the list of state officers and committees of the Women's Organization for National Prohibition Reform, the names were also overwhelmingly Old American. Meanwhile, the WCTU was losing some of its former elite status. In Washington State in 1910, according to Norman Clark, it "had attracted the wives of prominent physicians, lawyers, and men of commerce. In 1930, it could list only the wives of morticians, chiropractors, tradesmen, and ministers of minor distinction."

The rivalry between the two women's organizations went down to the grass roots. By 1930 the WONPR was able to challenge the WCTU for the allegiance of the same constituencies, and was placing booths opposite the time-sanctioned WCTU booths at state and county fairs. One industrious member of the WONPR's Kentucky branch scored a breakthrough in the dry South by discovering in a secondhand store a scrapbook of newspaper clippings dating from 1887 that disclosed the anti-prohibitionist views of the sainted Jefferson Davis. After verifying the sources, the *Louisville Courier-Journal* ran the story on page 1, and the action seems to have been helpful to the wet cause throughout the domain of the Old Confederacy. Mrs. Root suggested that her organization won support away from the WCTU in part because it presented a more attractive lifestyle—"Our women were more amiable and laughed with the crowd instead of preaching to them"—though a cynic might have concluded that the power elite had merely learned a softer sell.

In any event, despite the snipings of dry defenders like Gordon and Dobyns—who, in effect, dismissed the women opponents of Prohibition as barflies!—the activity of the WONPR clearly had destroyed a major component of the entire dry mystique: the notion that the women of America constituted a massive and undivided opposition to beverage alcohol. When Mrs. Sabin spoke on April 3, 1929, at a lunch given in her honor by the Women's National Republican Club and announced she had resigned as Republican national committeewoman because she wanted to work for a change in the prohibition law, she took note of that mystique: "It has been repeatedly said that the women of the country favored the prohibition law. I believe there are thousands who feel as I do." The president of the men's group, the Association Against the Prohibition Amendment, was quick to agree: "The women of America do not believe in prohibition," Henry H. Curran declared that same day. "They need only to be organized to make this perfectly clear." With the exasperating unconscious condescension so usual in the male, Curran conceded that the ladies could even be permitted to do the organizing themselves: "I un derstand that Mrs. Sabin's organization is to be independent, and that is right. Our association will help in every way possible."

Mrs. Root, who was official historian for the Women's Organization for National Prohibition Reform, noted that when the Nineteenth Amendment, giving women the right to vote, passed

Congress in 1919 "not a woman's voice had ever been raised against Prohibition," whereas the WCTU at that time had been in business for fifty years. The Anti-Saloon League—run, of course, by men—generally supported woman suffrage in the pre-Prohibition years, on the assumption that women would overwhelmingly vote dry. This assumption found literary expression as well. The idea that men—including drinking men!—ought to support woman suffrage because "when the women get the ballot, they will vote for prohibition" was picturesquely expressed by Jack London in 1913 in his semi-autobiographical, semi-fictional, somewhat Mailerish musings on alcoholism, *John Barleycorn:* "It is the wives, and sisters, and mothers, and they only, who will drive the nails into the coffin of John Barleycorn." As the news of Mrs. Sabin's defection became known, one can imagine political professionals all across the land heaving a collective sigh of relief.

V

The impact of the WONPR could be attributed, of course, not only to its leaders' marital ties to the power elite but also to the "emancipation" of women during the twenties. Part of the disrepute in which the old-time saloon had been held, wrote Herbert Agar in the *English Review* for May 1931, "came from the fact that the saloon was a man's world, from which women were excluded, and which they therefore distrusted. In the speakeasy women are admitted on an equality with men." But from the standpoint of women's liberation it could be argued that the political price women had had to pay for this act of personal liberty was disastrously high: the loss of any fear by politicians that their united support of Prohibition might be symptomatic of their potential as a bloc vote on *all* issues. In the words of Paul Conley and Andrew Sorensen, "As long as women kept a united voice in favor of Prohibition, no politician would dare cast a vote which would offend at least half his electorate. Now that most formidable united front had been broken."

Perhaps Ella Boole sensed that more was at stake than persuading American hostesses to serve unspiked fruit punch, although she engaged in that sort of activity also. But a shrewd feel for partisan organization underlay Mrs. Boole's bland churchy language. Throughout her book *Give Prohibition Its Chance*, published in 1929, readers were forcefully reminded that the author spoke for a *Woman's* Christian Temperance Union, which had engaged for many years in activities—caucusing, lobbying, electioneering, direct action—for which American men had traditionally deemed women temperamentally unsuited, perhaps even biologically unfit. Midway through the book Mrs. Boole played her trump card:

> A little girl . . . on returning from school one day said, "I don't like history." "Why?" asked the mother. The child answered, "It is all about men. There is nothing in it about women." It is a fact that until women organized in societies of their own, there was little to record of woman's work except where women ruled their countries as queens.

So far as direct political rule was concerned, two women were elected governors in the decade of the twenties—both drys. Is it entirely a coincidence that after that dry spell was broken, no woman would serve in her own right as governor of an American state for another forty years?

If "woman power" perhaps suffered a setback in the struggles of the Dry Decade, the same may be said—far more tragically—of the alcoholic, who in this debate was simply lost in the shuffle. "Once Prohibition was enacted," as Conley and Sorensen have put it, "the drys saw the alcoholic only as a reminder of a bad dream that would soon disappear; to the wets the alcoholic was an embarrassing source of dry propaganda." Nor did matters significantly improve after Repeal. Alcoholics Anonymous was founded in 1935, and enjoyed some spectacular successes with individuals who could be persuaded to go that route, but the appeal of that quasi-religious organization had some obvious built-in limitations. Otherwise, these authors concluded, "even today [1971], the care of the homeless alcoholic is still viewed in most cities as the exclusive province of the churches and missions." In other words, the care of these unfortunates has been relegated back to where it was prior to the

Volstead Act, and for centuries before that—to "the church and the jail."

Meanwhile, modern clinical psychology had begun to recognize that alcoholism was a public health problem, since individual therapy had been so staggeringly inadequate to the need. Conley and Sorensen cited one recent estimate that "if every psychiatrist and every social worker in the United States were to work in alcoholism there would not be enough to treat the alcoholics in the state of California." But Prohibition—for all its neglect of the individual alcoholic—paradoxically *was* an attempt to treat alcoholism as a public health problem, replacing individual treatment (for example, persuading people to "take the pledge") with a crude kind of preventive action.

Without forgiving or denying the mean-spiritedness, hypocrisy, legal repressiveness, and hysterical propaganda that so often marked the dry cause, perhaps today we can concede their point that Repeal overthrew this effort at prevention without putting anything in its place. In 1934, the year after the Noble Experiment ended, Deets Pickett wrote: "We come now face to face with the original problem, which is not Prohibition, but alcohol." Although the WASP churches had worked long and hard for Prohibition, and although the Anti-Saloon League had called itself "the Church in action against the saloon," in another sense the Eighteenth Amendment was an attempt to secularize a kind of social concern that had hitherto been left in private and religious hands, and to make it the responsibility of the state—a process which had long since taken place in education and would soon, during the 1930s, take place in public welfare.

As early as 1884 Archbishop John Ireland, one of the rare Roman Catholic advocates of Prohibition, told the Citizens' Reform Association of Buffalo that "the state only can save us," because it alone was competent to control the sale of liquor, as distinguished from its consumption. In 1926 the Methodist *Christian Advocate,* militantly dry, worked out the political logic of this from local option to national control, in terms not unlike those that wet political liberals would employ a decade later in dealing with other issues:

"If New York may legally define intoxicants so as to break through the Amendment which prohibits the liquor traffic, why might not South Carolina—should she so desire, as most assuredly she does not—define 'involuntary servitude' in such terms as would nullify that other Prohibition Amendment which outlawed slavery?"

Although perhaps overly generous to the motives of some South Carolinians, this judgment does contain echoes of the quick dismissal of Southern and Republican states'-rights claims during the thirties and forties by ardent New Deal advocates, and it reminds us that the Noble Experiment was among other things an enormous augmentation of the power of the Federal Government. Herbert Hoover noted in 1921 that "the crushing of the liquor trade without a cent of compensation, with scarcely even a discussion of it," certainly violated traditional notions of the sanctity of private property. Prohibition was also the occasion for the first constitutional test (*Olmstead* v. *United States*, 277 U.S. 438) of the government's power to tap the phones of private citizens, in this case bootleggers rather than radicals; and the Supreme Court's 5–4 decision upholding that authority drew not only a liberal dissent, on the ground that the government may not engage in activities which would be crimes if committed by private citizens, but also a conservative dissent, on the ground that privacy is part of what a telephone company sells to its customers. "Liberalism" and "conservatism," not only in the twenties but afterward, may have found common ground in opposition to "statism." From that standpoint, it may have been perfectly natural that Liberty Leagues would organize and work vigorously to secure one form of personal liberty, but then savagely oppose the national government in defense of another form. Questions were raised here that the New Deal's democratic political successes did not fully answer.

CHAPTER VI

The Governor and the Champion; or, the Forgotten Victories of Women's Liberation

WHEN THE business leaders of a south Florida community in the mid-twenties learned that the governor of their state and the governor of Wyoming were about to visit their city, they arranged an elaborate stag dinner for the two officials. The gracious but preoccupied hosts had overlooked one crucial detail: their Western guest was a woman.

Wyoming had been the first American political jurisdiction to grant women the right to vote, when it was first formally organized as a territory in 1869—back in the gaslight era when woman suffrage almost everywhere else in America was still considered either a threat or a bad joke. Appropriately, therefore, the aged Chief Justice of that state—a surviving delegate to the territorial convention that had drafted Wyoming's first constitution, with its equal suffrage clause—administered the oath of office in 1924 to Nellie Tayloe Ross as the nation's first woman chief executive. Two women were in fact elected governors of American states in 1924. But Miriam ("Maw") Ferguson of Texas hardly qualifies as an example; her husband, impeached in 1917 and removed from that same office, called the plays and did most of the talking during her nominal administration. In sharp contrast, Mrs. Ross was a widow at the time of her election, and by all accounts she governed Wyoming in her own right. But it is a strangely forgotten episode in American history. Although Mrs. Ross after her "first" did not simply disappear from the stage—in 1933 FDR named her Director of the U.S. Mint (another "first" for a woman)—her memory had virtually disappeared from our national consciousness. That fact tells us more about our era than about hers.

Unlike her formidable contemporary, Jeanette Rankin, whom the neighboring state of Montana elected in 1918 as the first woman member of Congress, Nellie Ross had never been active in the women's rights movement as such; nor, until it was suggested to her in 1923, had she cherished elective ambitions for herself personally. "My life had been made up of those domestic and social activities that engage the time of the average American woman," she confessed. Nellie Tayloe Ross had a strong sense of place and of identity; her own account of her strenuous political campaigns in Wyoming mentions the tang of the sagebrush, the brilliance of the Indian paintbrush, the tortuous mountain passes, the checkered fields of irrigated crops—and also the state's "exceptionally vivid and captivating personalities." To have captured the leadership of such a community seemed to her to have been a natural and logical process of growth.

Nellie Ross had come to Cheyenne as a bride in 1902; her young lawyer husband, William Bradford Ross, was at that time still heavily in debt for his education. Two years later Mr. Ross was elected county attorney (by twenty votes) and thereby launched upon a political career. But Mrs. Ross's energies in those years were spent in the care of three ailing children, one of whom died; later she recalled an hour spent "thrown prostrate upon the bed beside those wailing, colicky babies, and from sheer exhaustion and despair mingling her tears with theirs," with the feeling that although they "might survive the perils of infancy, their mother would never live to tell the tale." What sort of training was that for future public service? a male skeptic might have asked. "Simply this," said Mrs. Ross: "The demands of that day, which could not be ignored, evaded, or postponed, challenged every resource of which I was possessed." By that reasoning, the average American young woman might have been considered *better* trained for politics—or any other kind of executive responsibility—than the average American young man; and her mass participation in public affairs might have been expected to raise the level of national life just as women leaders such as Jane Addams had hoped it would. That such participation by and large did not take place—that women of Mrs. Ross's sort were exceptional, not typical—is one of the central tragedies of the twentieth century in America.

The Ross family eventually got on its feet. Husband and wife found the leisure to read aloud to each other (Dumas, Balzac, Dickens), and Nellie joined the Cheyenne Woman's Club, an experience she later described as "something like the training men receive in county boards, municipal councils, and legislative halls." But she was still no political activist. In 1922 she opposed her husband's running for governor, but capitulated on the ground usually expected of a wife: it would be improper of her to thwart his career. He filed for the nomination and was elected, a Democrat in an overwhelmingly Republican state. As chief executive, he got the state's royalty in Standard Oil's Salt Creek fields raised from 33⅓ to 65 percent, no mean achievement in a time when corporate power was plundering the American West of its mineral resources and driving from office those politicians who tried to check its march. And then, almost coincidentally with Warren Harding, William Bradford Ross died.

"I had begun to think that my individuality was almost submerged in his," Nellie Ross afterward testified. "But when all at once I found myself standing alone, facing an unknown future, I knew that there had been no submergence." Indeed, partly out of that very relationship with her husband, "there had been developed a more clearly defined and independent individuality with real self-reliance based upon convictions and experience." In that mood she was approached by the chairman of the State Democratic Committee, and other of her late husband's associates and friends, who asked her to run for governor.

Mrs. Ross, by her own account, had no doubt she was qualified for the office; her only question was whether she had the physical stamina to run. The Republican Opposition evidently shared her own confidence in her political potential, and some of them tried to get the Republican-controlled legislature to create a meaningless "job" for her, in effect granting her a widow's pension in order to prevent her from running. (Their own 1924 nominee, although a man "of high character and . . . personally popular," was a conservative identified with the oil interests and therefore—inevitably, in the public mind of that year, especially in Wyoming—with Teapot Dome.) Feeling a commitment to carry on her husband's unfinished work as well as a desire to find "a compelling interest that would absorb me completely," and angry with the G.O.P. for in effect having tried to buy her off, Nellie Ross consented to make the race.

Nationally, 1924 was a banner year for women candidates. For example, Mary Teresa Norton, already seasoned as a New Jersey politician—she had been vice-chairman of the Democratic State Committee since 1920 and an at-large delegate to the Democratic national convention of 1924—was elected to Congress. Significantly, although Mrs. Norton was a widow, her late husband had never been a Congressman. Congresswoman Norton was elected because she brought in the votes for Jersey City Mayor Frank Hague; she earned her political reward in the same fashion as any politically talented male. (On the other hand, given the authoritarianism of Boss Hague's machine, it could be argued that, after all, Mrs. Norton—unlike Mrs. Ross—spent her political career working for a man.) In contrast to most other women Representatives elected in the twenties, who would appear in one session of Congress only to be retired by the voters before the next, Mary Norton was destined for a long and distinguished career in the U.S. House. Before her retirement in 1951 she would chair three standing committees; one of them was Labor, a vital assignment during the New Deal years. Nor was she alone. Six months after Mary Norton's first successful race, a special election in Massachusetts sent Edith Nourse Rogers to join her in Congress on the Republican side of the aisle. Mrs. Rogers's career would last even longer than Mrs. Norton's—until her death in 1960.

Although there was some carping from the press, on the whole the media welcomed this new species of officeholder. Contemplating Miriam Ferguson's vast Texas realm from its own provincial New England perspective, the *Boston Transcript* noted that her authority would "extend over a region much larger than France, and more than five times as large as England, with a population greater than that of Ireland, and resources far beyond those of the German Reich . . . a position as proud as that of many famous queens of the past." *Current Opinion* ran a full-page portrait of Nellie Ross in its rotogravure section, along with such male notables of the day as Calvin Coolidge, Vice President-elect Charles Dawes, British Prime Minister Stanley Baldwin, the prominent Spanish writer and political rebel Vincente Blasco Ibañez, the new Secretary of Agriculture, and the new French Ambassador. (Mrs. Ross was shown in a big hat with veil, long dangling earrings, and a fox fur piece; one is struck by her large, compelling eyes.) But, typically, the news and opinion journals "feminized" their accounts of these women's triumphs: "The majority of women being natural-born housekeepers, why shouldn't the infinite detail of a governor's office appeal to the female of the species?" Pictures in *World's Work* showed Governor "Maw" Ferguson peeling potatoes or feeding the chickens on the family farm, with a ramshackle Texas outhouse not far away. Mrs. John I. Nolan, a Congresswoman from California between 1922 and 1924, was photographed in the kitchen in her apron busily at work with an egg beater—which proved, *The Independent* editorialized, "that official duties need not interfere with the rites of the home."

II

A somewhat similar folksy kind of public relations was expected of male politicians as well; there are, for example, those hilarious portraits of a glum Calvin Coolidge swamped under a Sioux warbonnet, and, from earlier in the century, an even funnier photo of a corpulent William Howard Taft wearing a top hat as he tosses out the season's first baseball. But Nellie Ross was not about to campaign, or govern, on any such basis. As a "first," she was inevitably subjected to a barrage of publicity; "my opinion was asked on absurdly irrelevant subjects." A movie cameraman wanted to take some footage of her making bread, sweeping, or engaged in other domestic activities, but she refused to play the game that way. In her reelection campaign of 1926, she laid down a first ground rule: "This is a business mission, not a social one." To be sure there were homely personal touches, as when she brought flowers for an elderly lady who lived at an inn along her campaign trail, or on another tour sat down at the piano and played "America" to open the meeting because the orchestra that was supposed to do so had left. But when she got up to speak, Mrs. Ross typically apologized for not telling funny stories because, she said, with all the issues facing the state there was no time for them. She also conscientiously kept up with her job; a reporter who accompanied her noted that during seven strenuous—one might say "man-killing"—weeks of campaigning across the vast stretches of Wyoming, the Governor did not miss a meeting of any of the state boards of which she was ex-officio a member, back at the state capitol in Cheyenne.

Nellie Ross also told her campaign workers: "I refuse to do anything myself that is low or unfair, nor will I allow any one else to do it for me, with or without my knowledge"—a shining exception to the general gamy political standards of the twenties, including those of her Texas contemporaries Jim and Miriam Ferguson. "If we do not always meet success at the hands of the people," Mrs. Ross explained, "at least we shall strive to deserve it." Cynics might have considered such a stand naïve, but the male politicians back at the capitol seem to have been impressed. If the legislative session "began with the feeling that a woman would think or act in some unusual way, that she would approach serious matters impulsively and hastily or timidly and indecisively, or even that she would upset all precedents, many were generous enough to say that it had disappeared at the end"; one who paid particularly generous tribute was the Republican Speaker of the House, whose party at the time held political control. She fought, skillfully and often successfully, for her own policies against those of the Opposition-controlled legislature and the equally G.O.P.-dominated state boards; one notable example was over the naming of the state's bank examiners. Unlike Mrs. Ferguson in Texas, she was extremely careful in her use of the pardoning power lest she be accused of being "soft like a woman"; in the same spirit of personal autonomy she even fired some of her own late husband's political appointees whom she thought unfit for office. All in all, the *National Cyclopaedia of American Biography* summed up her administration: "She sought so to acquit herself that it could not be said women were incapable of holding high executive positions in public life."

Nellie Ross had made a promising start, but all gubernatorial terms must one day come to an end. The "governor lady"—as *Good Housekeeping* was later to christen her—had to stand for reelection. Mrs. Ross refused to cultivate the "woman's vote" as such, but that did not save her from chauvinist reprisal. The campaign was fair enough on the surface, but its undercover slogan seems to have been "we need a man." (Still further beneath the surface may have been reprisal of a more crassly economic kind, from oil interests irked by the independence of both the Rosses, but that is a matter for conjecture.) The campaign's greatest irony was summed up in the action of one black male citizen of Wyoming who, as his wife indignantly told the Governor, had not voted in twenty years but now availed himself of the privilege specifically in order to vote against Mrs. Ross—on the ground "that the office was no place for a woman." But the Governor took her defeat with serenity. Issue-oriented to the last, she declared a year after that election that the greatest political service American women could now render would be to "restore meaning to party alignment"—to lead in a breakaway from partisan allegiance based on "tradition, association, or prejudice."

Her contemporary, Eleanor Roosevelt, when asked by *Redbook* magazine in 1928 to write on the subject of women and politics, responded with an article asserting that "Women Must Learn to Play the Game as Men Do." Nellie Ross would have emphatically agreed: "A woman will succeed or fail just as a man will succeed or fail," she declared in a memoir of her campaigns, "and it is difficult indeed to understand why a generation which has been brought up under the coeducational system of the American public schools should imagine that there is any real difference in the manner in which men and women approach intellectual or practical problems." The women's liberation movement of today has cautioned us about the subtle conditioning toward "men's" and "women's" roles that the school imposes on the child; girls do not play with chemistry sets, boys do not take "home ec." Nevertheless, in probing for the causes of the new freedoms of the flapper in the twenties, the historians may here have overlooked one of the most obvious of all.

Mrs. Ross's achievement was all the more impressive in the face of the powerful masculine prejudice against women playing "unwomanly" roles—a prejudice that did not disappear into the air merely because women had won the right to vote, important though that hard-won victory was. Nellie Ross, it must be remembered, was not only the first but also the *last* woman actually to govern an American state until Ella Grasso took the helm in Connecticut in 1975 (the mid-sixties regime of Lurleen Wallace in Alabama does not really count). Long after the twenties, as Betty Friedan has pointed out, "a woman was made to think she was crazy and needed psychiatric counseling if she didn't get total satisfaction from making peanut butter sandwiches and scrubbing the kitchen floor." We often think of the Freudianism and other psychological theories that were in vogue during the twenties as having had a "liberating" effect; on the contrary, they sometimes had an impact that was regressive. "The women who crowd the offices of nerve specialists," nerve specialist Louis E. Bisch pompously wrote in 1927, "are trying to side-track nature's decrees. That is why they are confused, morose, wrought-up, ill. Obstetricians, gynecologists, and psychologists will tell you that a woman is at her best—physically, emotionally, and mentally—when she is with child."

"The inferiority *does* exist," chimed in his contemporary John Macy, in two condescending *Harper's* articles, "Equality of Woman with Man: a Myth" (November 1926) and "Logic and the Ladies, with a Word about Their Other Mental Processes" (November 1928). "The reason that women are more subject to hysteria than men," Macy pontificated, "is in plain terms that their brains are weaker, more easily unbalanced." In politics they were typified not by the politically straight-shooting Eleanor Roosevelts and Mary Nortons and Nellie Rosses but by "the woman as kill-joy, as sneaking, malicious trouble maker, or innocently unconscious sadist [note again the popular Freudian language] enjoying the discomfort of others," who came to Senate hearings ostensibly on behalf of the homes and schools of America but in actuality "impelled by the desire to spoil man's pleasure, whether evil or innocent"—a judgment reflecting wet political ire at the highly effective partisan activities of the WCTU. James M. Cain, who frequently wrote in a "hardboiled" vein for H. L. Mencken's *American Mercury*, shared Macy's jaundiced view of the female politician; the most politically effective woman of their generation, he declared in 1924, was Alice Roosevelt Longworth, who succeeded precisely because she did not work through conventional political channels as did her arch-rival and cousin Eleanor. "Woman, indeed, like the harmonica, shines best as a solo instrument," Cain explained, missing the point that Eleanor achieved whereas Alice merely amused. "When she attempts to play *ensemble* the result is often disastrous." Politicking en masse, said Cain, she lost what would nowadays be called "glamour."

It is worth recalling here that Grace Coolidge, one of the most personable of all our First Ladies, had so little access to the political side of Calvin's life that she first learned of the President's decision not to run for reelection from a senator who had learned it from the press. Coolidge had taken the trouble to hand out to each of the reporters at his press conference a typed slip of paper bearing the famous statement "I do not choose to run for re-election in 1928," a decision of which he had not seen fit to inform his wife! With blatant male chauvinism so rife in the land during the emancipated twenties, not surprisingly some women who functioned effectively as politicians—perhaps indeed in order to function effectively in that role—picked up these prejudiced cues.

Few Americans, male or female, had the political "clout" during the Twenties of Mrs. Belle Moskowitz, for example, who was to Alfred E. Smith something like what Colonel House had been to Woodrow Wilson. ("He's growing," she said of Smith in 1927. "I no longer have to edit his speeches and messages as carefully as I did.") In fact, she was so powerful a member of Al Smith's state administration at Albany that when Franklin Roosevelt succeeded Smith in 1928 as Governor he had to fire her in order to run his own show. Yet at a forum held at Columbia University on April 27, 1926, when she was at the height of her power, Mrs. Moskowitz publicly endorsed female inferiority:

> Women have qualities of mind peculiarly feminine, but they are not the intellectual equals of men. Their intuitive sense is the biggest thing that they bring to politics. . . . Combined with the thinking ability of men, this makes a splendid working team. It would be better for women to use the abilities they have and not attempt to do what they can not do.

"Calls Her Own Sex Inferior Mentally," the New York *Times* captioned this statement the next day; "Men Ungallantly Applaud."

III

Even Governor Nellie Ross, who rejected the notion "that there is any real difference in the manner in which men and women approach intellectual or practical problems," yielded somewhat to the prevailing prejudice. "It is in the realm of the home, in wifehood and motherhood, that woman fulfills her highest destiny and finds her greatest happiness," she declared, almost apologetically adding that in her own case "Divine intervention" had changed the circumstances of her life, leaving her "in a position to assume public responsibilities." In short, the choice was still put as home and family *or* a "career"; as had been the case since colonial times, for a woman in America full personal autonomy was still reserved to widows and spinsters.

Women younger than Eleanor Roosevelt and Nellie Ross, in a society with the surface youth-orientation of the Jazz Age, sometimes were able to postpone facing that old dilemma. The flapper—independent, self-assertive, shocking to her elders in her newfound personal freedoms—might, if she chose, go to work for a living. Statistically, William H. Chafe has shown, the independent, self-supporting young working woman of the twenties is largely mythical; symbolically, however, her contemporaries may have been right in their assumption that in the booming economy of the postwar decade the formerly grubby image of the "working girl" had become transformed, even glamorized. A magazine illustration in 1925 captured the image of this new young woman on her way to work, straphanging on a streetcar; flung over her free arm was an impressive wrap, apparently of fur. Such women, Samuel Crowther wrote in an accompanying article, "can support themselves better than many of the men of their own age. They have awakened to the fact that the 'superior sex' stuff is all bunk." Consequently, the man who aspired to marry one of these "liberated" women must realize that she would not be contented as "merely an unpaid servant" to her husband; "and this in turn means that the men have got to work—than which nothing better could happen for the country." In short, the flapper's brief taste of freedom and conpctcncc, once she got married, would cause the wheels of capitalism to spin even more furiously than before.

The catch was that even in those social classes that were carefree and prosperous in the twenties—and we know that millions of working and nonworking men and women were not—eventually, more often than not, the young woman did marry. However great her independence and earning power had been up to that moment, she discovered that she was after all only a wife. Even so glamorous a wife as Zelda Fitzgerald learned—at the cost of sanity itself—that her own unschooled but powerful native talent could not be allowed to unfold; it must be crushed lest it undercut the work of her husband, who after all was earning their daily bread. Furthermore, had Zelda never met Scott, she probably would never have become aware of what she might be able to accomplish; a case of damned if you do, damned if you don't.

As one anonymous "ex-feminist" confessed in 1926, "In six years of married life I have gradually but surely descended from that blithe, enthusiastic, cocksure young person I was eight or ten years ago to the colorless, housewifely, dependent sort of female I used to picture so pathetically and graphically to my audiences—the kind of woman we must all have a chance not to be!" She considered herself, relatively, "a very fortunate woman"; she had "a splendid husband who, after six stormy years of matrimony, is still my lover as I am his," and they had "a beautiful daughter of four, radiant in health and spirits." But this splendid husband, when the chips were down, was like husbands in general, who, "while giving lip-service to our feminist creed, . . . feel, in any real crisis where sacrifice is demanded of them, that the best is for the male and the rest for the woman."

As wife, housewife, and mother, the anonymous author concluded, "I am a fairly complete success, but as an individual I have amounted to nothing." What is appalling to the present-day reader of these "Confessions of an Ex-Feminist" is that they sound so familiar; that in half a century so little has changed. And, regrettably, we can generalize from the individual to the collective: the Equal Rights Amendment was stalled in the legislatures of the mid-seventies by the identical arguments that had prevailed against it in the Jazz Age.

Still younger than the flapper in the Twenties was the schoolgirl. She too, in certain circumscribed ways, was permitted to discover her own individuality. After all, the flapper role was, fundamentally, little more than a new technique for the old purpose of catching a man. By playing it to the hilt a woman tacitly conceded the larger battle for selfhood. But the younger girl might be temporarily excused from that kind of role-playing. In refreshing contrast to the tendency in so many American women to become (in a sense) "stage mothers," neurotically prepping their daughters for wifehood from kindergarten if not from the cradle, one writer for *Good Housekeeping* in 1925 argued that "all girls should experience, between the time they are children and the time they become young women, the period of girlhood when romance is associated with heroes of history, with great living personages, with causes and ideas rather than with individuals of the other sex." They should study art, science, and history. Although their mothers should also train them for homemaking, their fathers should at the same time teach them the value of money, and not stand in the way of their youthful vocational enthusiasms.

Implicitly, if the growing girl was to have heroes, she might also have heroines. If a boy aspired to be Thomas Edison, a girl might aspire to be Madame Curie; if a boy dreamed of exploring the South Pole, like Admiral Byrd, a girl might dream of going off by herself to Samoa, like Margaret Mead. In that decade especially, if a boy identified with Babe Ruth or Red Grange or Johnny Weissmuller, a girl might identify with Helen Wills or Suzanne Lenglen or Gertrude Ederle. The twenties, as we all know, were a boom time for competitive and spectator sport. They were also a time of major breakthroughs in athletics for women. In the old days, as one woman professor of physical education, Elizabeth Halsey, pointed out in 1927, "nice girls did not play games in public"; now, increasingly, they did. "The tomboy ideal," declared Glenna Collett—who had won the women's national golf championship in 1922 at the age of nineteen—"is far more healthful than that of the poor little Goldilocks of the seventies and eighties, who was forbidden vigorous activities lest she tear her clothes."

There were resistances, to be sure, to this kind of emancipation also. Conceding that the modern girl was bound to play in competitive sports—"It is a part of their new feeling for liberty and equality of opportunity"—Henry S. Curtis urged in 1928 that their activities be kept intramural: "It is not good social policy to have girls travel about the country for inter-school contests." Fewer than ten percent of American colleges permitted them to do so, he pointed out; the Women's Athletic Federation itself was opposed. In his article, published in the American Medical Association's magazine *Hygeia*, Curtis suggested some masculine-biased reasons why: untrained in "the traditions of sportsmanship that have been impressed upon men's teams for generations," he declared, girls were "poor losers"; moreover, "remarks by the spectators are often discourteous or even insulting, and the publicity in the papers is usually not the kind that emphasizes feminine ideals."

The thought of women on the playing field inevitably prompted thoughts about their directly challenging the male. "Good comradeship in sport demands that women should be allowed to compete with men," declared Glenna Collett in 1924. The fact that the men would usually win should be no deterrent, added Helen Wills two years later; in any sport, competing against a better player is one of the best ways to improve one's game. However, tennis star

William T. "Big Bill" Tilden—who beat the best woman tennis player of the day, Suzanne Lenglen, 6–0, 6–0, allowing her only a scattered eight points—was politely skeptical. Having tried his "hand or foot at golf, baseball, football, hockey, soccer, tennis, and even in a rash moment cricket," Tilden complacently observed, "even in my worst moments I defeated decisively any members of the fair sex who attempted to compete with me." While conceding "the full equality of women in art, science, business, the theatre, music, and the movies"—a concession more generous, incidentally, than many men of his generation would have made—Tilden concluded: "Frankly, I hand down the verdict in favor of the man in athletics."

The tennis king of the twenties granted, however, that a historical and psychological factor mitigated this verdict: "Since time immemorial man has beaten woman. . . . The old bromide 'A team that won't be beaten can't be beaten' is more or less true here, for man won't be beaten by woman, that is until he has been a few times, so that it sinks in." Fifty years afterward another professional male tennis player, named Bobby Riggs, who wouldn't be beaten by a woman, was. Billie Jean King's victory over Riggs has had its detractors, some of whom felt that a young woman was picking on an old man. Still, the aging pro was well paid for his humiliation, and the victory of Ms. King shattered the psychological barrier to which Bill Tilden had pointed in 1922.

IV

A major step toward that breakthrough was taken at 7:08 A.M., August 6, 1926, at Cape Gris-Nez, when Gertrude Ederle slipped into the English Channel. The wind was from the southwest; the air temperature was 61 degrees; the sea was rough. The nineteen-year-old daughter of a German-American butcher, who had attempted the Channel the previous season and failed—not from physical exhaustion but from seasickness—swam powerfully and steadily; at 10:30 she paused to sip beef extract and gnaw a salt-washed leg of chicken. On board the tugboat *Alsace* nearby were her trainer, her father, her sister, and two other women swimmers; on its lee side they had printed the slogan "This Way,

Ole Kid!" and drawn an arrow. Below decks, a "wireless" flashed bulletins of her progress; not far off, another tug carried newsmen and photographers.

At an age when most girls were still playing with dolls—eight years old, according to the papers; nine, by her own account—Gertrude had watched the boys splash in the New Jersey surf, picked up and surpassed their strokes, and shortly was beating every other kid on the beach. At the age of fifteen she entered the three-and-a-half-mile swimming race between Manhattan Beach and Brighton Beach, and came in sixty yards ahead of the then American women's champion, Helen Wainwright. At seventeen, Ederle won a gold medal as a member of the American swimming team that made a clean sweep of the 1924 Olympics; International Newsreel footage showed her in the water that year, arm blurred in "the famous six-beat crawl stroke which has made her the fastest woman swimmer in the world." Before turning professional, Miss Ederle had broken every amateur women's swimming record on the books; now she was attempting something no woman, and only five men, had ever accomplished. Understandably, and properly, the media had a field day.

At 1:30 P.M., nine miles out from England, came rain and a heavy, wind-driven swell. To keep her rhythm up she sang "Let Me Call You Sweetheart"; at 3:00, although the rain continued, she received a respite as the incoming tide carried her toward Dover. At 5:00 she sipped hot chocolate through a baby's bottle. The sea turned "choppy and angry"; there was talk of quitting. At 6:05 Gertrude's trainer, a man named Burgess, told her father and sister they should take her out of the water. Someone yelled, "Gertie, you must come out"; according to the *New York Daily News* "Trudy looked up in amazement and said: 'What for?' " (wild cheers). By 7:15, the coach had come around to her point of view: "God Almighty! I never saw anyone so marvelous. She has done everything." The day faded, and at 9:39 the American girl made it to shore and was greeted by a bobby who (seriously, she still believes) asked her for her passport! Time, 14 hours, 31 minutes— better than the records of any of the few men who had completed that treacherous thirty-mile course. Ironically, while she was in the cold Channel water a London newspaper was setting in type for publication next day "a calm and scholarly editorial commenting on the futility of competitive athletics for women, on the ground that they must ever remain athletically inferior to men."

Gertrude Ederle's iron constitution was none the worse for wear. After a hot bath at her hotel, she reported, she was not even stiff the next morning. The only ill effect of the crossing was a hurt wrist afterward from shaking a great many hands. She—and the media—seem to have understood clearly the symbolic significance of what she had done. "All the women of the world will celebrate, too," she had told W. O. McGeehan, sports editor of the *New York Herald Tribune*, before making her supreme effort. "It was spoken lightly, 'a little shyly,' " the *Literary Digest* reported, "but with evident realization that her triumph over the choppy, chilly, changeable, treacherous tide-riven, squally, fog-haunted English Channel, supreme challenge of aquatic heroes and baffler of supermen, would be hailed as a battle won for feminism"—the "unanswerable refutation of the masculinist dogma that woman is, in the sense of physical power and efficiency, inferior to man."

A woman who achieved in any area, observed the *Boston Globe* editorial writer "Uncle Dudley," was likely to have her achievement put down as atypical. If she managed a business, people said she had a man's knack of administration; if she became eminent in science or literature, they said that she had a masculine brain; if she attained a new athletic record, those on the sidelines declared she was strong or skillful—for a girl. But her triumph over the men at one of their own competitive games had torpedoed that rationalization. "The Channel has been the means of giving to women new physical dignity," the *Globe* columnist concluded. "In the larger sense, that is what the victory of Miss Gertrude Ederle means."

"Fourteen hours and a half with no lunch hour is overtime even for white-collar men—most of whom couldn't swim for fourteen minutes in a mill-pond," said the *Jersey Journal* (of Miss Ederle's native state). "Well, women got the vote . . . , and now they hold the greatest of all swimming records, despite the fact that their champion, Miss Ederle, still lacks two years of voting age. The feminists are surely having their innings, despite 'Ma' Ferguson's defeat." And Carrie Chapman Catt, the veteran and victorious leader of the woman suffrage movement itself, declared: "It is a far cry from swimming the Channel to the days to which my memory goes back, when it was thought that women could not throw a ball or even walk very far down the street without feeling faint." She also recalled that a suffrage leader in Boston forty years earlier had predicted that "Woman's freedom would go hand in hand with her bodily strength. The first necessity in the battle for equal rights, she said, was equal health," and that battle, Mrs. Catt believed, had now been won.

The modern American woman had not only physically but psychologically triumphed over the "weaker sex" image that had oppressed her Victorian forebears. Gertrude Ederle's feat would not have been possible thirty years before, according to Northwestern University swimming instructor Tom Robinson. Physical education had "brought about an evolution of common sense that has wrought a complete turnover, not only in woman's physical condition but in her whole mental attitude." Freed from the "corsets, and other ridiculously unnecessary clothing" that had formerly hampered her movements, the modern young woman might find in sport not only exercise for the body but also exercise in what women's liberationists today would call consciousness-raising. The erosion of this possibility, as women's "p.e." became an easy target for educational budget-cutting, is one of the sadder by-products of the social process in more recent years.

V

But civilized males had long since realized that in order to maintain their supremacy over women it was not usually necessary to beat them into submission. Instead, one could put them on pedestals and worship their "superior" qualities, as Victorian men had done, and discount their effectiveness in the decision-making "real" world just as effectively. In Queen Victoria's world, the pedestal had been labeled Motherhood; in Warren Harding's world, it was more likely to read Sex. The same summer season in which

Gertrude Ederle won her first long-distance race, 1922, saw the inauguration of the Miss America contest; annually thereafter, from that day to this, despite increasing static from women's liberationists, the swim suit queens have paraded across the Atlantic City boardwalk with their standardized smiles and bodies and their equally standardized conversations. The younger swimmers, typed as "mermaids," escaped some of this sexist ballyhoo only to be equally stereotyped as its exact opposite: "A strapping, wholesome, fun-loving creature is Gertrude," the *Brooklyn Eagle* moralized in 1924, "with muscles of steel and a great chuckle in her throat, and honest, wide-set brown eyes that would never lure a good sailorman on the rocks when there were a wife and children waiting for him on shore." But as they grew toward womanhood, the System was ready to annex and exploit them in the modern way. The "weaker sex" had been dethroned; the "bathing beauty" reigned in her stead.

"Swim and Grow Beautiful," wrote Helen Wainwright, at that moment the "all-round woman swimming champion of the world," in an article published the very week of Gertrude Ederle's Channel triumph. The article was appropriately embellished with fetching photos of girl swimmers. Still more pointedly, a *Collier's* double-spread ad in 1925 asked: "How well can you look in a swimming suit?" The accompanying picture showed three girls, and two men in the (to our eyes) ridiculous topped bathing suits men used to wear, happily tumbling in the surf. And yet, the advertising copyist had to take account of other values besides simple sex appeal. Most of the copy dealt with the physical sensation of wearing the suit itself: "You feel like an Olympic champion the minute you put one on." The coupon in the lower right-hand corner, so typical in advertisements of the 1920s, could be clipped and sent in with a quarter to the A. C. Spalding Company, the swimming-suit manufacturer—not for a manual of glamour on the beach but for a businesslike booklet on "The Science of Swimming," by Frank J. Sullivan, swimming instructor at Princeton; or, if one preferred, "Swimming for Women" by L. de B. Handley, coach of the New York Women's Swimming Association. In the same spirit Jantzen, Spalding's leading competitor in the swimsuit business, advertised its product as "the suit that changed *bathing* to *swimming*." Even in a sexist culture, it seemed, an activity taken up as a mere means to an end (becoming attractive to the opposite sex) could subversively become an end in itself and thereby a way out of the modern woman's (or man's) self-pitying subjectivism. And again, since the bold and free twenties there has been erosion; have you seen a Jantzen ad lately?

Helen Wainwright's article, also, despite those swimsuit snapshots, was not primarily an essay on how to be sexy. "I learned to swim when I was a baby," she began, "and in Florida last winter I taught an 84-year-old man the six-beat crawl." She then discussed the history of the crawl, and raised that most frightening of male-chauvinist bugaboos—that women might actually be better at something physical than men. "Over a period of six to twelve hours a woman can cover a greater distance than a man," Mrs. Wainwright asserted, because of lighter bones and greater buoyancy. "Even in the shorter distances women are not overshadowed by men as they are in other sports"; the women's swimming record at that time for the mile was just about two minutes behind the men's record of 23 minutes, 34.5 seconds. "That's a difference of about 100 yards." Half a century later, as Gertrude Ederle lived to testify in 1973, both the male and the female sports records of the twenties would be in eclipse; "The way the kids swim today, you'd think we were tied to the pier." The Channel-crossing times had been cut by an incredible five hours, but the match between the sexes in this event remained even. Despite the erosions of women's self-esteem in America since the twenties, there had lately been a rallying; nobody was suggesting to the female swimmers that it would really be more prudent and womanly of them to let the boys win, either in the archaic spirit of "Annie Get Your Gun" or in the more modern spirit of Lucy in the "Peanuts" comic strip, with her complacent observation: "Love is letting him win even though you know you could slaughter him."

It was a far cry, perhaps, from winning a race to governing a state. How fast could the president of any major corporation swim the English channel? one critic of this chapter has already asked. Nevertheless, rightly or wrongly, our society *does* draw inferences about people's individual worth from the physical and psychological stamina shown in athletic success, and other discriminated-against castes have had to learn the same bitter lesson: *first* Joe Louis making money with his fists, *then* Ralph Bunche making peace for the U.N.; *first* Jackie Robinson running the bases, *then* Shirley Chisholm running for President; *first* Althea Gibson on the tennis court, *then* Thurgood Marshall on the Supreme Court. It remains to be seen whether the parallel will hold for the largest of all the castes, the "minority" that is numerically the majority; whether, before many of its members can expect to become governors, more of them will first have to win acceptance as champions.

CHAPTER VII

The Folklore of Advertising

SPEND A RAINY AFTERNOON sometime browsing through the popular magazines of the twenties, and you will quickly be distracted by their ads. You will discover curious gaps and omissions; from a present-day point of view some emphases are strikingly different. (An Aqua Velva ad promises "After-Shaving Comfort on the Hottest Day," but the accompanying photo shows only a straw-hatted, middle-aged man holding the opened front passenger door of a closed car—no dashing sportsman in a convertible or on a motorcycle or water skis, and no smashingly tempting blonde to croon "There's something about an Aqua Velva man.") The colored illustrations are paintings, the photographs only black-and-white; the typography and layout seem old-fashioned; and to modern ears the copy often sounds quaint. Nevertheless, for a person raised in modern mass society these advertisements have a haunting familiarity.

The advertisers' index for a single fat (200-plus pages) weekly issue of the *Saturday Evening Post*—taking, at random, March 26, 1927—discloses name after name that would still be familiar to most Americans. American Express; American Tobacco, and the brand names "Half and Half" and "Lucky Strike"; Buick ("When better automobiles are built, Buick will build them"); Burroughs Adding Machines; Cadillac and Chrysler and Chevrolet; Cyclone Fences and Fisher Bodies; Florsheim Shoes and Fuller Brushes; Goodyear Tire & Rubber ("It outperformed them all!

For months the hard-driven road cars of the Goodyear test fleet had been roaring night and day . . ."); Hammermill Paper and Kohler Plumbing; Metropolitan Life, with the same kind of "institutional" advertising that the same company sponsors today; Pet Milk and Pittsburgh Plate Glass; Procter & Gamble and Raytheon; Three-in-One Oil, with a coupon for a free sample; Timken Roller Bearings. Long before, in the Gilded Age—when Rockefeller, Carnegie, Westinghouse first became household names—the broad entrepreneurial outlines of American capitalism had been laid down; we had then begun to ride up and down in Otis elevators, take Kodak pictures, and shave with King Gillette's throwaway blades. By the 1920s, such products and trade names were part of the daily landscape of Everyman. Many of those exact signs and shapes and slogans have continued with remarkable stability, despite economic disruption, civil strife, and war, to dominate his landscape from that day to this.

We have long been taught the dogma that advertising is one of the great, seductive evils of American capitalism. Begotten of an illegitimate union between Machiavelli and Freud, it cons people into buying what they do not want, and into mortgaging the future in order to satisfy the induced urges of the present. It pushes products that corrode the teeth, bloat the tissues, and shorten life. It reduces the rational discourse that ought to pervade society under a republic down to a yammering repetition of mindless slogans. It appeals to envy, greed, fear, snobbery, and lust.

To say there is no truth in this indictment would be to deny the obvious. Nevertheless, something is missing from the foregoing philippic. The converse of the advertiser's moral world—an ethic of gratify now, pay later—would presumably be an ethic of restraint, conservation, prudence, self-discipline; in short, exactly the Protestant or bourgeois ethic so often disliked by the same kind of critic who doesn't like advertising. Ironically, it was a capitalist economy infused with all those old prudential virtues— "waste not, want not," "a penny saved is a penny earned," "don't pay too much for your whistle"—that created advertising; and advertising seems destined to sweep those older values away. Marxists have often said that capitalism contains the seeds of its own destruction, but this overthrow of Ben Franklin by P. T. Barnum is not usually what they have had in mind.

Moreover, the power of advertising has certain psychological limitations. It upsets the old "law of supply and demand" by creating demand where none had existed, but it cannot—not yet, at least—create that demand entirely *ex nihilo*. If it panders at times to extremely low desires, it nonetheless builds upon desires that are already potentially there. Feedback from those desires conditions the messages it sends to arouse them. In a sense, therefore, advertising is a *product*, not simply a molder, of modern mass society. The story has been told elsewhere of how the producers of Listerine in 1922 discovered in a British medical journal the forbidding word *halitosis*, and vulgarly popularized it to the enormous profit of the company. In full-page ads with titles like "They Say It Behind Your Back," the Lambert Pharmaceutical Company exploited the anxiety of middle-class Americans about personal hygiene. But it did not *invent* that anxiety; it had not required advertising to make people buy and use bathtubs in nineteenth-century America, just as it did not take propagandistic urging to make people put on surgical masks during cold and flu seasons in twentieth-century Japan.

As the distinguished economist Wesley C. Mitchell wrote in 1929, "Changes in taste are in large part merely the consumers' response to the solicitation of novel products, effectively presented by advertising. But that is not all of the story; the consumer . . . sometimes reveals traces of initiative." For example, Americans in the twenties were consuming fewer calories per capita; they were eating less wheat and corn but more dairy products, vegetable oils, sugar, fresh vegetables and fruit. More families than ever before were sending their sons and daughters to college; young children, girls, and women were wearing lighter and fewer clothes. Surely, Mitchell argued, these were not entirely triumphs of high-powered salesmanship.

Furthermore, success in promoting one line of goods sometimes implies failure in marketing another; as Mitchell put it, "In a sense, every consumer's good, from college to candy, is a rival of every other consumer's good." Consider for example a copywriter's saga of Eric the Surveyor, composed in 1926 for Dutchess Trousers & Knickers ("10¢ a Button, $1.00 a Rip"— sums that would be paid to the wearer should the garment give way). The pitch made by the manufacturer of work trousers to the consumer of his homely product logically clashed with the snob appeal inherent in clothes made for the likes of Scott Fitzgerald:

> Don't talk to Eric about wide open spaces.
> His idea of a thrill is a Saturday night once a month in a tank town where there's cactus on Main Street and perhaps one place where they've got ice enough to get a drink, good and cold. Sometimes when he gets a week-old newspaper from the coast, he has a lot of fun reading "What the Well-Dressed Man Will Wear." But his own scarred and work-stained wardrobe is eloquent testimony of what should be worn where there are bridges to build, mountains to scale, rattlesnakes, alkali and sage brush.

To be sure, Eric and the Well-Dressed Man might never meet to compare notes, and the same corporation could therefore presumably peddle its wares to both. But sometimes the conflict between one consumer good and another was more direct. In the 1920s, for example, streetcar manufacturers presumably wanted to sell their product just as much as Henry Ford wanted to sell his. But an advertisement in 1928 pointed out that these two aspirations were highly incompatible: "The street car passenger occupies six square feet of traffic space. The automobile passenger requires an average of 44 square feet." Streetcars were carrying more than thirty million passengers daily in thirty of America's largest cities; "Attempt to put them in automobiles, and the street—which cannot easily expand its curbs—would be too narrow to hold them." It is an argument used regularly today by advocates of urban mass transportation who decry the private automobile. Radical city planners of the seventies, anticommercial in outlook, can thus accept the commercially motivated logic of a business corporation in the twenties: "The electric street car is our most efficient means of moving masses of people." (Today the copywriter might add also that it does not pollute.)

But, as every harassed commuter and death-defying bicyclist

knows, that argument did not prevail, and it would be oversimple to contend that it failed only because pro-streetcar propaganda was less effective than the sales pitch for private automobiiles. The mass-media advertising out of Detroit, strident and mendacious though it has been—and irresponsible, in its tacit encouragement of reckless driving—has to some degree been the beneficiary of genuine if wrongheaded consumer choice.

The same may even have been true of a product for which there was initially no spontaneous demand because it did not yet exist. Coca-Cola, that ultimate symbol of consumer capitalism, has so defended itself; "Coca-Cola's popularity rests upon the free consent of the thirsty," a magazine ad proclaimed in 1926. "It had to be good to get where it is"—whatever happened to its users' teeth, nerves and digestion along the way.

H. L. Mencken's *American Mercury* regularly scoffed at the lame-brained George F. Babbitt with his narrowly commercial vision of the Good Life and his cultural imbecility. But the *Mercury* also carried advertising. Like the colorful spreads in today's *New Yorker,* its ads celebrated many of the same values its sophisticated fiction writers and essayists professed to scorn. As the *New York Sun* put it in 1926,

> The academic essayist may tell you that the material things of life are negligible; "money isn't everything," etc. His essays, however, are written with advertised pens on advertised paper, the author resting his feet on an advertised rug and looking forward to an evening of surcease with his books, motor-car, radio outfit, phonograph or player-piano—all advertised, all material. He will tell you, perhaps, that his years of poverty were happiest. What he means is that the successful struggle against poverty was enjoyable. Straight poverty is pleasant only to persons like St. Francis of Assisi; and the census taker could not find many of these today.

The pursuit of happiness, whatever Jefferson originally intended it to mean, had long been interpreted by Americans in material terms. And the special, hedonistic twist taken by that pursuit during the 1920s was to a great extent compatible with the advertiser's intentions.

Advertising's greatest influence, Professor Mitchell suggested, may not have been what it made people consume, but how it made them produce:

> Desire for new goods, or the pressure of installment purchases once made, may lead people to work harder or more steadily, and so get more dollars to spend. Presumably the enticements of automobiles and radios, of wrist watches and electric refrigerators, of correspondence courses and college, have steadied many youths, set many girls hunting for jobs and kept many fathers of families to the mark.

So much, then, for the image of carefree, irresponsible flaming youth in the twenties; in order to obtain all those good things, the youths had to do something else besides flame. Even that hero of high living Scott Fitzgerald from time to time had to chase away the party-crashers and engage in drudge work in order to keep the wolf from the door. The American variant on capitalism thus had begotten two mutually inconsistent and unsatisfiable demands: a desire for unlimited pleasure-seeking, but at the same time a need for unlimited self-denial in money-getting in order to have the wherewithal for the pleasure. On this point the advice of socialists was of no avail; Stalin's grim Five Year Plans, just then getting under way, were not conceived of as a way of enabling workers to get their personal kicks without being in bondage to the bill collector.

II

A ghostly naked giant emerges from a relay panel, both of his great hands tugging at lines that reach to cranes, ships, factories, derricks, steel mills, dynamos, rotary presses, smelters. "Confident, precise, powerful—a giant rears his head above the incompetence of Man and gives to Industry an automatic control of electric motors which knows no error and no fatigue." The ad appeared in *Scientific American* in 1921, but its theme of the animated mighty machine was an old one in America. As early as 1840, railroad locomotives were described as "dragons of mightier power, with iron muscles that never tire, breathing smoke and flame through their blackened lungs, feeding upon wood and water." The earth-moving machine has impressed generations of young (and older) Americans with its clamorous dinosaurian eating habits. Typically, a steam shovel looms up in a 1924 advertisement in the *Literary Digest.* "Out, out swings the heavy scraper way beyond the end of the boom and drops to earth," says the accompanying narrative. ". . . The scraper digs its sharp beak into the earth. Steadily, relentlessly, it begins to move, gathering speed, and soil, as it comes in."

The machine has freed man from slavery; it is a familiar-enough theme of both American and Soviet poster art. But in celebrating the prowess of the machine, and more specifically of the machine that controls other machines, did the copywriter really intend to assert "the incompetence of Man"? Another advertisement from the twenties, in the mass-circulation *American Magazine,* depicted a powerhouse, with its great boilers, pipes, and valves, surely a man-dwarfing environment. But the illustration of this colossus is surrounded by a blueprint; man is after all superior to his creations. "Carved in stone above the Gothic doorway of the School of Commerce, Northwestern University," the advertisement explains, "are these words of Benjamin Franklin's: *An investment in knowledge always pays the best interest*"—a thought "doubly apt," since the same door leads also to the power-house shown in the picture. "Man's mastery of his metals and his influence over their texture and quality are the interest on just such an investment in knowledge."

The manifest purpose of all three of these ads was, of course, to publicize something for sale: General Electric Industrial Controllers, Yellow Strand Wire Rope, Crane Piping Materials. But they carried also a latent message, which the anti-capitalists in the Kremlin could also have accepted as sound doctrine: knowledge is power; it is not, as some literary intellectuals of the twenties were saying, an ironic recognition of man's powerlessness.

Knowledge is power, and power is deployed not only through wires and pipes but also—and increasingly—by the spoken and written word. "There is a mistaken idea in many men's minds that hard work is all that is necessary for success," said a 1926 ad for the Harvard Classics. "Horses do hard work and get nothing but their board." Fifteen minutes a day, publisher P. F. Collier promised, would eventually take you through the 418 books on Dr. Eliot's Five-Foot Shelf, and hopefully acquaint you with Plato, Epictetus, Marcus Aurelius, Augustine and Cicero; with Homer, Beowulf, and the Song of Roland; with Marlowe's *Faustus* and Goethe's *Faust;* with Bacon, Shakespeare, Milton, Bunyan, and Burns; with Adam Smith, Darwin, Burke, Hume, and J. S. Mill; with Cervantes, Lessing, Molière, Schiller, and Browning; with Pascal, Machiavelli, Luther, and St. Thomas More. At a less elegant level, an advertisement for a Funk & Wagnalls course on "How to Become a Master of English" asked: "Do you fumble simple words like these?" The fumbled words were those grade-school teachers' favorites, *quick–quickly, me–I, can–may, who–whom, shall–will.* No notion, in this copy, that linguistics is merely a matter of usage; there is axiomatically a right and a wrong way to say it, and the English teachers and grammarians in their endless losing battles against semantic imprecision may have found here on Madison Avenue an unwitting ally.

The major appeal was, of course, commercial: *"The big jobs* always go to men who have the ability to express themselves clearly. . . . Fortunes, literally, have been built upon words." But the command of the language could also enhance one's personal life. "Many an opportunity is lost because the power of speech is lacking. Many a friendship is shattered because of an ill-chosen word," the advertiser ominously warned; but also, more constructively, "The person who makes the real, lasting impression is the one who reveals high ideals and great thoughts when he speaks." As always, in such cases, the copy promised too much: A NEW COMMAND OF ENGLISH IN 30 DAYS. Can high ideals and great thoughts be learned in thirty days? Still it was something, in an era supposedly drenched with the ideals of Babbitt, to affirm that great thoughts can be learned at all.

In an era we often think of as marked by consumer passivity, such an advertisement was not an invitation to passive consumption. However simple it made the task sound, it did invite the

customer to attempt to *do* something. (Indeed, it ran the incidental risk that a person who took the course and learned to make
exact verbal discriminations, however rudimentary, might in the
process begin to educate himself to see through the claims of advertising!) There was also during the twenties, to be sure, a constant litany of "buy and use up," but in frequent counterpoint was
this other theme of self-improvement. Robert and Helen Lynd, in
Middletown (1929), lamented that in that Midwestern city the
spontaneous musical activities of the nineties (community sings,
for example) had faded away under the influence of the phonograph and the radio, but they seem to have overlooked other currents of the twenties flowing in the opposite direction. For example: "Music! You love it. Why don't you learn to play!" a band
instrument ad invited, under a photograph of a young woman at
the piano, a man with a saxophone, and another couple hovering
nearby. Though the copy, as usual, hedged in the direction of
ease—"simplified fingering . . . you don't have to favor and fuss
for certain notes"—nevertheless it was an urge to achievement:
"The pleasure of listening to good music is not to be compared to
the pleasure of making it." And, it may be added, such refinger-
ing also revolutionized the way musical instruments were played
by professionals, thereby greatly expanding the corps of competent musicians.

"Are you among the 30,000,000 who play musical in-
struments?" asked John Howe in the *American Magazine* for
November 1924. Howe's article was based on an interview with
Rudolph Wurlitzer, the piano and organ manufacturer, who was
entirely sanguine about the future of "live" music in the United
States: "Many people have an idea that the radio and the phono-
graph will supplant the local orchestras. But these increase as the
radio and phonograph spread." Thirty years previously in
America only five major symphony orchestras had existed: in New
York, Philadelphia, Chicago, Cincinnati, and (of course!) Boston.
Now nearly a hundred cities had them; Wurlitzer singled out
Minneapolis, Pittsburgh, St. Louis, Rochester, San Francisco,
Los Angeles, New Orleans, and Atlanta. Many of these communi-
ties to this day remain justifiably proud of their orchestras, al-

though perhaps some of this symphony-endowing reflected civic rivalry in pecuniary emulation and had little to do with music. Wurlitzer regretfully told the story of one woman who "neither knew nor cared anything about music," but who walked into his firm's New York store to buy, purely as interior decoration, a $3,500 piano to match her Louis XVI living room. However, the piano tycoon thought this exceptional. There had been a great breakthrough, he insisted, not only in musical performance but also in mass music appreciation:

> "You know more about music every year," Rudolph Wurlitzer said, leaning back in his chair.
> "Possibly," I admitted. "But I am a long way from being a musician."
> "That doesn't matter," he replied. "Just look back five years, and realize how much more good music you have heard in those years than in the five that went before. Think how many more names of composers you know, how many more compositions you recognize, and this without any study or particular attention. You simply could not help it, because music has been on the increase at such a rate that everyone who listens must learn."

Between the manufacturers of musical instruments and the manufacturers of phonographs and records there was inevitably a little fratricidal warfare: "There is a personal thrill in *hand played* music that reproductions cannot give," asserted the "learn-to-play" band instrument ad cited above. But the re-producers of music were bringing in on their side of the battle some enormous improvements in their technology—which would, in turn, compel improvement in standards of performance. A new loudspeaker marketed in 1927, said an RCA advertisement, "has brought *reality* to radio. It reaches the full volume, even of an orchestra, without blurring or altering the tone. It captures the quality of beauty that makes great music great." And precisely the greatness of the music was what the company chose in this instance to advertise: "Thousands of people everywhere are getting something more out of radio than just dance music, entertainment, speeches." How infrequently, in the usual stereotype of the "Jazz Age," have we heard it referred to as "just" dance music! Of course, RCA managed to have it both ways. Above the advertising copy the illustration shows a young woman kissing an older one goodbye, while behind her a tuxedoed young man waits with their coats. Near the old lady's chair is a radio speaker, and beneath that picture is the caption "At home but never alone." Perhaps the younger generation is about to go out dancing to a jazz band, and leaves the older generation parked beside the radio to listen to classical music. Yet the young also, as Rudolph Wurlitzer pointed out, were both hearing and playing classical music as never before.

And in this field, quite as much as in stock and bond selling, novel-writing, or stunt flying, it was possible in the twenties to hold up standards of excellence. "Music is only as good as each performer can make it," declared a full-page Victrola ad on the coveted page 1 spot in the *Ladies' Home Journal* for August 1925. It offered records—at $1.50 or $2.00 for no more than ten minutes of 78 rpm playing time—by John McCormack, by the Metropolitan Opera's Maria Jeritza, and by the violin master Fritz Kreisler. McCormack's light tenor is not so highly regarded now as it was in the twenties, and these advertised recordings were somewhat on the slushy side ("Drink to Me Only with Thine Eyes," "Moonlight and Roses"). But one could also purchase Kreisler's performance of his own *Liebeslied* and *Liebes-freud* and, if one preferred opera, there was Jeritza singing "Dich, teure Halle" from *Tannhäuser*, "Divinités du Styx" from Gluck's *Alceste,* and the stunning (when well performed) "Voi lo sapete" from *Tosca.* "Waiting to sing and play for you—Christmas day or any day," said another Victrola ad in the December number of the same magazine. Such an appeal might be considered an invitation to sit and listen rather than to get up and act, but it was also an offer of emotional enrichment. The phonograph lid is raised; a young woman places the needle. Behind her hovers a crowd of phantom figures, most of them in opera costume; one is surely Caruso. Only the most antiseptic of activists would have found fault with her for thus lapsing into "escapism."

III

"I have seen the future, and it works," exclaimed Lincoln Steffens upon returning from the Soviet Union in 1919. But the spirit of "futurism" was not confined to revolutionary Russia in the twenties; it swept also through capitalist America. "It's the new and better thing that stirs the people's heart," declared a full-page ad in the *Saturday Evening Post* for July 3, 1926:

> On Broadway a new play triumphs; and for months great crowds vie to witness it.
>
> In Miami there appears a chic new fashion; and the country immediately takes it to its heart.
>
> In Chicago, a new invention revolutionizes an industry; and the entire nation pays eager tribute.
>
> Out of Los Angeles comes word of a remarkable scientific discovery, and people everywhere thrill to the achievement.
>
> *This is America!* Ever seeking to improve upon the past. . . . Those who would appeal to America, and win and hold America's favor, must keep pace with America's desire for progress.

As the pace of invention and discovery—and of their exploitation by advertisers—quickened, many would come to find this argument giddy and unsettling. Alvin Toffler has argued in *Future Shock* (1970) that a society in constant flux and turmoil, with not only science and industry and fashion but also ethics and lifestyles and philosophies forever being revolutionized, is more than some are humanly able to take. Inevitably, therefore, an effort is made to anchor the revolution in nostalgia. Thus in the twenties the *Ladies' Home Journal* ran its ads for the new electric kitchen equipment in pages which also carried handsomely illustrated historical costume dramas, or Westerns like Zane Grey's *The Vanishing American*. *Saturday Evening Post* short stories ever and again celebrated life in an old-fashioned rural or small-town setting. Best-sellers of the twenties included books that took their readers to the far frontier or to the historic or legendary past: *The Thief of Bagdad*, by Achmed Abdullah; *Captain Blood*, by Rafael Sabatini; *Clothes Make the Pirate*, a humorous travesty on the same buccaneering theme, by Holman Day; *The*

Covered Wagon, by Emerson Hough; *Rustler's Valley,* by the creator of "Hopalong Cassidy," Clarence E. Mulford; *Rugged Water,* a tale of pre-tourist Cape Cod, by Joseph C. Lincoln; *The Alaskan,* by James Oliver Curwood; and *Show Boat* and *Cimarron* by Edna Ferber. *Show Boat,* with its show-stopping "Old Man River," became one of the greatest of Broadway musicals; the same book, along with several others on this list, were made into highly successful movies.

Magazine advertisements often reflected a similar turn to the past. By the twenties the products themselves were, in some instances, old enough to be marketed as much for their nostalgia as for their technological modernity. Singer advertised a search for "the 100 oldest sewing machines, regardless of make, in family use in the United States and Canada," and offered to swap them for new ones ("electric or treadle, as preferred"). Coca-Cola noted that it had been available "through all the years since 1886": the picture showed an elderly gentleman in a Palm Beach suit and hat with a cane, handing a coke glass to a lady of similar vintage. "Were your watch and your sweetheart both young together?" an Elgin Watch ad asked, depicting a couple who were obviously at least middle-aged. Their competitor Gruen Watch contrived to have it both ways, in an advertisement that simultaneously celebrated both the antiquity and the progressive improvement of their wares. Illustrated with a Cruikshankish drawing of gartered, ruffled, and bewigged Old World aristocrats, the copy told the story of "how the jeweled toy of princes became an accurate timekeeper"; it traced the process back to inventions in the sixteenth and seventeenth centuries by the Swiss watchmakers Zech and Gruet and in 1770 by Lepire, who created "essentially the type of movement used in the best watches when the Gruen Watch Makers Guild was founded, more than fifty years ago."

Or, if the appeal was not to the past, it might be to the outdoors, itself in an urban era increasingly a thing of the past. A hand holds a frying pan over a wood fire; "Just to taste it" (Swift's Premium Bacon) "makes you long for the woods." Similarly, Baby Ruth Candy Bars were offered not only to over-consuming children but also to "rugged grown-ups with hearty appetites." In the accompanying picture, grouped with a mounted fish, a gun, and a hunting dog, we see mackinawed men, rosy-cheeked from tramping outdoors.

In all this nostalgic appeal, however, there was an element of tease, of make-believe. For example, under the caption "Two ways to keep cool," a light sailboat in a sudden gust heels over almost to the gunwale. One man tugs at the tiller. Opposite him another hugs the rail. Forward, a young woman struggles with the jib (why doesn't her hat blow off? a skeptic might ask). Beside the mast, another flapper clutches the cabin door and looks out at the choppy sea with apprehension. "Down to the sea in ships in one way," lectures the advertiser. "Down in front of a Graybar Electric Fan the other—this way more convenient and quite as refreshing." The moral: Outdoor adventure is something one thinks about with pleasure, but it is not necessarily something one actually does.

As with the Great Outdoors, so with the romantic past: one may praise it without really wishing to return to its rigors. A fine 1925 Norman Rockwell painting beautifully makes the point. A woman in an Old American kitchen with wide floorboards is cleaning a kerosene lamp wick, with a pile of other lamps and chimneys awaiting her care—but, dear reader, "*you* have light at the touch of a finger," said the copywriter for Edison Mazda Lamps. "Remember the lamps you had to fill and trim and polish each day? You knew they were dirty and dangerous; but perhaps you think they were cheaper. *They were not!*" Furthermore, a 75-watt bulb gave more than four times the illumination of a 40-watter but averaged only a third of a cent more an hour for current. "*So use light freely,*" the ad concluded—words which readers in a later, energy-conscious era can hardly read without wincing.

But in the twenties the presumable alternative to squandering kilowatts was to go back to polishing those lamp chimneys. And drudgery, the advertisers implied, is not really a synonym for virtue. Quite the contrary, said the makers of Luco-Lac Brushing Lacquer in 1927: "If you enjoy colorful things, you may now have them with slight effort." A slim young woman in a sleeveless, deeplyV-cut lounging robe relaxes in a comfortable chair with many pillows; around her we see a bird cage, a Japanese lantern, a box of growing flowers, and two big, sunny windows. The message is ambiguous. Has she been liberated from the monotonous and exhausting toil her mother endured for no other purpose except to lounge around? Or is the proper emphasis upon the color, thanks to the chemistry of modern paint mixes, with which she will easily be able to brighten an older America's drab and dingy walls?

IV

"In a thundering power station at Niagara, on a wall of the dynamo-room, there hangs an arresting and startling placard. It reads: 'Tradition is the enemy of progress.' " Thus spoke Julius Klein, President Hoover's Assistant Secretary of Commerce, as the twenties came to their close. The wisdom of the Founding Fathers might still be invoked on points of economic and political doctrine: the protection of private property, the limitation of government, the conduct of foreign policy without "entangling alliances." Sometimes, in counterpoint to the decade's anti-clericalism and bohemianism, an "old-time religion" or an old-fashioned sexual morality might also be affirmed. But the period's recurrent themes of scientific achievement and technological prowess made it hard for even the most diehard of conservatives to affirm that the wisdom of our fathers and mothers had been quite universal. "Don't let your great-great grandmother tell you what to eat!" warned a *Ladies' Home Journal* advertisement in 1925.

> Read the cook-books of great-great grandmother's day—and marvel! Plenty of rich, heavy food for every meal. . . . Her family survived, it is true. They ate at her groaning board and got away with it.
> But life was different then.
> Nowadays, diet must be carefully adapted to the strain, the sedentary work, the nervous intensity of modern living. Fortunately, the wives of this generation are learning more about food and food values than the wisest men of great-great grandmother's time ever dreamed of.

The sales pitch this time was for Grape-Nuts, "one of the Post Health Products." The outraged eater of today's so-called breakfast foods, those confections of sugar, air, and cardboard laced with a few vitamins, is likely to forget that dried cereal began at the turn of the century in all seriousness as a health food, even as something of a health fad. And the didactic theme of "eat what is good for you" was a prominent feature in the advertisements of the twenties.

"Soup provides real, nourishing food," said its best-known American manufacturer. A sumptuous painting—even more mouth-watering than the color photograph which would be its equivalent today—depicts a head of cabbage, whole tomatoes, potatoes, an onion, peas in the pod, an ear of corn; and, in the foreground, the familiar Campbell can, which has undergone some redesigning since the twenties but to the modern reader (or eater) is still recognizable. The specific customer aimed at this time is "the prettiest girl in the office," whom "you don't find . . . eating just anything she sees. She is Little Miss Careful . . . in taking care of her complexion and her figure. Trust her to follow every hint about eating the right things to keep her trim and attractive." The tone is in sharp contrast to the savage essay Bruce Bliven wrote for the *New Republic* in 1925 on "Flapper Jane" whom he described as "frankly, heavily made up, not to imitate nature, but for an altogether artificial effect—pallor mortis, poisonously scarlet lips, richly ringed eyes. . . ." This bizarre image of the "flapper" has crept into all our textbook stereotypes of the Roaring Twenties, but the advertising copywriter at the time seems to have assumed that a different standard of sexual desirability was available. It is hard to imagine anyone achieving the effect Bliven described by diligently eating vegetable soup!

The health appeal was aimed not only at the single office girl but also at the scrupulous young mother. "6,000,000 children in our country—one out of every three—are suffering from undernourishment," warned a Borden ad in 1924. "Hardly a family—well-to-do and poor alike—escapes the menace of malnutrition. Your own child may fall victim to this insidious evil." (It is scare talk, but it has been abundantly confirmed by subsequent medical opinion and research, despite—or in addition to—the fact that we also already had a national trend toward obesity.) What should the reader do about it? Clip the coupon and send for Borden's Three Little

Books, on how to recognize malnutrition, on menus and recipes, on calory and vitamin tables; check up on her children's daily health habits; let her doctor examine them thoroughly for any organic defects—and put them on Eagle Brand condensed milk, a dreadful enough conclusion from the standpoint of a present-day child (or mother!). If they won't drink it straight, spread it undiluted on bread, or mix it with fruit or egg; "The food value is the same in whatever form you give it." Other products took a similar line. Thus Eleanor Roosevelt in 1930—by which time Franklin was Governor of New York—was persuaded to endorse Cream of Wheat, which their son John had eaten since he was a baby. "I think Cream of Wheat has undoubtedly played its part in building his robust physique," Mrs. Roosevelt declared. Given the general public knowledge of her husband's gallant battle against polio, and the terror inspired by the ravages of that and other diseases upon children, such testimony must have hit home.

Much of the advice on calories and vitamins may have been misinformation from the standpoint of a later day, and no doubt the primary purpose was merely to sell Cream of Wheat or Eagle Brand. But great-great-grandmother, and other mothers not so far removed in time, *had* stuffed their guests with five or six different kinds of starch at a sitting. Advertising of this kind—reaching a reader who might have treated the same advice from a school hygienist or nurse with the condescension we are told was reserved for schoolteachers in those days, or who (considering the dropout rate then prevailing) might never have gotten the school's health message at all—may have accomplished some incidental good.

For infant feeding, the food processors and the electrical industry in effect joined forces. "One Day of Life" was the way one *Saturday Evening Post* ad put it in 1926. "Six little bottles of milk? No, not merely that. Six little bottles of strength, of growth, of health—of Life itself." And the life was to be safeguarded by the "constant cold" of electric refrigeration. It comes as a bit of a shock: yes, there were enough old-fashioned iceboxes in use across the land in the mechanized, urbanized twenties to make such an advertisement a worthwhile investment. Not everybody could afford to replace them, even on the installment plan; and thus, in discontented icebox-using Americans, were planted a few of the germs of the New Deal.

Food was not the only component of this health appeal. "Health has few allies, disease few enemies more powerful than the paint brush," said a 1926 ad under the title "save the surface and you save all." "Where people are crowded together, as in schools and trains, public buildings, ships and hotels, there paint and varnish are invaluable guardians":

> Disease lurks in dirt and darkness. Paint and varnish bring light and cleanliness. Disease most fiercely attacks those who neglect hygiene. Paint and varnish strongly influence personal cleanliness. The philosophy of the paint brush is inseparable from the philosophy of mental and bodily well-being. When you save the surface, you act to save not property alone, but that which makes it worth while to own property—good health.

The implications of such an appeal are far-reaching. Perhaps the classic antithesis between "human rights" and "property rights" is one of those plausible but misleading abstractions; perhaps capitalism, not only for the consumer but for the capitalist himself, was only a means to another end; perhaps the material god most ardently worshiped in America, even in the money-mad twenties, was not the sound dollar so much as the sound body.

In 1929 Charles Atlas, "The World's Most Perfectly Developed Man," began to publish—in the humbler pulp fiction and mechanics monthlies rather than the slick-paper mass-circulation magazines we have been examining—his now-famous testimonial, "I was a 97-pound weakling." Another chapter was begun in American folklore, as you too, gentle reader, learned that through a regimen of "Dynamic Tension" (Atlas's advertiser's name for what we now call isometric exercises) you could find your way to "Everlasting Health and Strength."

For the more affluent citizen, too much caught up in the business whirl to take time out for exercises, shortcuts were available, as one *Saturday Evening Post* ad grimly pointed out under the title "The Survival of the Fittest." A businessman is standing in a busy office, hand in pocket, with a glum expression. To the left, a secretary bends to confer with a man at a desk; on the right another man, hat hastily dropped on his briefcase, topcoat still on, hunches over a telephone. The atmosphere is one of furious, competitive haste. "One of the most important allies of success is health," the copywriter explains. "Guard it well if you have your eyes fixed on the top of the ladder. . . . Business is a stern taskmaster. Only the fit survive." Eventually, the narrative gets to the point; our hero's problem, it delicately explains, is "faulty elimination." But "now, thanks to a delicious cereal food, he can ward off this danger without recourse to habit-forming drug laxatives." And then the brand name: Post's Bran Flakes, for "Everybody—every day—as an ounce of prevention."

A homily against habit-forming drugs, however quaint from the standpoint of a later, stoned generation, is in refreshing contrast to the pill-popping inducements of present-day drug companies' advertising. Perhaps the epithet "Aspirin Age," as applied to the twenties and thirties, is a misnomer. Nerve-wracking enough the commuters' grind and office jangle of the 1920s may have been, but it does not seem to have prompted an impulse remotely comparable to that of our times to peddle and consume headache relievers and nerve soothers, products to wake you up and products to put you to sleep. The total absence of liquor advertising because of the Eighteenth Amendment—and thus also of hangover remedies!—reinforces this aura of healthful innocence, and it probably reinforced also the social standards of those Americans in the twenties (more numerous than some students of Prohibition are yet aware) who had never tasted bathtub gin. The pursuit of happiness in the twenties may have been a matter of eye-gouging competition and involved the reckless purchase and lavish display of sometimes useless consumer goods, but at least—outside of Scott's and Zelda's social circles—it did not have to be chemically induced.

V

The Crash came and the glow faded. Suddenly people did not have money enough to buy what they read about in the magazines. Campbell's Soup was no longer a health food; it was what you ate, with a few plain crackers, because you couldn't afford anything else, and it is so remembered—sometimes with affection, but also often with loathing—by multitudes who grew up during the Depression. As they scrambled for the shrinking supply of customers' dollars, according to one student of the subject, the advertisers' entire game seems to have turned more dirty, downright, and crass. Surely no words from the twenties today have a more bitterly ironic ring than Calvin Coolidge's before the American Association of Advertising Agencies in 1926: "There can be no permanent basis for advertising except a representation of the exact truth."

Inevitably, the cessation of the glut of consumer goods prompted some moral hair-shirting, of the same sort that would be prompted later by the energy crisis of the seventies. A preacher-cartoonist in the early thirties drew a picture for his parish bulletin of a muscled gym instructor labeled "The Depression," administering calisthenics ("One! Two! Bend down!") to a scowling pot-bellied citizen who is presumably Mr. Middle American. But the artist had an afterthought. Looking in through the gym window is a gaunt, ragged scarecrow of the kind made familiar to us in countless New Deal documentary photographs, and attached to him is the label: "Some do not need it."

The pent-up desires held in check by the Great Depression were only partially appeased by the full-employment war economy of the forties, with its rationed abundance; and then, after the war, the dam broke. A tidal wave of consumer goods rolled across the land, trumpeted by the new advertising medium of television, and another tidal wave of Americans born in the "baby boom" scrambled after it to consume them. By the tail-finny fifties some were beginning to complain of psychic indigestion, and by the marching sixties the more radical of the affluent young, never having known any lifestyle except one of overstuffing, had become so jaded that they rejected the advertisers' wares and values altogether. This put them at cross-purposes, to the great injury of the radical movement, with rising minorities such as the blacks who had never enjoyed such goods, even in the booming twenties, and who would be denied them no longer. (Perhaps here is a clue also to the mutual contempt and hostility felt between the college generation of the sixties who took those goods for granted and the middle-aged non-college whites who had struggled so hard during the Depression to get them.) "Our society has told us to want certain kinds of things very much," said Frederik Pohl—co-author of a well-received fictional satire on advertising, *The Space Merchants* —toward the end of 1968. "And it's no accident that during the looting in America's urban riots, the first things taken are the commodities most heavily advertised on TV."

The riot impulse faded after 1968, but the basic situation Pohl had described remained: "They [the poor] know what we [the affluent] have got," thanks to the instantaneousness of modern communication. "What they see we have, they want. . . . If they can't earn it, they'd like someone to give it to them. If [we] can't give it to them, perhaps they'll take it." There has been much discussion in recent years of a "revolution of rising expectations," not only in America but even more sharply in the Third and Fourth Worlds. As a prologue to that revolution, the twenties may have been far more radical than that decade's business-minded political leaders ever realized. For who has contributed more to those expectations than the advertiser? Far from having hammered the consuming public into a passive mass, the copywriters may have unwittingly goaded it toward mass action; far from having diverted people's attention from political and economic reality, they may have fanned unquenchable flames of discontent. For a time in the late sixties it appeared that in those flames Madison Avenue itself might be consumed.

But as that abortive revolution flickered out and gave way to an ecology/energy crisis the advertisers had also helped beget, it appeared that for the foreseeable future we were stuck with this social institution. Advertising in a modern corporate world had come to play an energizing, morale-building role comparable to that of a Cotton Mather in a smaller, more communal world. If age-old, life-denying assumptions of scarcity and deprivation are to be overcome throughout our planet, and if at the same time the provision of abundance and gratification shall not plunder the planet's resources beyond recall, surely whatever policy is evolved for these high and perhaps inconsistent purposes will have to win public support. For that purpose, one way or another, it will probably be advertised—unless those in authority simply decide upon the policy and tell the rest of us what to do. Our former standardized values of display, luxury, and power were easily translated into advertising copy, and our new, or old, countervalues—don't waste, turn down the furnace, turn off the light, form a car pool— have proved equally advertisable: "Smokey Bear says, 'Only you can prevent forest fires.' " Unfortunately any instrument of persuasion is a two-edged sword; Cotton Mather could preach to men to hang witches, and he could also preach to them to accept smallpox inoculation.

It will not do to say that we could get rid of advertising under socialism, unless we can assert that *any* organization should abstain from peddling its wares—which historically no business, or political party, or government, or church, or educational institution has shown itself willing to do. A public-ownership society has its own priorities and values to publicize: if possible through a Great Cultural Revolution; if necessary through a "Ministry of Truth." Can we somehow learn, all of us, to send up in concert from the grass roots an uncoached signal of our own so powerful that it drowns out the copywriter's message? Even in America's most innocent years that would have seemed an unlikely Utopian hope, but perhaps tomorrow is a time when necessity must become the mother of Utopia. Of course, the laissez-faire solution is also available: we can go on riding our ungovernable horse into the future, shouting contradictory slogans into his ear. In his confusion at the conflicting messages he hears, the outcome may well be as forecast in the Apocalypse: famine and pestilence, war and death.

CHAPTER VIII

"Horatio Alger Doesn't Work Here any More"

"AIM HIGH." That, in 1885, was the kind of advice the steel magnate Andrew Carnegie gave the students in a commercial college in Pittsburgh. "Do not rest content for a moment in your thoughts as head clerk, or foreman, or general manager. . . . Say each to yourself, 'My place is at the top.' *Be king in your dreams.*" Thirty years later, for business tycoons counseling a new crop of rising young men, the dream seems not to have dimmed. The mass-circulation *American Magazine*—the most popular periodical, among both working-class and business-class families, in the Lynds' Middletown—regularly ran inspirational interviews with successful men, written in a manner implying that you too, dear reader, can go and do likewise:

——"Don't fear to attempt a thing just because it looks big," George Washington Goethals ringingly declared in 1922 in a typical *American Magazine* interview. "Nothing is ever as hard as it seems to be." At the age of fourteen Goethals had been a cashier and bookkeeper in a market at five dollars a week, working after school and all day Saturday. At the age of fifty-four he had built the Panama Canal.

——Charles W. Brown told another writer for the *American* in 1926 that he had received his original business training on

board a sailing ship, amongst a tough, salty crew: "A thrashing administered by a hard-boiled mate taught him, while he was still a
boy, not to argue about work, but to do it." Later, as a ship captain himself, he had learned "to act on his own responsibility, to
handle men, and to make advantageous business trades." At the
time of the interview, Brown was President of the Pittsburgh
Plate Glass Company.

——A. E. Lefcourt in 1924 described for still another
American Magazine interviewer how he had started out at
the age of eight as a newsboy and bootblack on New York's
Lower East Side. "There was apparently nothing to distinguish
him," according to the magazine's account, "from the thousands
of other ragged, yelling little sons of foreign immigrants with
whom he dodged under the feet of the dray horses in the narrow
streets." When he liquidated his manufacturing interests in 1923
to go into real estate, Lefcourt was the unquestioned leader of the
city's garment industry.

From testimonies like these we may infer that in the twenties
the spirit we usually associate with Horatio Alger was alive and
well. For some uninhibited operators, even Andrew Carnegie's
caution to the young man starting out in business that he "make
the firm's interest yours" was to confining. One such individualist, fired twenty times during the previous twelve years by
bosses who never had had the feeling he was really working for
them, proclaimed (anonymously) in 1923: "The only person a
self-respecting man can work for is himself."

Indeed, to be fired, in a booming entrepreneurial economy,
rightly considered was not a disgrace but an opportunity. "Firing
is as much a normal part of business as hiring," mused one successful businessman, who had himself once lost a $23-a-week job
after a fifteen-minute fist fight with a sadistic boss, in the course
of which they smashed a showcase in the store where they
worked. However, the firing need not take place in so traumatic a
way. Instead, the boss should call in the employee and tell him:
"My boy, there really isn't any job here that is going to satisfy
your particular sort of talents. . . . Take your youth and go and

lick the world. I like you too well to coddle you. Here's a month's wages. You're fired."

It is hardly a line of approach that either an employer or an employee would take today, when a record of frequent dismissals would routinely be fed into the patient and inexorable computers, whence it would follow a man until the crack of doom. But the twenties had little inkling of the oncoming era of electronic surveillance. To be sure, one might be blacklisted for joining a labor union. But otherwise, the prevailing private enterprise gospel affirmed, whether one were hired or fired individual merit would win out in fair and free competition, one way or another. "Most men who fail at their work, fail by only a little," insisted E. D. Stair, publisher of the Detroit *Free Press,* in 1926. "They give almost, but not quite, enough. Another ounce of steam and they would have turned the trick." A decade later, advice such as this would be remembered with bitterness by men who during the Depression years gave all that they had and found it was nowhere near enough. But hindsight is not foresight. In 1923, that free spirit who had thumbed his nose at twenty employers in a dozen years looked to the future with serenity: "I tackle the next fifty years with light heart, sure hope, and resolute faith."

So hopeful was the prospect of success, in the opinion of one aspirant, that it was worth a detour through blue-collar ranks; he had quit an advertising agency job to enroll in an auto mechanics school. "Didn't you get sick of the dirty, grinding work?" a concerned friend asked him after he had signed on as a helper in a garage.

Not half as sick of it as he had been of his former pallid pencil-pushing, the new repairman replied.

"How about your friends the girls, and your social position?" the friend persisted.

"I wasn't caring a fig either way," the mechanic insisted; it didn't bother him even when erstwhile white-collar associates would come into the garage for service or repairs and "nod coldly to me in recognition." Besides, in due course such problems would solve themselves. His boss had just told him that after the first of the year he would be the manager of a branch garage, and share in the profits.

One popular stereotype of the business world of the twenties conceives it as a nation of earnest, bumbling Babbitts, economic individualists in the marketplace but social conformists at their Chamber of Commerce breakfasts and Rotary luncheons, where they smothered all personal uniqueness or distinction under a blanket of boosterism, optimism, and good-fellowship with the boys. On the contrary, some business leaders were saying, it is not enough merely to scramble after success. One must do so in one's own way. "All Ford cars are exactly alike," said Henry their maker,

> but no two men are just alike. Every new life is a new thing under the sun; there has never been anything just like it before, and never will be again. A young man ought to get that idea about himself; he should look for a single spark of individuality that makes him different from other folks, and develop that for all he is worth. Society and schools may try to iron it out of him; their tendency is to put us all in the same mould, but I say don't let that spark be lost; it's your only real claim to importance.

The paradox here is that in all likelihood nobody was doing more to iron out the differences—class, regional, ethnic—in American society than the archetypal mass-producer of those exactly-alike automobiles. Henry Ford, moreover, was a rugged individualist even by rugged individualism's own standards. The Ford Motor Company had financed its initial expansion essentially out of its own earnings; it had never, therefore, been brought to book by the investment banking forces symbolized in the House of Morgan and thereby disciplined into its proper place in America's corporate structure. Thus the head of that family firm—whose stock was not yet even traded on the Exchange— might be indulged in his quirky personalist views.

But after Henry came Edsel and Henry II, and their mere biological existence posed a problem. "There is but one way to produce a man," Professor Gus W. Dyer told the 1920 annual convention of the National Association of Manufacturers, "and that is to pitch him out and give him the reins and let him make himself." By the logic of that argument, all well-to-do fathers would have had to disinherit their sons, for the sons' own good! No less a self-made man than Andrew Carnegie had once declared: "The almighty dollar bequeathed to children is an almighty curse. No man has a right to handicap his son with such a burden as great wealth." (Carnegie's only immediate heir, incidentally, was a daughter.)

Inheritance was a serious logical obstacle for any doctrine of laissez-faire, and in particular for the Darwinist variety Carnegie had always espoused. Public discussion of that problem continued after the steel magnate's death in 1919. According to an editorial in *Collier's* for September 29, 1923, "Born wealth stops the process by which earned wealth is made." The point was illustrated with a cartoon by J. N. "Ding" Darling that showed one man in a boat on the open, choppy sea, casting in sportsmanlike fashion for fishes labeled "Big Fortunes," while another placidly angled for his prey from the shore of an enclosed private fish pond, with a butler standing by to serve him a drink.

"Four-fifths of the American fortunes with incomes of over a million dollars per year have been accumulating for two generations or more," warned William G. Shepherd, another *Collier's* writer, in 1922. "Five hundred fortunes between $5,000,000 and $10,000,000 have been handed down within thirty years." The point was not so much economic as moral: "Unearned dollars have changed many a fine boy into a dangerous fool." In effect agreeing with a "soapbox socialist" he had lately heard denouncing "those lapdog Americans who inherit their wealth," Shepherd suggested the same remedy the capitalist Andrew Carnegie had proposed: a heavy, confiscatory inheritance tax. The federal government and the states could and should "take these dangerous dollars and put them into road building and park making and into carrying out all the dreams of a better future . . . that every American citizen cherishes."

England had long since been taxing its dead for public purposes, the author pointed out—and, he might have added, without markedly diminishing the Establishment's economic, social, or political power. As a matter of record, Congress in fact took a long step in just that direction, in a bill signed by Coolidge on June 2, 1924, which raised the tax on estates valued at over $10 million to a maximum of 40 percent. (It was a step, however, of which the Coolidge Administration soon repented; under Treasury Secretary Mellon's prodding, Congress set about rolling that tax rate back.)

II

For all their bumptious after-dinner individualism, in their more reflective moods successful Americans in the twenties sometimes admitted that the art of making it could no longer be pursued in the manner of that archetypal bourgeois Robinson Crusoe. "No man ever made a fine record in anything entirely through his own efforts," testified Arthur L. Humphrey, President of Westinghouse Air Brake, in 1928. "Show me a man in a responsible position, and I'll show you a man who has had help." More help, perhaps, than an independent-minded executive really wanted; a medium-sized plant in the twenties employing between 1,000 and 5,000 people typically might have an Advertising Committee, a Cost Committee, a Budget Committee, a Design Committee, a Management Committee, an Inventory Control Committee, a Personnel Committee, a Safety Committee, a Standards Committee, a Sales Committee, and if all else failed a Suggestion Committee. The top boss himself was not immune from these committees' relentless scrutiny; by 1926 it was possible for management and personnel people to speak of "the illusion of final authority."

"More men are being brought within managerial responsibilities," according to the government-sponsored survey of *Recent Economic Changes* (1929), "and the co-ordinated group, each member of which has his own share in the total of responsibilities, is replacing the absolute 'big boss.' " In those *American Magazine* interviews the voice might be that of the self-made, self-directed entrepreneur, but the hands were those of Organization Man. Small wonder, then, that some sardonic ob-

servers of the corporate process doubted whether all this commit-
teemanship in the name of enterprise added up to real employment. "The men get up about eight o'clock and go down to New
York to Business," says a character in Ring Lardner's *The Big
Town* (1925). "They don't never go to work."

Even so earnest a high priest of free enterprise as the advertising magnate and amateur theologian Bruce Barton could occasionally admit that the self-made man in America was becoming
a myth: "Every man in a big position knows in his own heart that
forces entirely outside himself have played a large part in his
making," Barton conceded in 1928. Granted, such a man personally could influence the precise way those forces operated
upon him. A multimillionaire Barton knew had recently remarked
in confidence that his life had been "just a series of accidents"—
"but," said Barton, "he was always on his toes to take advantage
of them." Nevertheless, those accidents did happen. "Did you
ever watch oranges being assorted in a packing plant?" asked
Charles F. Stern, president of a combination of ninety-one West
Coast banking firms, in 1926. "They are dumped into a conveyor,
and carried along over a series of holes. Gradually, each orange
finds its particular-sized hole and disappears. . . . It's like that
with men."

To be sure, Stern catechized, some free play for individual initiative remained:

> A man has this advantage over an orange: he doesn't have to re-
> main in the groove into which he has been dropped unless he
> wishes to. By the exercise of his brain, his grit, and his determina-
> tion, he can so increase his girth that he is forced out of his groove,
> is caught up again by the conveyor, and deposited into a hole bet-
> ter fitting to his new size.
>
> Thus, a man sets his own limitations. . . . He alone is to blame
> if he is permanently dumped from the conveyor before he reaches
> his goal.

In a sense, then, a man remains individually responsible for his
destiny, in accordance with the true American laissez-faire tradition. And yet, all he can really do by means of brains, grit, and

determination is to find out what his limits are! We are a long distance indeed from the rousing activism implied in the titles (less
so in the actual plots) of Horatio Alger's novels: *Bound to Rise,
Helping Himself, Making His Way, Strive and Suc-
ceed, Do and Dare.* In the real world of modern business,
socially as well as mechanically automated, man proposes but ultimately the conveyor disposes.

"There was a time when it was considered up to the young
man—and up to him alone—to show what stuff was in him,"
wrote G. M. Eaton, a Westinghouse engineer, in the journal *Industrial Management* for March 1923. "Today the existence
of a joint responsibility is recognized. The mist must be pene-
trated by both the man and the establishment." That establishment in the twenties was bigger and more complex than ever
before. Although the number of small industrial units (employing
between six and twenty persons) remained remarkably stable—
53,954 in 1914, and still 54,609 in 1923 after a short but severe
recession—the larger plants were doing the lion's share of the
production; the 4 percent of American manufacturing establish-
ments each having more than 250 employees accounted for 4.5
million wage earners, or slightly more than half the entire industrial labor force. At the same time there were continuing waves of
mergers and holding-company consolidations; "banking," writes
David Shannon, "experienced a concentration in the 1920's that
made the old 'money trust' seem juvenile." And hundreds of
shiny new outlets for Walgreen, J. C. Penney, Safeway, and O.
P. Skaggs dramatically overshadowed the surviving Mom-and-Pop
stores.

"The family-owned, one-man-controlled type of business today
is a relic of the past," Pennsylvania Railroad president William
W. Atterbury observed in 1928. ". . . More and more is the
ownership of business passing into the hands of large groups of
stockholders," who in turn devolve responsibility upon a hired
professional manager. There were certain conspicuous exceptions
to that rule; the Rockefeller dynasty was in its second generation,
and at the outbreak of World War I Pierre du Pont and a corps of

brothers, cousins, and in-laws remained in undisputed operational control of their century-old family firm. Yet even that close-knit Wilmington, Delaware, clan had had to adapt to the new order. A bruising intrafamily fight during the War, in which one group of du Ponts hauled its sibling rivals into court charging that a $14 million stock sale between two of the cousins was illegal, literally set brother against brother, mother against son. In the view of the business historians Alfred Chandler and Stephen Salsbury, this ruinous suit of *du Pont v. du Pont* dramatized the lesson that "if [a] company is to continue as a force in its industry, the needs of the enterprise must come before those of the family."

In 1917 the anciently established Du Pont Company, with a strong assist from the House of Morgan, made a heavy investment in the young and swiftly growing automobile industry. Pierre du Pont won the chairmanship of the board of directors at General Motors, and in the sharp automotive recession of 1920 he took over its presidency as well. But the measure of his achievement there was precisely Pierre's ability to bring together in an effective operating force a group of strong-willed men to whom he was *not* related by marriage or blood. When, in 1924, Pierre du Pont turned the leadership of General Motors over to Alfred P. Sloan, the automobile firm had undergone a sweeping managerial reorganization (largely proposed by Sloan); it was now an impersonal modern corporate colossus, all primed for its impending successful challenge to the still patriarchal Ford. "General Motors," Sloan wrote in his *Adventures of a White-Collar Man* (1941), "had become too big to be a one-man show."

From examples like this, and without passing upon the merits of James Burnham's controversial thesis of a "managerial revolution," we may at least concur in the judgment of Henry Dennison in 1929 that the old unmanaged era, when "sheer power and drive could win almost every time over finesse," had passed. "There is to-day," Dennison concluded his chapter on "Management" in *Recent Economic Changes*, "not only more production per man, more wages per man, and more horse power per man, but more management per man as well."

III
The sociology of the new management dictated some changes in the ways businessmen related to their peers—and to the public. Even if a man were a rigidly archaic exemplar of the strong, silent, inner-directed, wooden-faced Gary Cooper American, all at once he had to learn to smile, to engage in groupthink, to deal not only in production and sales figures but in personal and verbal relationships as well. (Philip Armour, the meat-packing tycoon, said after he had amassed his millions that he "would rather have been a great speaker than a great capitalist.") In this new situation some of these men made the panicky discovery that they were tongue-tied. One day a man might be called on to make an impromptu address, and—for all his wealth and power—fail in embarrassment and humiliation. Into this unforeseen breach in the ramparts of capitalism stepped Dale Carnegie, a man quite different in style and temperament from Andrew.

After an obscure career as a regional sales representative for Armour and for the International Correspondence Schools, this younger Carnegie (no relation) had come to New York in 1911, where he at once found his vocation: teaching inarticulate business and professional men how to talk to a live audience. Dale Carnegie offered his courses to businessmen in the Advertising Club and the Rotary Club of New York, the Manufacturers' Club and the Penn Athletic Club of Philadelphia, the Brooklyn Chamber of Commerce, and the Federal Reserve Bank of New York; under YMCA auspices he took the classes also to Trenton, Philadelphia, Wilmington, and Baltimore. Seven thousand men had taken the course by the time Carnegie developed it into a book, which the Y's Association Press published in 1928: *Public Speaking, a Practical Course for Business Men.*

The author drilled his readers at the end of each chapter with lists of words often mispronounced, errors in English, and correct usage of words; but this was more than a simple "how-to" book. It was an evangelist's gospel. Against the American masculine deadpan ideal, Carnegie quoted a Chinese proverb: "He who cannot smile ought not to keep a shop." Somewhat more crassly, he offered an exercise:

> Try this: say "thirty million dollars" quickly and with an air of triviality so that it sounds like a very small sum. Now, say "thirty thousand dollars"; say it slowly; say it feelingly; say it as if you were tremendously impressed with the hugeness of the amount. Haven't you now made the thirty thousand sound larger than the thirty million?

The potential for moral disaster implicit in such behavior is self-evident. Moreover, Donald Meyer in *The Positive Thinkers* ominously warns, the Dale Carnegie smile-your-way-to-success formula entails a real risk of "the disintegration of one's own awareness of reality." But to the student taking Carnegie's course, its message may have been more than simply manipulative. Suddenly the unreflective, extroverted, things-oriented American businessman was being asked to do what he had so often faulted the intellectuals for doing: to indulge in self-examination, to introspect the inner recesses of his own soul:

> The preparation of a speech, a real speech, does not consist in merely getting some mechanical words down on paper. . . . Neither does it consist in lifting a few thoughts second hand from some book or newspaper article. No, no. But it does consist in digging away down deep into your own mind and heart and life, and bringing forth some convictions and enthusiasms that are essentially yours. Yours! YOURS! Dig. Dig. Dig. It is there.

Was the smiling YMCA teacher fully aware of the unconscious Emersonian yearnings that could be tapped within the reader of such words? Perhaps the harried entrepreneur, enmeshed economically in the omnipresent Organization, in his very efforts to cope with people in the new managerial way was also rediscovering an ancient but perennially fresh source of individual expression and fulfillment. What did all this actually have to do with inventories and stock quotations? the tired businessman might have asked himself, as he lay flat on his back following Carnegie's instructions to improve his breathing, or stood up to perform another kind of exercise:

> Relax; feel in the throat the cool, delightful sensation of an oncoming yawn; drink in a deep breath of air. . . . Now let us try con-

trolling, by means of the diaphragm, the release of this air. Hold a
lighted candle close to your mouth. See if you can empty your
lungs now so slowly, so evenly, that the flame of the candle will
not flicker in the slightest even though it is held quite close to the
mouth. You should practise this until you can exhale steadily for
thirty or forty seconds without disturbing the flame of the candle.

Was it really the thought of how to win friends and influence
people—the theme of a later, more widely-read Carnegie book—
that prompted a busy capitalist to take time out for such behavior? Or was it an impulse more akin to that which impels some
people to take up Yoga?

The young countercultural rebels of the early 1970s, practicing
transcendental meditation on street corners or on college cam-
puses, might have been disconcerted at the thought that, physically at least, they were thus linked in common activity with
Grandfather Babbitt half a century ago. But there were nonecono-
mic implications for the 1920s in Dale Carnegie's breath-control
exercises also. He described them with a gusto that was partly the
put-on of a salesman, no doubt, but also with echoes of quite
another theme of that decade: its heedless, joyous hedonism. For
contrast with the classic model of an earlier capitalism, imagine
Ebenezer Scrooge heeding advice to "take a deep breath. . . .
Start to yawn as you drink it in, deep, now, deep; feel your
porous lungs expanding like a toy balloon. . . . Now, before the
yawn breaks, with your throat open, sing 'ah.' "

IV

How was the outsider to the business process, in position neither to bully nor to sing his way to power, supposed to view the
new situation? Under Andrew Carnegie's regime in America, as
distinguished from Dale's, the "little man" had been asked to identify with the great ostensibly as a model for his own behavior: you
too may become a capitalist, or a President of the United States.
By the twenties the plausibility of that model had begun to fade,
despite the *American Magazine*'s urgings. The testimony of
that white-collar advertising man turned garage mechanic to the
contrary notwithstanding, all contenders on the economic battle-

ground were *not* equal; education alone, with the cultural and economic class advantages it implied, conferred status upon the young businessman quite independently of his personal worth. "I would say that a college-trained man attains an executive rank about ten years sooner than does the man of similar ability and initiative but limited schooling," the Pennsylvania Railroad's William Atterbury acknowledged. In what sense, then, could a member of the "silent majority" who was not even on the bottom rung of the business ladder identify with the new breed of businessman?

"Me and Rockefeller." "All of you wish you could say it," wrote Stuart Mackenzie in 1926. "Well, perhaps you can." As a matter of fact, Mackenzie claimed, more than fifteen million Americans—roughly 12 percent of the entire population!—were entitled to use that expression already: the holders, great and small, of stocks and bonds. Three hundred fifty thousand stockholders—three-fourths of them having twenty-five or fewer shares—owned American Tel & Tel. The employees of Standard Oil of New Jersey (the corporate ancestor of Exxon) owned half a million shares in that company. One-fourth of the New York Central Railroad's employees were buying stock on the installment plan, at $10 to $15 below the market price. "I like to think that millions of us still own part of the work we have been doing," Mackenzie wrote; shareholding thus was not only an answer to the question of how an individual succeeds in a complex corporate society but also an easement of the much-remarked alienation between the worker and his work.

Rather than go to work for a company and rise within it by proving his worth, by this reasoning, young Horatio Alger could instead use the pennies he had earned as a newsboy to buy his way into it. Stuart Mackenzie's figure of fifteen million shareholders is almost certainly inflated; the economist John Kenneth Galbraith in *The Great Crash* cites figures indicating no more than a tenth that many people had active accounts with brokerage firms in 1929. But mere inaccuracy of arithmetic is not enough to deflate a legend. "The striking thing about the stock market speculation of 1929 was not the massiveness of the participation," Galbraith concludes. "Rather it was the way it became central to the culture."

So central was it becoming to the culture, before the disaster in the fall of 1929, that some even foresaw the goals of socialism achieved through capitalism's own processes. George E. Roberts, vice-president of New York's National City Bank, predicted that "the great organizations for production, transportation, and distribution will be practically owned by their employees and by the people whom they serve." "In other words," journalist Stuart Mackenzie added, "they will be owned largely by wage earners." Clutching his or her handful of shares in Mr. Rockefeller's company, the man in the street or the woman in the kitchen could then claim the common bond of ownership, and legitimately speak of "me and Rockefeller." Furthermore, anyone could play the game. As John J. Raskob, a General Motors and former Du Pont executive who was also chairman of the Democratic National Committee, explained, "Everybody ought to be rich," and the way to become rich was to invest in stocks and bonds. According to Raskob's calculation $15 a month wisely invested, if you did not spend your dividends, would be worth about $80,000 in twenty years, a return on the investment of over 400 percent.

Not everyone, of course, could afford the initial $15, and occasionally some spoilsport warned that even for those able to pay for such a venture, getting rich might not be quite so easy as Raskob suggested. "The Ticker says *Nothing* about To-Morrow!" cautioned a 1926 advertisement for the Adair Realty & Trust Company, citing one university-sponsored survey of a large number of men who had speculated in stocks over a period of years—97 percent of whom had lost money. According to that survey 2 percent broke even and only 1 percent came out ahead. But Americans in the twenties were about as likely to heed such a warning as they are today to pay attention to the Surgeon General's statement that the cigarettes they are about to consume are hazardous to their health. Anyhow, Adair Realty's caution was on behalf of a sales pitch of its own, urging the purchase of guaranteed 6.5 percent bonds secured by first mortgages upon "carefully selected income-producing properties"; and real estate, in the general debacle after 1929, would prove as dubious an investment as any other.

But Pollyanna is always more fun to listen to than Cassandra. John J. Raskob's exhortation to everybody to get rich was printed in the *Ladies' Home Journal* two months before the Crash. The historians and social critics have had fun with it ever since, and unfortunately once a myth has been destroyed it becomes difficult if not impossible to recapture the emotions which that myth once compelled. Frederick Lewis Allen, however, writing in 1931 when the memory of that promised horn-of-plenty was still green, could still describe how it had fired the imagination of the pre-Crash American:

> He saw a magical order built on the new science and the new prosperity: roads swarming with millions upon millions of automobiles, airplanes darkening the skies, lines of high-tension wire carrying from hilltop to hilltop the power to give life to a thousand labor-saving machines, skyscrapers thrusting above one-time villages, vast cities rising in great geometrical masses of stone and concrete, and roaring with perfectly mechanized traffic—and smartly dressed men and women spending, spending, spending with the money they had won by being far-sighted enough to foresee, way back in 1929, what was going to happen.

This pre-Crash American was not quite America's Everyman, and his angle of vision as described in Allen's *Only Yesterday* was narrow. From a rural potholed road leading to a farmhouse lighted by kerosene, or from an ugly company-built house tottering at the edge of an open-pit mine, or from a garbage-reeking airshaft surrounded by noisy tenements, the view would not have been the same. Yet the lure of that magical new Jerusalem probably extended beyond the ranks of the smartly dressed spenders described by Allen. As Scott Fitzgerald was to write in retrospect of the twenties, "Even when you were broke you didn't worry about money, because it was in such profusion around you." In the bleakest of circumstances, the lightning might strike; that hope fueled not only the stock market but also the ineradicable Harlem numbers game.

But wealth and good living, however desirable in themselves, were not all that Horatio Alger was supposedly striving for. The "me and Rockefeller" promise implied not only profit but also participation; those fifteen million American shareholders were expected to regard themselves not only as spectators of Wall Street's gaudy show but also—at least by proxy—as actors. However, in this game, to put it mildly, if all men were equal some were more equal than others.

Prematurely, Internal Revenue Board figures released in 1922 seemed to show that "millions of persons of moderate means are becoming wealthier and the so-called rich are becoming poorer." But over the course of the twenties quite a different trend developed. According to the *Literary Digest*, "Our 1926 crop of multimillionaires was a record one"; the number of persons reporting incomes of more than $5 million had doubled over the previous year. The unsleeping Internal Revenue Bureau counted taxable incomes in the fiscal year just past at $21.5 billion, of which wages and salaries had accounted for less than half; interest on investments was reported at $2 billion, and dividends—much the fastest-growing category—amounted to $4 billion. (In 1924, significantly, the four Americans reporting the highest aggregate income for the previous year claimed comparatively modest salaries, averaging $70,000 each—but acknowledged combined dividends of $30 million!) Soberly considered, the United States at the end of the twenties was hardly a land of fifteen million incipient Rockefellers.

V

"Me and Rockefeller," then, did not really mean making decisions like a captain of industry although on a more modest scale. Rather, it meant *benefiting* from those decisions. Business oratory, Dale Carnegie–coached or otherwise, often sang of "productivity," "initiative," and "free enterprise," but it also dwelt at length upon "the American standard of living." Somebody up there might still be obeying Horatio's admonition to Do and Dare, but the goal for the non-Algers here below was to Receive and Enjoy.

A curious double standard pervaded the media when they discussed "prosperity" and "success." On the one hand, a rhetoric persisted that said: young man, work hard; don't squander on luxuries the surplus you could invest; keep your eye on the ball and mind the main chance. But at the same time, as businessmen and their prophets contemplated the national future, they welcomed a predestined *end* to many time-honored forms of hard work and self-denial. "Days of Drudgery Will Soon Be Over," said Walter S. Gifford, President of A.T.&T., in a 1928 *American Magazine* interview:

> The housewife, more and more, is going to see her labor lightened and shortened by electricity. The farmer, who not so long ago toiled twelve and fourteen hours a day, is going to find himself with plenty of time on his hands in which to do other things than run his farm. Every one of us will have more chance to do what he will, which means greater opportunity, both materially and spiritually.

In a more folksy vein, a 1926 General Electric advertisement showed a young father with pipe, fishing pole, and creel, walking beside a rosy-cheeked son who holds up his hands in a fisherman's classic space-measuring gesture for "this big":

> These are wonderful days for Dads. They have bought homes; they have bought cars; they have money saved; they have time to spend with their sons. . . .
> The tired worker, worn out by his labors, is ceasing to be. In his place is a new man, commanding power, providing more easily for the needs of his family, and having time for the duty and joy of being a pal to his son.

But a less-than-joyous reaction to this ad can well be imagined. A father comes home from the exhaustion and monotony of a speeded-up assembly line, which that very day has broken all existing production records. Too tired to do anything but sink into a broken-down old armchair, or a new one on which not all the payments have yet been made, he irritably waves away the excited little boy who wants Daddy to play, and picks up the September *American Magazine*. It opens to the G.E. advertisement just described, and his eye is caught by the half-inch block-letter caption: "DAD." What does he think, let alone say? Or is he too weary to think at all?

"Even in the relatively prosperous year 1919," Irving Bernstein writes in *The Lean Years*, "a majority of workers' families failed to enjoy an 'American standard of living.'" On the other hand, the *content* of that standard was changing so rapidly, with the advent of the movies, telephones, radio, vacuum cleaners, and all the rest of the technological cornucopia, that all but the most severely hard-pressed could feel that their situation was improving. In Bernstein's judgment this hopeful attitude had important political implications. "Ownership of a Model T, even if shared with the finance company, was more than entertaining: it inclined one to accept things as they were." That worker too worn out by the daily grind to go fishing with his son apparently was not thereby "radicalized"; in the Lynds' Middletown, his historical real-life equivalent seems in many cases to have voted for Coolidge.

Along the white-collar sector of the labor front, the rat race took a somewhat different form. As Gilman Ostrander succinctly puts it, "Living standards went up for millions of Americans who did not improve their positions much economically." To document the point, Eunice Fuller Barnard in *Survey* magazine for November 1, 1928, described "What our parents didn't pay for":

> Today, the Department of Commerce estimates, the average American family has more than a third more purchasing power than it had just before the War. Yet it is a question whether the crushing load around the middle-class wage earner's neck has been appreciably lightened. For during the interval he has come to live in a new world filled with new things for the family to buy.

Then she tabulated some representative examples:

Schedule of 1928		Offsets of 1900	
1 automobile	$700	2 bicycles	$70
1 radio	$75		
1 phonograph	$50		
1 washing machine	$150	wringer and washboard	$5
1 vacuum cleaner	$50	brushes and brooms	$5
1 sewing machine (electric)	$60	sewing machine	$25
other electrical equipment	$25		
telephone (year)	$35		
	$1,145		$105

In addition to which, the author argued, the mounting cost of education had to be reckoned in, and its greatly lengthened term; likewise the far higher price of health—tonsillectomies, orthodontics, and (ironically) paying for the fresh air and sunshine that had once been free. Eunice Barnard in these judgments was not being a nostalgic reactionary; she acknowledged that the twenty-eight cents a quart paid for certified milk, in contrast to the six or seven paid by the previous generation "for the then unanalyzed and unclassified product," was no doubt worth the difference. "When some of us bewail the higher cost of living we may be talking about the higher cost of *better* living," she concluded.

But are we really living better? The anonymous author of a *Scribner's* essay on "How the American Middle Class Lives" was not so sure. For many, the increment perhaps was soaked up in rent, food (more healthful, better-balanced food to be sure), life insurance, and especially medicine. Some members of this category of Americans had, for example, "witnessed the tragedy of the father, told that he had cancer, who blew out his brains rather than use, to prolong his own life, the money saved to put his son through college." And there were other crises, less extreme but even more prolonged, and in quiet ways almost as tragic:

> The handling of every penny till the skin is worn off your fingers kills, in many of us, what is most individual and worth saving. It is this that gives to the middle-aged women among us . . . that suggestion of pressed flowers from whom the pages of the book of life have squeezed out all the juice.

This is a far cry indeed from the free-and-easy American "new woman" who remains one fond stereotype of the Jazz Age. We sometimes forget that there *were* middle-aged women during the twenties, and for some of them the very existence of that new, younger woman would have been galling. Edna St. Vincent Millay—herself a suburban housewife—might urge that her generation burn the candle at both ends, but some among her audience had not the surplus energy to light it: "We crave adventure, experimentation, drama, beauty; only we know that for ourselves they cannot be bought save at the expense of our daily bread." Despite the promises of the President of American Tel and Tel, this subspecies of Middle Americans doubted that the days of drudgery, for them, would soon be over.

Yet these petit-bourgeois citizens seem no more to have been radicalized than Bernstein's workers. These were the people, the anonymous author of "How the American Middle Class Lives" insisted, who punctually paid their bills and taxes, affirmed a quiet patriotism—and voted Republican. In fact, nothing more irritated the dissenters and critics of the twenties than to realize that the G.O.P.'s favorite ploy—the notion, as the *New Republic* put it in 1928, that "prosperity is a prerogative which God has bestowed, subject to certain limitations, upon the American people if they remain Republican"—was a political success. And if by fluke some Democrat should make it into the charmed circle, the liberal weekly continued, "he would have to pay for his election by behaving as Al Smith is now behaving," i.e., as a conservative.

In desperation, such liberal opponents of the System looked forward to the time "when the American organism slows down" in a tone implying that they almost hoped there would be a depression; *après nous, le déluge,* and the sooner the better:

> There is, so far as we can see, no reason why the Republicans should not continue to control the mechanism of American secular salvation until economic discontent becomes a much more positive and permanent fact in American life than it now is. They are confronted at present with little conscious opposition. Almost all politically effective Americans worship success in the person of men like Mr. Raskob, and they will continue to do so until there is less success to pass around.

"The only thing we have to fear is fear itself," FDR would say in 1933; but what the liberal editorialist of 1928 seemed to fear politically most of all was the continuation of the prevailing optimism.

In due course the bubble broke, and the "prophets of gloom and doom"—as Republicans were still calling them a half-century later!—turned out, for the time being at least, to have been right. Occasionally a business tycoon tried to affirm the old, bold virtues in the old, bold spirit. J. G. Lonsdale, who had started out in business during the depression of 1893 and was President of the American Bankers' Association during the depression of 1929, told an *American Magazine* interviewer in 1930 that there was positive value in such periods: "Muscles get tough. Fat doesn't form. Coats are off. Eyes are to the future. . . . Habits form that make whatever may come later seem like a bed of roses." But such testaments were becoming more rare; in hard times that was no way for a periodical to build circulation. Shortly after the Crash the *American Magazine*'s new editor, Sumner Blossom, sent his staff a memo in which the magazine's "success" formula was redefined away from personal prowess and toward a more socialized concept: the idea of achievement which is "successful" in that it improves the welfare of large numbers. As Mr. Blossom explained, "Horatio Alger Doesn't Work Here Any More." The growth of Organized America during the twenties suggests that actually, with isolated exceptions, that kind of youth had not been working there for quite some time.

Chapter IX

A Republican Form of Government

WE SPEAK of an Age of Jackson and an Age of Roosevelt; an Eisenhower era and a Kennedy era. "At any time and under any Presidency, the state of mind of the country is largely influenced by the state of mind of the man in the White House," said Will H. Hays in 1921. "The country is colored by his personality[,] what he does, what he thinks, what he feels. Intangible and imponderable though it is, it is one of the Presidency's most important functions." For better and for worse, in the United States the 882 days between March 4, 1921, and August 2, 1923, were the age of Warren Gamaliel Harding.

A scant two months after Harding's death in office, the now well-known scandals began to unfold: the little green house on K Street, and influence-peddler Jess Smith humming "My God, How the Money Rolls In"; an Attorney-General obstructing justice, and a Secretary of the Interior taking a bribe; poker games around the corner, and clandestine sex behind the back stairs; good intentions vitiated by ignorance, and kindness debased by corruption. Not in half a century, since Grant's time, had anything comparable happened to the American government; and not for another half-century, until Nixon's time, would anything comparable happen to it again.

But to understand what those days meant for the people living through them, we must for the moment forget Teapot Dome and all that it implies. If the misdoings of Cabinet officers and White House confidants unearthed by Senator Thomas Walsh's Teapot Dome committee bear comparison with the similarly unsavory deeds disclosed by Senator Sam Ervin's Watergate committee, there are at least two crucial diferences.

In the first place, although politicians were among those involved in the Harding scandals, what they engaged in was not in the strict sense *political* corruption. Except for Attorney-General Harry Daugherty's inept effort to frame Senator Burton K. Wheeler as a "radical," which was primarily an attempt by Daugherty to discredit Wheeler's Senate investigation (and perhaps thereby save Daugherty's own skin), the Harding White House family never fell into the trap of regarding the government as "we" and its opponents as "they." There were no "enemies lists," no burglarizing of psychiatrists' offices or party headquarters, no IRS harassment of politically troublesome persons. Nobody from the White House gumshoed around on the trail of potential Democratic presidential candidates trying to get something on them, or to stir up their partisans against one another. (Nor was it necessary; as the 103-ballot 1924 Democratic national convention demonstrated, their partisans were perfectly capable of stirring up themselves.)

In the second place, and in contrast to the landsliding 1972 voter—who had already been told a little about Watergate, but who seemed too frightened of George McGovern to care—the voter in 1920 who helped give Warren Harding a majority comparable to Nixon's in 1972 did not knowingly condone foul play. To that voter, and afterward in 1923 to the thousands of ordinary Americans who filed past the President's bier or quietly waited along the route of the slow funeral train, as their grandparents had waited for Lincoln and as their grandchildren would wait for Robert Kennedy, the "Age of Harding" meant something considerably more respectable than Teapot Dome.

It also meant something altogether different from the "imperial presidency" Arthur Schlesinger, Jr., has discerned in more recent Cold War regimes. The high style of the sixties would have been out of place in the White House during the twenties. Some members of Harding's administration—some among "those temporarily charged with official responsibility," as he modestly called them—had private and ulterior reasons for hiding certain of their own actions from public scrutiny; nonetheless, no "Camelot," no monarchical mystique, shrouded their ill-fated regime. In fact, the government's remoteness from the people in the artificial environment of the nation's capital (what we nowadays term "Potomac fever") seems to have troubled Warren Harding. "Those of us who are in Washington live in an atmosphere of officialdom which often hinders our knowledge of the thoughts around the American fireside," he told an audience in St. Louis two months before his death. "You know the President is not any different from anyone of you," Harding assured the people at a lunchtime whistle-stop on June 21, 1923, also in the course of that last "swing around the circle." "He is just an ordinary citizen of our common country until you clothe him with authority to speak for you."

Properly, critics have pointed out that extraordinary times may call for a leader who is not just an ordinary citizen clothed by his fellows with authority to speak for them. If during Harding's presidency there was some popular disappointment in his performance, "a feeling on the part of the public of expectations unfulfilled," as the thoughtful journalist Mark Sullivan wrote in November 1922, it was precisely in this area of effective governance: "The public expects leadership in the White House, and it is not a part of Harding's temperament . . . to provide that leadership." Theodore Roosevelt had led vigorously (or had seemed to), and so had Woodrow Wilson; "The experience of half a generation of leadership from the White House has led the public to look for it permanently." (Suppose for a moment that Theodore Roosevelt had not dropped dead in 1919; with the conservative Henry Cabot Lodge as an ally and his own Progressive support he would probably have been a shoo-in for the Republican nomination in 1920. In that case, would we now be saying that the American public in the twenties craved the stimulus of leadership rather than the soothings of Normalcy?)

On the other hand Theodore Junior, defeated for Governor of New York in 1924 by Al Smith, was not able to carry forward the family mystique. And the forceful wartime rule of Woodrow Wilson seems to have generated a backlash that helped put Harding in the White House. That backlash is usually interpreted as having been a mandate for conservatism. Still it was a liberal, not a conservative, who later proposed the slogan "the Century of the Common Man"; and a faith that even very common men may be able to govern had traditionally been one of the meanings of American democracy. During Harding's presidency, out in western Missouri, a plainspoken county judge, just then beginning his political career with the blessing of a gamy local Democratic machine, was destined to carry that traditional faith forward into a new generation. In doing so, Harry Truman would necessarily have to work out his own difficult balance between statesmanship and corruption—a more satisfactory balance, many would now say, than that achieved by either Harding or Nixon.

To be sure the Harding twenties, like the Truman forties, were extraordinary times for an ordinary citizen to attempt to govern. The month of March 1921, when Warren Harding was inaugurated, saw strife and commotion throughout the rest of the civilized world. In southern Italy peasants rose against their landlords; in Egypt socialists and nationalists rose against British rule. In Ireland an Associated Press correspondent was led, blindfolded, to an underground hideaway so that the revolutionary leader Eamon De Valera could grant him an interview. In Turkey another revolutionary leader, Mustafa Kemal, formally broke with the Sultan's moribund regime; in Russia the three-year-old Bolshevik government suppressed a sailor's mutiny at Kronstadt and other risings in Minsk and Petrograd. Just over history's horizon were Hitler's Munich beer-hall putsch and Mussolini's march on Rome.

Worldwide revolution was in fact not quite so imminent as such events made it appear, but the situation was quite serious enough from the standpoint of the American President-elect. "If revolution insists upon overturning established order let other peoples make the tragic experiment," Harding declared in his inaugural address on March 4, 1921. "There is no place for it in America." That

would have been news indeed to our Founding Fathers, whom
Warren Harding regularly and fervently praised. Yet by the time of
Harding's nomination and election America's own "Red Scare," a
by-product of the pathological last months of the Wilson Administration, had largely run its course. Harding's Attorney-General,
Harry Daugherty, was not above crying "Bolshevik" as a convenient strikebreaking ploy, but Harding himself was too good-
natured to engage convincingly in Red-baiting. It was the "liberal"
Woodrow Wilson who had regarded Socialist leader Eugene Debs
as too dangerous a radical to be let out of jail, even after the war
Debs had conscientiously opposed was over; and it was the conservative Warren Harding who reversed that policy and granted Debs
a pardon.

In a speech prepared for delivery at San Francisco on July 31,
1923, but never made because of his final illness, President Harding insisted that there was "an unfailing friendship in the United
States for the people of Russia." Although he continued to oppose
recognition of the Soviet government, he had "gladly recommended an appropriation of $20,000,000 by Congress for the relief
of her famine-stricken people." In contrast to the militancy of many
other American conservatives, Harding's opposition to "Bolshe-
vism" was couched not in righteous anger—or in fear—but in regret, coupled with a skeptical note of "show me." His oratory, as
usual, was wretched; but his intention was reasonably clear:

> If the fundamentals of our boasted civilization are based on twenty
> centuries of maintained error, if the Russian conception of the social
> fabric is the true revelation, tardily conceived after forty centuries of
> evolution and development, the truth will ultimately assert itself in
> the great experiment. I can see Russia only as the supreme tragedy,
> and a world warning, the dangers of which we must avoid if our
> heritage is to be preserved. If the revolutionary order is the way to
> higher attainment and greater human happiness, Russia will com-
> mand our ultimate sanction.

In short, despite his abhorrence of revolution, whose "dangers
. . . we must avoid," Harding was inclined to let nature take its
course: "No one seriously questions the continuation of the present

government [of Russia], or wishes to direct the expression of Russian preference." No inflammatory talk here of "liberation," or of an American mission to marshal the forces of a "free world" against an "international Communist conspiracy." Wilson's wartime regime *had* intervened in the Russian Revolution, and there is now some evidence that despite a rhetoric of "self-determination" Woodrow Wilson conceived of his cherished postwar world order, with its League of Nations as the capstone, to some extent in counter-revolutionary terms. But Warren Harding, as is well known, rejected American entry into the League, and his successor, Calvin Coolidge, proposed normalizing U.S. relations with Russia—but backed away with his customary caution from the resulting furor.

Yet if "anti-communism" does not fully describe the foreign policy of Harding's government, neither does "isolation." Moved by an abhorrence of war that seems to have been patently sincere, the President fully supported his Secretary of State's bold initiatives toward international disarmament; and, risking the division of his own political party in the process, he came out for U.S. adherence to the World Court, a body almost as unpopular in some quarters as the League. While Cabinet secretaries Herbert Hoover and Charles Evans Hughes were endorsing the Court, John T. Adams, Chairman of the Republican National Committee, was publicly denouncing it. Such a situation, in which "the responsible administration . . . boldly commits the party to one policy, and the party organization . . . is just as boldly advocating precisely the opposite," was without political precedent in America, said the news monthly *World's Work* in its issue for August 1923. Note that this "Impending Republican Split" prophesied in the month of the President's death, this "crisis in the Harding Administration," had nothing to do with scandal. Rather, it had to do with basic national goals.

II

All such speculation was cut off sharply at 7:30 P.M., Pacific time, on August 2, 1923. In their suite at the Palace Hotel in San Francisco Mrs. Harding was reading to the ailing President a favorable article about him from the *Saturday Evening Post*. She paused to prop up his pillows. "That's good, read some more," the patient urged, and in that moment Warren Harding died.

What might have happened to U.S. foreign policy—or domestic, for that matter—had he lived will now never be known. (How would history have remembered Richard Nixon if he had departed this life after 882 days in office, which would have been on June 20, 1971—with the *New York Times* Pentagon disclosures one week old and the "plumbers' " operations under way, but with the President's momentous trip to Peking not yet taken?) Along with the windbaggery expected along the campaign trail, in the speeches Warren Harding delivered in his last weeks on earth a tone of resolute advocacy as well as a coherent rationale for his administration, perhaps even a platform upon which to run for reelection in 1924, began for the first time to emerge. The historian Robert K. Murray believes that many options which remained flexible and open under Harding froze afterward into dogma under Coolidge. If Murray is right, then perhaps the Babbittish Midwesterner with his preposterous rhetoric had potentially more to offer America and the world than the flinty-faced New Englander who succeeded him—notwithstanding the scandalous mess Warren Harding left behind for Calvin Coolidge to clean up.

Coolidge's accession to power is itself an American legend. The news of Harding's death flashed across the country at the speed of light—and stopped twelve miles short of its goal. Between the sleeping Vice-President and the roaring modern world stretched a rutted country road. Incredibly, the modern world had to wait an hour and a half while a telegraph messenger traversed that road. At last, "after midnight into the graveyard quiet of the town of Plymouth, Vermont, came a chugging automobile. . . . A man dashed around the headlights and pounded on the door of the Coolidge house. A match flared out, a coal oil lamp was lit, and a head appeared at a bedroom window." The President's father demanded to know "What's wanted"; the messenger told him. In the small hours of the morning John Coolidge, by his authority as a country notary, administered the presidential oath of office to his son; and afterward, as the roads and parking spaces at last began to fill up with cars bearing newspapermen and politicians and the curious, the new President blew out the lamps and went to bed. Thus in its metropolitan age did America observe the ancient ritual: "The king is dead; long live the king."

Weeks after Harding's death, the persistent Senate investigators who were tracing the relationship between Harry Sinclair's Mammoth Oil Company and Interior Secretary Albert B. Fall began at last to get results. The media had begun by treating the oil controversy simply as a policy question, with "conservationists" lined up against "developers" of the nation's natural resources; now at last they frankly assessed the actions of the oil barons and their political allies as crimes. But rather than be stampeded into removing Harding holdovers from office without proven cause, Calvin Coolidge dug in his heels, waited for the inevitable turn in public opinion, and then moved vigorously. As a result, the scandals which otherwise might have brought on a Republican Administration's downfall redounded to the new Republican Administration's credit. Although two Democrats, Thomas J. Walsh and Burton K. Wheeler (both from Montana), conducted the Senate inquiries, the Democrats as a party derived no glory from the committees' revelations; one of their own presidential hopefuls, William Gibbs McAdoo (Wilson's son-in-law), turned out to be as spattered with raw petroleum as were the Republicans.

"Four years from now," a writer in *Collier's* for March 5, 1921, had predicted with unknowing irony, "President Harding will know who his friends are." Four years from that date the Yankee from Plymouth, Vermont, was installed in Washington as President in his own right, after a triumphant 1924 election campaign, and some of Harding's friends were on their way to jail. From time to time through the later twenties an aspiring young lawyer named John J. Sirica sat in court watching the shabby spectacle of those presidential friends on trial—a liberal education Sirica never forgot.

Cleaning up the government—"turning the rascals out"—is a time-honored, if often futile, American rite of moral purgation. Calvin Coolidge hinted that it might also be a sound economic investment. As he informed the New York State Chamber of Commerce on November 19, 1925, "It is notorious that where the government is bad, business is bad." Coolidge's definition of "bad" was narrower than Franklin Roosevelt's, or even Woodrow Wilson's; if he opposed the cruder kinds of business interference with government, as for example when an oil company bribed an official, he also usually opposed government interference with business, even when that interference might have helped people in need or redressed an old and entrenched wrong. "When government comes unduly under the influence of business, the tendency is to develop an administration which . . . becomes narrow and selfish in its outlook, and results in an oligarchy," Coolidge lectured his Chamber of Commerce audience. "When government enters the field of business with its great resources . . . , having the power to crush all competitors, [it] likewise closes the door of opportunity and results in monopoly." So much for New Nationalisms and New Freedoms, for Fair Deals and Great Societies. But by the same token Calvin Coolidge also opposed any fusion of political and industrial power into one great social monolith, of the kind some liberals in our own time have also come to fear. The national government had begun operations in 1789 within walking distance of Wall Street, but President Coolidge was pleased that it had not remained there:

> The great cities of the ancient world were the seats of both government and industrial power. . . . In the modern world government is inclined to be merely a tenant of the city. Political life and industrial life flow on side by side, but practically separated from each other. When we contemplate the enormous power, autocratic and uncontrolled, which would have been created by joining the authority of government with the influence of business, we can better appreciate the wisdom of the fathers in their wise dispensation which made Washington the political center of the country and left New York to develop into its business center. They wrought mightily for freedom.

Political life and industrial life ideally flowed on side by side in their separate channels, but apparently one channel was a narrow rivulet and the other a broad and mighty stream. "After all," Coolidge told the American Society of Newspaper Editors on January

17, 1925, "the chief business of the American people is business. They are profoundly concerned with producing, buying, selling, investing and prospering in the world." The great majority, he strongly believed, would "always find these are moving impulses of our life"—impulses not only to individual achievement but to collective development as well. "True business," Coolidge told the New York Chamber of Commerce, "represents the mutual organized effort of society to minister to the economic requirements of civilization. It is an effort by which men provide for the material needs of each other." The American economic creed had never been more sweepingly expressed. For Coolidge, "true business" was not merely the best, most logical, or most humane way to cope with civilization's economic requirements; it was *the* organized effort of society for that purpose. From where the Yankee President sat, capitalism was not a beleaguered ideology; it was literally the only game in town. Alternative ways by which men tried to provide for the needs of each other, as in Russia, were not even a tragic error as Warren Harding had argued; in effect Calvin Coolidge denied their very existence.

But what kind of capitalism? Here there seems an inconsistency in Coolidge's own point of view. At bottom, he held personally to a penny-squeezing ethic of scrimp and save. When New York's Federation of Jewish Philanthropic Societies invited him to address them by telephone from the White House in 1924, he listened with perfunctory politeness until their spokesman explained that they were to devote an evening to the consideration of a budget. Then he began to take real interest, the President confessed; for the budget idea, he had to admit, was for him something of an obsession:

> I believe in budgets. I want other people to believe in them. I have had a small one in my own home; and besides that, I am the head of the organization that makes the greatest of all budgets—that of the United States Government. . . . Yes, I regard a good budget as among the noblest monuments of virtue.

In 1926, in a still more exalted mood, he declared: "It is not through selfishness or wastefulness or arrogance, but through self-denial, conservation, and service, that we shall build up the American spirit. This is the true constructive economy, the true faith on which our institutions rest."

But if Will Hays had been right in his dictum that the state of mind of the country is largely influenced by the state of mind of the man in the White House, then during those boom years Americans must have been getting also from their President a message of quite another sort; an admonition not to save but to spend, not to serve but to plunge, not to deny oneself but to indulge oneself, not to budget but to buy on time. Coolidge's 1926 tribute to the American advertising industry—"The uncivilized make little progress because they have few desires. The inhabitants of our country are stimulated to new wants in all directions"—hardly squares with his other ethic of self-denial and conservation. Similarly, his treatment of the Wall Street boom seems strangely out of phase with his WASP New Englander's aversion to gambling. In fact, one great irony in Coolidge's historical situation is that his "Jekyll" inclination to watch that budget probably fanned the nation's "Hyde" impulse to squander its inheritance. One purpose of the government budget-cutting and debt retirement at which Calvin Coolidge worked so diligently and effectively throughout his presidency was precisely to liberate private capital, which had more than enough internal expansive urge as it was.

The President may have known (as many a Coolidge anecdote attests) that the big bull market must one day tailspin down out of control, but he never publicly said so. Instead, whenever the stock market wavered, he reassured the public that all was well. As he told the Congress in his annual message of 1927: "If the people will maintain that confidence which they are entitled to have in themselves, in each other and in America, a comfortable prosperity will continue." Perhaps Coolidge had no choice but to say such things; his biographer William Allen White argues that had he not given forth that assurance—had he not informed the stock investor, at least, that the only thing we have to fear is fear itself—the President would have been checked by "a raging populace roaring at the White House to let the carnival go on." Indeed, since the survival of any bull market is so largely a function of ever-expanding investment, had the quiet Vermonter succeeded in outshouting that chorus and in doing so deflated this particular American dream, he might only have brought on more swiftly the very depression he sought to avoid. In repeating to the people the tales they were all telling each other, White concludes, "Calvin Coolidge was democracy functioning at its best, which sometimes is its worst."

Still, the American government had been designed in the first place to weather the worst. "It is in vain to say that enlightened statesmen will be able to adjust these clashing interests, and render them all subservient to the public good," James Madison had warned in Federalist Paper Number Ten. "Enlightened statesmen will not always be at the helm." By implication, the Founders *expected* that the ship of state would be piloted not only by Wilsons and Roosevelts and Kennedys but also by Coolidges and Hardings—and Nixons. Quietly and almost unnoticed, the 150th year since the Declaration of Independence passed during the twenties; commenting on its observance, President Coolidge remarked that although the United States still had the reputation of being a "new" nation, it was quite old enough as governments went nowadays.

Considering the international setting, of hysterical nationalist demagoguery, it may have been just as well that in America democracy chose at that moment to pursue its own narrowly conceived interests rather than play follow the leader. The hypothetical news vendor or shoeshine boy who, we are told, spent the twenties speculating on the Big Bull Market—or wishing that he could—might, under different incitement, have cheerfully foregone his dreams of personal gain and cheered for a president who promised him national glory instead; and rather than the droning normality of Harding and Coolidge we might have had the excitement of a charismatic American Mussolini.

Some apologists for America's own power elite leaned in exactly that direction. "Fascism," wrote Isaac Marcosson in the *Saturday Evening Post* for July 3, 1926—illustrated with photos of gleaming new dams and hydroelectric plants backed up by spectacular Italian Alpine scenery—had "promulgated a gospel of effort, economy and discipline that has balanced the budget, increased production, galvanized industry and inspired an intensive national-ism that is little less than a miracle." The writer uttered no senti-mental nonsense about leaders as ordinary citizens clothed by the people with authority to speak for them (as Harding had viewed them) and he expressed no misgivings about the creation of enor-mous and uncontrolled autocratic power by joining the authority of government with the influence of business (of which Coolidge had warned). "Big business in Italy is squarely behind the Fascist movement," Marcosson affirmed, on the ground that "discipline always pays, even when it is enforced with a big stick." In one for-merly ailing European nation "the strong arm and the mailed fist have been translated into terms of productive awakening"; was there a lesson here for isolated America? Or was America's poky political "Old Order" of the twenties— cavalierly dismissed by so many American historians—perhaps after all the best available bargain?

III

"The strength and hope of our civilization lies in its power to adapt itself to changing circumstances," President Coolidge once told the National Council of the Boy Scouts of America. If Ameri-can civilization during the "Coolidge boom" of the mid-twenties showed any inclination so to adapt itself, it got little help from the White House, where the President took his regular afternoon naps and rode his mechanical exerciser—and conducted his politics in much the same way. In stark contrast was the situation over at the Department of Commerce, a formerly obscure government bureau which Herbert Hoover took over in 1921 and fired into unwonted activity—an endeavor meticulously reported to the nation by his own image-building public relations personnel.

Knowing there was no logical (or ideological) reason for a plumber given the task of fixing a kitchen sink to have to go back—every time—to the shop for a spare part, or else bring along a ten-ton truck with enough parts to fit the variety of connections he was likely to find, Secretary Hoover prevailed upon industry in general to standardize; to simplify; to eliminate thousands of mismatching or superfluous shapes, sizes, dimensions, and threadings. Perceiving that radio was no toy but the most important communications breakthrough since Gutenberg, Hoover battled successfully to unsnarl the chaos of competing frequencies and to define broadcasting as a public forum. Aware that American export capital was going to go overseas regardless of any formal political and military commitments to "isolation," he expanded his department into a major engine of foreign policy, so that U.S. commercial attachés in many a nation abroad came to count for more than the men who carried on America's conventional diplomacy.

Later years would cast Herbert Hoover politically in the role of an "isolationist," but in the twenties few Americans seemed more internationally minded. Certainly Hoover's horizons were wider than Coolidge's; even in the years before the war, a contemporary biographer pointed out, "Hoover boarded an ocean liner as casually as you or I take a trolley-car to our daily jobs." He had traveled, seasick, on camel-back in western Australia, and dodged Boxer shellfire in Tientsin. He had rescued the American tourists stranded in Europe by the outbreak of the First World War, and then fed the hungry Belgians—on a budget larger than that of the entire United States government in Grover Cleveland's time. He had overcome anti-Bolshevik hostility in the West and anti-capitalist suspicion in the Soviet Union to minister to the victims of Russia's famine.

Then, in April 1927, the Mississippi River crested into a cataclysmic flood, "and at last his own country turned to Hoover the Reliever." Seven hundred thousand flood refugees had to be cared for, and the organization of this relief work gave Hoover dramatic public visibility at a most propitious political moment. Since the campaign of 1920 Hoover had from time to time been mentioned as a presidential possibility; as soon as President Coolidge in the late summer of 1927 uttered his cryptic "I do not choose to run," skillful public relations management proceeded to ignite popular sentiment into a Hoover boom. In less than a year following the Mississippi flood the veteran war correspondent and antiwar journalist Will Irwin, who had known Hoover since they were both undergraduates at Stanford, brought out an admiring sketch entitled *Herbert Hoover: a Reminiscent Biography*.

Livelier in style than most such books, it was in form a classic campaign biography, stressing pioneer ancestry, childhood adversity, and boyhood indications of future greatness. But Herbert Hoover was also an ideal campaign biographer's subject. Details of his childhood—"sliding down Cook's Hill in snow-time, ranging the spring fields in vain pursuit of baby rabbits, gathering wild strawberries in summer, the sonorous roll of the English Bible at family prayers," and even such singular details as playing with "hordes of little Indians, running wild as pup coyotes"—were real; Irwin had not had to make that boyhood up. And the rest of the story, combining success in the "self-made man" tradition with a moral scruple quite untypical of Darwinian self-made men (for example, Hoover's decision to divest himself of all his war-related business ventures—which might have made him a fortune—in order to engage unencumbered in Belgian civilian relief) was a transcript, however partisan and selective, from the real Herbert Hoover.

True, the society into which he had been born, where people "manufactured their own butter and cheese, slaughtered and dressed their own meat, raised their own fruit and vegetables, carried their grain to mill and . . . returned it to their cellars as flour, . . . made their own clothes, . . . boiled their own soft-soap, tried out their own lard," by Hoover's own admission had largely disappeared by the time of his mature public career. But, as our first chapter reminded us, such a milieu was not so far behind the consciousness of Americans in the twenties as to be totally incomprehensible, even if "self-reliance" in a modern urban situation necessarily had to take a different form.

Will Irwin's narrative reached its own dramatic crest in its account of the Mississippi flood. Psychologically, Irwin was still the lowly freshman looking up to the puissant senior; from his point of view the orphaned farm boy from West Branch, Iowa, had naturally evolved into the nation's wonder-worker:

> Hoover touched flood-relief with his magic hand. Immediately, lifeboats and crews were speeding westward from the Atlantic coast, aëroplanes winging from the army and navy fields, coast guard vessels speeding up the river-flood, carpenters in a hundred yards

throwing together emergency boats, Red Cross units entraining for the Mississippi. Then, like one of those trick moving pictures, lines which signified nothing by themselves jumped together into coherent meaning. Ahead of the flood moved Hoover's forces in perfect coördination. . . .

I, who have followed Hoover on his great European jobs, would like to leave him as I saw him one May morning of 1927—standing on the tottering Melville levee, his aëroplanes scouting overhead, his mosquito-fleet scurrying below, a group of prominent citizens about him listening to the wise, quick, terse directions which were bringing order out of chaos. It symbolizes the man, that scene— "The one tranquil among the raging floods," the transmuter of altruistic emotion into benevolent action.

This is, to say the least, a highly partisan view. It could almost have served as the peroration of a convention speech placing Hoover's name in nomination. But it may also be read as a corrective on the equally partisan portrait we have inherited from the Depression, of Hoover the Great Obstructionist, brutal to protesting demonstrators, cold to the cries of the poor—and, above all, able to work no wonders. So quickly do historical circumstances alter reputations! In 1927, the available contrast was not between a frightened, property-minded Old Order and a cheerful, people-oriented New Deal. It was between the closed, coercive new order promised abroad by dictatorships, whether Right or Left, and an open, voluntaristic society at home. "Hoover does not make anyone do anything," his biographer summed up. "He inspires volunteers. . . . He is engineering our material civilization as a whole; and that without goose-stepping the human spirit, blue-printing the human soul."

IV

In his own memoir, published in 1942, Will Irwin reminisced of the presidential campaign that followed: "Now we had Al Smith to fight. I would rather have fought a worse man." Irwin had no sympathy with the "underground religious argument" being used against Smith. Moreover, he agreed with Smith's stand for Repeal, and only on the promise that he personally would not have to defend Prohibition did Irwin consent to go on the stump for his college hero.

In the course of the campaign the reporter found himself seated at a dinner beside "the admirable Mrs. Moskowitz, 'the conscience of Al Smith,' " and instantly they plunged into argument. Despite all odds, she seemed confident that her candidate was going to win:

> "Your man appeals to the intellectuals," she said. "The college-graduate class. The highbrows. They're a minority and always will be. They have no wrongs to right. They can take care of themselves. Look at New York City! Al has never won in the district between the Third Avenue L and the Sixth Avenue L. He simply ignores it. But he understands the people—and he gets them. You'll see!"

In those pre–New Deal days the image of the liberal intellectuals as unanimous Hoover-haters obviously had not yet jelled. Not that Al Smith lacked for intellectual support; he had around him his own highly effective "brain trust," a precursor of Roosevelt's. One of its most effective members for ten years—despite her public disavowal of female intellectual ability—was Belle Moskowitz herself. In the 1928 campaign her husband Henry was, quite literally, Will Irwin's opposite number; in collaboration with Norman Hapgood, Henry Moskowitz produced an Al Smith campaign biography, *Up From the City Streets*. The thesis of the book was an extension of what Belle told Will on the campaign trail: Al understood and got the people because he was one of them. At least, he was one of them in New York.

The book was published in November 1927, before a single convention delegate had been chosen by either party. But we may infer from its opening paragraph its authors' realization that nationally Herbert Hoover, with his traditionally rural political and personal heritage, was the man to beat. The lower-Manhattan section where Al Smith had been born, actually in the shadow of the Brooklyn Bridge, was a far cry from the silent green hills of Hoover's Iowa: "The Fourth Ward and the parish of St. James in which he lived were surrounded by poverty and vice in terrible forms," and Smith was "the first of our national heroes to be born amidst din and squalor." Nevertheless, Alfred E. Smith's "story suggests that in the future our vast cities may do better by humanity than we have feared," Hapgood and Moskowitz argued. "It is possible that their evils may be reduced, and that their sons may show not less energy, persistence, and initiative than have come heretofore from the silences and the long labor of ax and plow."

The streets and tenements of lower Manhattan had been at least as tough a proving ground for young Al Smith as the sun-parched and snow-swept fields of Iowa had been for young Herbert Hoover. Bad enough even in the affluent twenties, "life on the East Side of New York when Alfred Smith was born was an even fiercer struggle than it is now." Within that environment, however, were "many elements tending to favor activity, independence, quickness of mind, and persistence"—the very values Middle America had long cherished in its heroes. In fact this sample of urban American society was not so divergent from rural culture as both ruralists and urbanites sometimes supposed.

"A person who knows this sea of human beings does not think of them as all alike." The mass broke down into a collection of neighborhoods, composed of Italians, Germans, Jews, Greeks, or Slavs; and the activities of the Tammany organization that wove them all together could be construed as "neighborliness, which on election day is translated into votes." Beset though it was on its borders by the derelict resorts on the Bowery (one of them named McGurk's Suicide Hall) and by the sailors' dives along Water Street, the neighborhood in which Al Smith grew up was composed in the main of "God-fearing, home-loving, upright people"—in Robert Coles's sense, Middle Americans. Although "no boy could grow up in that region and not be familiar with the harshest that life afforded," that harshness did not extend to the youthful Al Smith's own existence among the 18,000 souls who constituted the parish of St. James:

> The differences were not fundamental between them and the kind of people who would have made up a town of 18,000 in the Middle West. They were unquestioning, like the people in the Middle West. A point of view of life had come to them and they accepted it. The people in the Middle West might be Presbyterians; these were Catholics. The people in the Middle West might have come from

England and Sweden and Germany; all of these came from Ireland. But there was no dissent in either case. Virtue was virtue, vice was vice. The ideas of the parents did not differ profoundly from those of the children.

The parallels between Hoover's world and Smith's could be pushed still further. In these metropolitan neighborhoods, as Hapgood and Moskowitz described them, "life usually centered around the church, just as it does in a smaller place." If Herbert Hoover had "thee'd" and "thou'd" with his parents and waited for the movings of the Spirit in the silence of a Friends' Meeting, altar boy Alfred Smith had gotten up early on Sunday for seven years to serve the seven o'clock Mass. On weekdays, also, Smith's people lived by as rigorous a work ethic as Hoover's. "There was nobody in that family, and there were few if any in the neighborhood, who conceived of life as anything except an existence based on individual effort," the biographers continued. "Theories about what society owes to the individual were not topics of conversation. Everybody worked, and everybody took work for granted." So much for the received 1920s stereotype of a hidebound, pious, tribalized rural America confronting a liberated, skeptical, sophisticated metropolitan public—or the 1960s equivalent, of a frightened, status-conscious, "law-and-order"-haunted suburban America facing an atomized, alienated, insurgent crowd of urban revolutionaries!

Of course Norman Hapgood and Henry Moskowitz had created a highly selective portrait of Al Smith's America, as selective in its own way as Will Irwin's portrait of his fellow Stanford alumnus. Nor was Al Smith's America all of urban America. There *were* Americans in the twenties who rejected the values of their parents; there were some, among the ranks of trade unionists, social workers, and academic sociologists, for example, who rejected individualism as the basis for existence; there were at least a few who did not take work for granted. Even within Smith's close-knit, familial, God-fearing milieu there were jarring divergences from some of the mid-American norms, for example over Prohibition. But campaign biographers, like the politicians they serve, aim for the center. Quite understandably Hapgood and Moskowitz stressed Smith's congruences with the American electorate, not his dissimilarities. Those congruences included a commitment to freedom such as Warren Harding had never displayed, as in Al Smith's valiant battle for the seating of five properly elected socialists in the New York state legislature, and a commitment to public over private interest such as Calvin Coolidge had never manifested, as in Smith's vigorous challenges to the electrical energy trust.

In spite of all his provincialisms, the New Yorker succeeded in finding and winning a national audience. Between the Coolidge landslide of 1924 and the election of 1928 the Democratic presidential vote nearly doubled; Smith got nearly as many votes as Coolidge had received four years earlier. In 1928 Herbert Hoover defeated Alfred Smith; but it was a defeat like that of Frémont in 1856, foreshadowing a new national realignment, rather than a defeat like that of Bryan in 1896, signaling an era's end.

Although each had strong ties in the business community, both Herbert Hoover and Al Smith were "progressives," as that term was still understood in the twenties. Both mobilized peoples and innovated social structures, and both limited themselves as to how much mobilization and innovation their common ground rules would admit, perhaps realizing—as William Appleman Williams has so well said of Hoover—"that you let the system come apart at the seams rather than violate the principles by saving the system *for* the people. . . . For when you do that you *rule* the people instead of serving the people."

Came the Crash, and the system did come apart at the seams. A disheartened Hoover and an embittered Smith retired to the sidelines, crying out against a third political figure carrying over from the twenties, FDR, who attempted to save the system for the people—but who had not the temperament for iron rule. Meanwhile the tragedy of Europe, interrupted for the duration of the twenties (partly by the interposition of American loans), proceeded to its crashing Wagnerian climax. Only then, as they picked up the pieces of the evil empire established by Roosevelt's screaming, black-cowlicked adversary in Berlin, and turned to face a more profound world revolution than Warren Harding ever dreamed of, did Americans begin to understand what it really means to rule—and be ruled.

The Sources for This Book

I. Towns and Roads

An earlier version of this first chapter was pruned and disciplined into publishability by the expert editorial hand of Erik Wensberg for the *Columbia Forum*, 2 (Spring 1973). In preparing that essay to be part of a book I have restored a few of Mr. Wensberg's cuts, but the chapter still shows, and benefits from, the effect of his fine work. (I much regret that journal's subsequent demise; it was civilized, it was provocative, and it had style.)

The first direct quotation in the chapter, and in the book—the comment about the machine-rhythms of jazz—is from a long-winded, elitist, but also intelligent and musically knowledgeable essay by Paul Fritz Laubenstein, "Jazz—Debit and Credit," *Musical Quarterly*, 15 (October, 1929). For an example of the unthinking stereotyped use of the year 1920 as a rural-urban population watershed, rather than embarrass fellow historians by singling any of them out for citation I confess its use in a previous work of my own, *The Decline and Revival of the Social Gospel* (Ithaca, New York: Cornell University Press, 1956), p. 36; the error stands uncorrected in a revised edition (Hamden, Connecticut: Shoe String Press, 1971). Other examples may be found in abundance by flipping through the pages dealing with the twenties in any standard assortment of U.S. history textbooks.

August Derleth's *Three Literary Men: a Memoir of Sinclair Lewis, Sherwood Anderson, Edgar Lee Masters* (New York: Candlelight Press, 1963), essentially a record of personal conversations, was a useful and thought-provoking source for this chapter. The other Derleth quotations are from the story collection *Country Growth* (New York: Scribner, 1940) and from the nonfictional *Village Year: A Sac Prairie Journal* (New York: Coward-McCann, 1941). I had prepared a list of questions for Mr. Derleth about his personal perspective on the twenties when his untimely death intervened (1971). Even without that hoped-for commentary, however, this exposition has insensibly been influenced by my own prior correspondence with Derleth, begun long before this book was conceived.

I used a paper edition (Bantam, 1964) of Ray Bradbury's *Dandelion Wine*, which was first copyright in 1957; it has since been re-issued in hard covers (New York: Knopf, 1975). The reference to the car that "blew tires and flung fan belts like lost garters down Route 66" is from the short story "The Inspired Sick Chicken Motel," in Bradbury, *I Sing the Body Electric* (New York: Knopf, 1969). Biographical material on Ray Bradbury may be found in James M. Ethridge and Barbara Kopala, eds., *Contemporary Authors*, first revision (Detroit: Gale Research Co., 1967), and in Sam Moskowitz, *Seekers of Tomorrow: Masters of Modern Science Fiction* (New York: Ballantine, 1967). But Ray Bradbury is his own best biographical source. He responded most generously, as he does with all serious inquirers, to an earlier draft of this chapter in a two-page single-spaced letter to me on February 27, 1963, and afterward to the published magazine version of the chapter, in a letter printed in the *Columbia Forum*, 2 (Summer 1973). The portions of the former letter appearing here are used by the kind permission of Mr. Bradbury. That version also elicited an incisive comment by Professor J. W. Smurr of Stanislaus State College, Turlock, California, written on June 19, 1973, which the *Forum's* editors kindly forwarded to me. Portions of the letter that appear here are used by kind permission of Mr. Smurr.

The information on highway development before and during the twenties was drawn especially from the Brookings Institution study by Charles L. Dearing, *American Highway Policy* (Washington, 1941) and also from [Lincoln Highway Association] *The Lincoln Highway: the Story of a Crusade That Made Transpor-*

tation History (New York: Dodd, Mead, 1935). The quotation from Anne O'Hare McCormick in the *New York Times* was reprinted in Allan Nevins and Frank Ernest Hill, *Ford: Expansion and Challenge 1915–1933* (New York: Scribner, 1957). The automobile advertisement from the *Saturday Evening Post* was described in Robert S. and Helen Merrell Lynd, *Middletown: a Study in Modern American Culture*, first copyright 1929; I used a more recent, but identical, edition in paper (Harcourt, 1956).

Vernon Parrington's essay "Sinclair Lewis: Our Own Diogenes" was included in Parrington, *Main Currents in American Thought* (New York: Harcourt, 1930), III. Sinclair Lewis's *Free Air*, probably because it was published before Lewis made his reputation, has become a "rare book" in some university libraries. I was able conveniently to use a copy of the 1919 edition off a regular stack shelf. *Dodsworth*, copyright 1929, is available now in several paper editions. *Main Street* itself, although not cited in the text, has obviously shaped my judgments; it also is available in many editions, some of them with misleading scholarly introductions. For biographical detail on Lewis, Mark Schorer's massive *Sinclair Lewis: An American Life* (New York: McGraw-Hill, 1961) is indispensable, although it should be noted that my own assessment of *Free Air* is not the same as that of most of the critics cited by Schorer.

The George McGovern quotations are from an interview near the scene of the 1972 Democratic National Convention with Richard Meryman, "I Have Earned the Nomination," published in the lamented news magazine *Life*, 73 (July 7, 1972). That viewpoint was reinforced in a New York Times News Service essay by Christopher Lydon, "McGovern: a Profile of a Dedicated Man," which, appropriately, I read not in the *Times* but in the *Daily Missoulian* (Missoula, Montana) for July 17, 1972.

II. War and Peace

Ray Stannard Baker described what he saw during a flight over war-torn northern France in "My Wild Ride With Youth in an Aëroplane," *American Magazine*, 89 (January, 1920). William Allen White wrote his account of the trans-Rhine occupation zone in *The Autobiography of William Allen White* (New York: Macmillan, 1946). A recent account of that occupation, and of the demobilization of the AEF, is in Burl Noggle, *Into the Twenties: the United States from Armistice to Normalcy* (Urbana: University of Illinois Press, 1974), chapter 2. George S. Patton has received a careful and scrupulous editing by Martin Blumenson in *The Patton Papers*, I: *1885–1940* (Boston: Houghton Mifflin, 1972) and II: *1940–1945* (Boston: Houghton Mifflin, 1974). It is devoutly to be hoped that these volumes will totally supplant as a historical source the sprawling, gossipy book by Ladislas Farago, *Patton: Ordeal and Triumph* (New York: Obolensky, 1963), from which the motion picture *Patton* was apparently made.

Barbara Tuchman has written of Patton's contemporary, Joseph Stilwell, in *Stilwell and the American Experience in China, 1911–45* (New York: Macmillan, 1971). More broadly—and, in the judgment of this reader, more persuasively—she has written of the onset of World War I in *The Guns of August* (New York: Macmillan, 1962), which I read in conjunction with Will Irwin's account of the German invasion of Belgium, in Irwin, *The Making of a Reporter* (New York: Putnam, 1942). Warren Harding's horrified recoil from an army war game is described by Irwin.

Calvin Coolidge's thrifty comments on the defense establishment were contained in a letter to the National Council for the Prevention of War, July 23, 1924, as quoted in Edward Elwell Whiting, *Calvin Coolidge: His Ideals of Citizenship as Revealed Through His Speeches and Writings* (Boston: W. A. Wilde, 1924) and (at greater length) in an address to the American Legion, October 6, 1925, as printed in Calvin Coolidge, *Foundations of the Republic: Speeches and Addresses* (New York: Scribner, 1926). Senator Thomas J. Walsh's comment that a war with Japan was about as likely as a war with Mars is quoted in Gerald Wheeler, *Prelude to Pearl Harbor: the United States Navy and the Far East, 1921–1931* (Columbia, Missouri: University of Missouri Press, n.d. [1963]). Admiral Yamamoto's benign rebuttal to Billy Mitchell is quoted in John Deane Potter, *Yamamoto: The Man Who Menaced America* (New York: Viking, 1965). The Kobe *Japan Chronicle*'s more ominous forecast, made prior to the successful

Washington Disarmament Conference, was reported in the *Literary Digest*, 63 (November 8, 1919).

The prophetic short story by F. Britten Austin, "When the War God Walks Again," appearing in the *Saturday Evening Post*, 197 (January 17, 1925), was the harbinger of much more of the same to come, particularly after the founding of the science fiction pulps in the second half of the decade. One of the better examples of such stories, Carl W. Spohr's "The Final War," serialized in *Wonder Stories*, 3 (March, April 1932) was clearly modeled upon Remarque's *All Quiet on the Western Front*. But also as straight nonfictional speculation, "next war" literature was abundant during the twenties.

An incisive comment on that literature from the end of the decade is Roland Hugins, "That Notorious Next War," *World Tomorrow*, 12 (July 1929); that essay is reprinted in my anthology of magazine articles from the twenties entitled *The Uncertain World of Normalcy: the 1920s* (New York: Pitman, 1971). The statement that chemistry could wreck the world, by Leo Baekeland—who, incidentally, was the inventor of "bakelite," from which derives the entire plastics industry—appeared in the *Literary Digest*, 83 (October 4, 1924). Will Irwin's satirical "Heroic Ballad: 1976" was reprinted in *ibid.*, 80 (February 9, 1924). My reading of Will Irwin, *The Next War: An Appeal to Common Sense* (New York: Dutton, 1921) was undoubtedly colored by awareness of my father's personal and intellectual acquaintance with Irwin during the crisis-ridden late thirties.

The bitter denial by Will Irwin that war improves men's character appeared in a public address, "The Churches Can Stop War!", published in the *Christian Century*, 41 (March 13, 1924). See also James M. Ludlow, "End war; now!", *ibid.*, January 24, 1924, and editorial in *ibid.*, January 31. That liberal Protestant journal is also the source for Ambassador Matsudaira's optimistic assessment of U.S.–Japanese relations: "Japanese Ambassador Decries War Talk," *ibid.*, 42 (May 7, 1925). My rejoinder that the churches were too ineffective as a social force during the twenties to dream of stopping war is based on Robert T. Handy, *The*

American Religious Depression, 1925–1935 (Philadelphia: Fortress Press, 1969). The anecdotes about warmongering clergymen during the First World War are drawn from the reminiscences of clergy known to me personally.

In considering the peace movement of the 1920s I have profited from a paper by David McReynolds, "Alternative Peace Strategies in the Twenties," which was read at a panel sponsored by the Conference on Peace Research in History during the annual meeting of the Organization of American Historians, April 16, 1971. I am indebted to Professor Alfred Young of Northern Illinois University for an advance copy of that paper in mimeograph. Oliver LaFarge's assessment of collegiate pacifism in the twenties, "Colleges and War," appeared in *Scribner's Magazine,* 78 (July, 1925); his own personal "dropout" from the public concerns of the twenties is implicit in the 1962 Foreword to LaFarge, *Laughing Boy* (Boston: Houghton Mifflin, first copyright 1929).

The 1924 Student Volunteer Movement world convention was discussed in "Youth's Decision Against War," *Literary Digest,* 80 (February 2, 1924). The 1927 National Student Conference was covered in *ibid.,* 92 (February 5, 1927), under the title "Students' War on Mars." Despite the eclipse of the *Literary Digest* after— but *not* as a result of—its heroically inaccurate forecast of the 1936 presidential election, that news weekly's thoughtful reporting and conscientious samplings from other news media make it an invaluable source for all aspects of the public life of the twenties; see William C. Capel, "Polls and the Birth of a Literary Digest Myth," *The Quill,* 54 (July 1966).

The education journals, often (and understandably!) neglected by historians, can be a treasure trove for anyone exploring the Jazz Age. William H. Kilpatrick's address "Our Schools and War," and H. C. Wegner's essay "Education vs. War," both appeared in the *Education Review,* 61 (March, 1921). John F. O'Ryan, "Teachers and World Peace," was published in the *NEA Journal,* 12 (May 1923). The 1924 study of hyperpatriotism in American history textbooks was discussed in *The Nation,* 119 (September 17, 1924); compare "ABC of Hate: International Hatred is Fostered in the Public Schools," *New Republic,* 62

(February 19, 1930). But take account also of the letter in *ibid.*, March 19, from the historian James Harvey Robinson, who argued that by comparison with Europe's hysteric national chauvinisms U.S. textbooks and teachings were not so bad after all.

The Havelock Ellis piece, originally an article in the (London) *Nation*, was condensed in *Current Opinion*, 66 (April 1919). Its American title was "War To Be Ended, Not by Love, Nor by Reason, But by 'Sublimation.'" H. L. Mencken's editorial "The Charm of War" appeared in the *American Mercury*, 19 (February, 1930); his remark that any man who has not stood in battle has missed the most colossal experience possible for his sex appears in Mencken, *In Defense of Women* (New York: Knopf, 1918). Sigmund Freud's wartime comment, "Thoughts for the Times on War and Death," is available in Freud, *Collected Papers* (New York: Basic Books, 1959), IV; his reply to Einstein, "Why War?", is in *ibid.*, V.

III. Ways of Worship

Nothing is more dead than last year's religious book. Happily for students of the history of religion in America, hardcover reprinting for libraries has revived some of the better books of that kind for a new generation of readers. The quotation which begins this chapter is taken from one such reprinted work, Willard Sperry, *Signs of These Times*, which originated as the Ayer Lectures at the Colgate-Rochester Divinity School in 1929 (Freeport, New York: Books for Libraries Press, 1968). Another book of this sort from which I have quoted is Charles Fiske, *Confessions of a Puzzled Parson*, first published in 1928 (Freeport: Books for Libraries Press, 1968). But inevitably it was also necessary to consult works long out of print with no prospect of resuscitation. The dialogue between the American soldier and the "Y" worker was recorded in such a book by Allyn K. Foster, *The Coming Revival of Religion* (Philadelphia: Judson Press, 1929). James M. Gray, "What the Bible Teaches About War," was published as a short-lived pamphlet (Chicago, [1917]). Alfred McCann's anti-Darwinist interpretation of the war appears in McCann, *God—or Gorilla?* (New York: Devin-Adair, 1922); that book achieved wide distribution and can still be found in many libraries, often with outraged marginal annotation.

The Darrow–Bryan quotations are taken from the abridgement of *State of Tennessee* v. *John Thomas Scopes*, in Sheldon Grebstein, ed., *Monkey Trial* (Boston: Houghton Mifflin, 1960). William Jennings Bryan's folksy Biblical literalism must be set alongside J. Gresham Machen's ably argued case for Fundamentalism, *Christianity and Liberalism* (New York: Macmillan, 1923). I have quoted also from the first chapter of Machen, *What Is Faith?* (New York: Macmillan, 1925). The reference to students who hissed their professor for his incautious use of the word "evolution" is in William H. P. Faunce, "Freedom in School and Church," *World's Work*, 45 (1923); it is quoted also in my essay "The Fundamentalist Defense of the Faith," a chapter in John Braeman et al., eds., *Change and Continuity in Twentieth-Century America: The 1920's* (Columbus: Ohio State University Press, 1968).

My inference that Judaism had to contend with a doctrinaire conservatism analogous to that of Protestant Fundamentalism is derived from Abba Hillel Silver, *Religion in a Changing World* (New York: Harper, 1931). Granville Hicks conducted his interview with Hillyer Straton, "The Son of a Fundamentalist Prophet," for the Universalist denominational paper the *Christian Leader*, 106 (March 10, 1927). It is reprinted in my magazine-article anthology *The Uncertain World of Normalcy: the 1920s* (New York: Pitman, 1971). Correspondence in 1968 with Hicks and Straton, both of whom recalled the interview, proved most helpful. The same anthology contains Allan Armstrong Hunter, "Why We Are Silent: the Problem Facing Young Ministers," first published in the *Forum*, 70 (October, 1923). From that essay came the quotation which opens Part IV in the present chapter. Mr. Hunter, like Granville Hicks and Hillyer Straton, generously responded to my request for comment upon what he had said in his youth from the perspective of longer experience. *The Uncertain World of Normalcy* also made available for present-day readers the article by Myron Stearns, "Gentlemen, the President! A Study of Calvin Coolidge," originally in *McClure's Magazine*, new series, 1 (June 1925). From that journalist's account came the anecdote of President Coolidge in church.

Joseph Wood Krutch mentioned the student hostility to religion he was told to expect as a visiting lecturer at Caltech in his autobiography, *More Lives Than One* (New York: Sloane, 1962). See also Krutch's own contribution to the "God is dead" literature of the Twenties, *The Modern Temper* (New York: Harcourt, 1929), and Harry Elmer Barnes, *The Twilight of Christianity* (New York: R. R. Smith, 1929). I have discussed the larger historical context of such writings in a paper read before the American Historical Association, December 30, 1971, published as "Science and the Death of God," *American Scholar*, 42 (Summer 1973). Sidney E. Mead, dean of American church historians, gave that essay the benefit of his typically incisive criticism before it was published, and he and Mary Kelley have further explored this question—concluding that the main lines of the "death-of-God" controversy were laid down in the twenties, not the sixties—in an article "Protestantism in the Shadow of Enlightenment," *Soundings*, 58 (Fall 1975). See also chapter 6 of my book *The Decline and Revival of the Social Gospel* (Ithaca: Cornell University Press, 1956; Hamden, Connecticut: Shoe String Press, 1971), whence came the quotation in the present chapter from Edwin Slosson.

The 1923 manifesto on science and religion, signed by leading scientists and churchmen, is in the collection of documents edited by E. C. Vanderlaan, *Fundamentalism vs. Modernism* (New York: H. W. Wilson, 1925); the statement was first published in *Science*, new series, 57 (June 1, 1923). The lectures at Union Theological Seminary by J. Arthur Thomson were published as *Science and Religion* (New York: Scribner, 1925). A harsh but effective comment on the religiosity of the physicist Robert A. Millikan appears in Daniel J. Kevles, "Millikan: Spokesman for Science in the Twenties," *Engineering and Science*, 33 (April 1969). The reference to the stained-glass church window depicting Albert Einstein is in Harry Emerson Fosdick, *The Living of These Days: an Autobiography* (New York: Harper, 1956); see also Lincoln Barnett, *The Universe and Dr. Einstein*, 2d. rev. ed. (New York:

Sloane, 1957). The interview with Shailer Mathews by Neil M. Clark, "Putting Religion to the Test," appeared in the *American Magazine*, 109 (June 1930).

Lloyd C. Douglas's complaint of "mendicancy, sycophancy, servility, and general self-abasement" in the churches is in an article by Douglas, "Increasing the Church's Self-Respect," published in the Methodist weekly *Christian Advocate*, 101 (July 1, 1926). Douglas's novel *Magnificent Obsession*, published in 1929, continues in print. Biographical material on Lloyd Douglas in the standard reference work by Stanley Kunitz and Howard Haycraft, *Twentieth Century Authors* (New York: H. W. Wilson, 1942), was augmented by correspondence in the early 1940s between Douglas and my late father, Manfred A. Carter, whose unpublished manuscript autobiography *Broken Spires* is the source for the ironic description of "making contact" in an urban church.

The anonymous criticism of church people for failing to realize that their pastor was human appeared in the *American Magazine*, 103 (March, 1927) under the title "Things I Wish My Congregation Wouldn't Do." The comment by Mamie Williams, Topeka schoolteacher, that the average minister was unqualified to present his message to the advancing intelligence of the new generation was quoted in a news story, "Churches Lose Influence Over College Youth: Kansas A. M. E. Meet Discusses Issue," *Chicago Defender*, January 12, 1929. The quotation from Stanley Walker of the *New York Herald Tribune* may be found in Charles Francis Potter, *The Preacher and I: An Autobiography* (New York: Crown, 1951), which is the source also of an unnamed layman's description of the minister up in the stands explaining the game to the ladies while the men are down on the field fighting.

Christopher Morley's cryptic confessional essay "Religio Journalistici" appeared in *Century Magazine*, 108 (July, 1924); it was published also as a small book (New York: Doubleday, 1924). Hal Bridges, *American Mysticism from William James to Zen* (New York: Harper, 1970) is a pioneering monograph on that subject. The idea that Zane Grey might be considered as a *religious* writer was first suggested to me by a student at the University of Arizona, Mr. Forrest Wilcox. (Other students in colloquia on the twenties, both at Arizona and at Northern Illinois University, in the give-and-take of the classroom doubtlessly have influenced this book in ways of which neither they nor I have been aware, not only in this chapter but elsewhere.) Data on Grey may be found in Kunitz and Haycraft, *Twentieth Century Authors,* and in Frank Luther Mott, *Golden Multitudes* (New York: Macmillan, 1947), a comprehensive historical study of American best-selling books. See also Burton Rascoe, "Opie Read and Zane Grey," *Saturday Review of Literature,* 21 (November 11, 1939). Two nonfiction items by Grey dating from the same period in which he wrote *Wanderer of the Wasteland* (1923) may be read as context for that novel: "What the Desert Means to Me," *American Magazine,* 98 (November, 1924) and *Tales of Lonely Trails* (New York: Harper, 1922). See in the latter work especially the conclusion to his first chapter, dealing with the Rainbow Bridge, and the final chapter, recounting an expedition of his own in 1919 to Death Valley. Perhaps it is time we gave popular writers of this sort the same kind of systematic attention we have long accorded to Fitzgerald and Hemingway.

Background for what is said in this chapter as to the implications for the future of religious developments in the twenties may be found in my article "The Pastoral Office of the President," *Theology Today,* 25 (April, 1968); in Arnold Toynbee's essay "Marxism, Socialism, and Christianity," an appendix to Vol. V of Toynbee, *A Study of History* (London and New York: Oxford University Press, 1939); and in two short, deeply thoughtful books by Sidney E. Mead, *The Lively Experiment* (New York: Harper, 1963) and *The Nation with the Soul of a Church* (New York: Harper, 1975).

IV. Science and Democracy

An earlier version of this chapter, under the title "Science and the Common Man," appeared in the *American Scholar,* 45 (Winter 1975–76). The present draft has been greatly improved by that journal's tasteful and meticulous editing. David Dietz, science editor of the Scripps-Howard newspapers, responded to a quotation from him in the *Scholar* article by writing me directly, on February 16, 1976, to share with me his own impressions of Albert Einstein's first visit to this country, deriving from an interview he had with Einstein and Weizmann when they came through Cleveland; Dietz's firsthand assessment strikes me as in accordance with my own secondhand one. Mr. Dietz was also kind enough to enclose two reminiscent articles on the early days of science writing for the American press, "A Bit of History About the Science-Writing Art By an Early Practitioner," *Scripps-Howard News*, 18 July 1964), and "Science, Newspapers and the Future," *The Quill*, 54 (July 1966).

News stories on that first Einstein visit may be found in the *New York Times*, which chronicled his sojourn with its usual detail (see the *Times* Index for April and May 1921); in the *Washington Post*, especially for April 3, 6, 19, and 27, 1921; and in the *Literary Digest*, 69 (April 16, 1921). The *Congressional Record*, 67th Congress, 1st Session, for April 18, 1921, took oratorical note of the Einstein theory. News coverage of Albert Einstein continued after his departure from this country, though of course less intensively than during the 1921 visit. The *New York Times*, for example, noted his temporary flight from Germany (August 6, 1922; editorial, August 9) and his denunciation by the Communist Party of the Soviet Union (November 16, 1922). From time to time during the twenties the weekly and monthly media continued to take notice of "the wizard of Württemberg," as one of them named him; see the *Independent*, 117 (July 10, 1926). The contrasting image of the American scientist as a good Rotarian, entitled "Must Scientists Wear Whiskers?", was an editorial in *ibid.*, 115 (November 28, 1925).

Edwin Slosson's judgment that Max Planck's equally revolutionary ideas had not had the same popular impact because Planck was not personally so picturesque as Einstein appeared in *ibid.*, 108 (May 13, 1922). I found particularly helpful for understanding Einstein's continuing popular appeal—not just in celebrity-conscious New York but in the rest of America as well—the article by M. K. Wisehart, "A Close Look at the World's Greatest Thinker," *American Magazine*, (June 1930). A more philosophical assessment of Einstein as a public figure in the early twenties, in Europe rather than in America, may be found in Alexander Mosz-kowski, *Conversations With Einstein* (New York: Horizon Press, 1970; first translated and published in 1921). An opinion of Einstein's American reputation that differs somewhat from my own may be inferred from Ronald Tobey, *The American Ideology of a National Science, 1919–1930* (Pittsburgh: University of Pittsburgh Press, 1971). The relevant quotation from Ralph Waldo Emerson is at the end of the *Divinity School Address*.

The Stafford Little Lectures Einstein gave at Princeton during that first visit to the United States in 1921 comprise the first four chapters of Albert Einstein, *The Meaning of Relativity*, 6th rev. ed. (London: Methuen, 1956). The historian of science David Corson, of the University of Arizona, helpfully criticized my wording of a point made by Einstein in those lectures. The solar eclipse of 1922, important as an empirical test of the general relativity theory, was chronicled in the *New York Times*, September 22, 1922. A preliminary report on the Lick Observatory expedition to Australia to observe that eclipse appeared in *Scientific Monthly*, 14 (March 1922), and a writeup of that expedition's findings appeared in *ibid.*, 16 (June 1923). The disclosures did not end the argument; pro-and-con discussions of relativity abound in the magazines of the twenties. An outstanding example is the symposium "Is Einstein Wrong?" published in 1924 in the *Forum*, 71 (June) and 72 (July, August). See also the comment by T. J. J. See, as reported under the title "Is the Einstein Theory a Crazy Vagary?", *Literary Digest*, 77 (June 2, 1923), and a letter to the editor, *New York Times*, November, 23, 1922. No less a science establishment journal than that of the American Association for the Advancement of Science published a Dutch savant's "decisive disproof of Einstein's theory"; *Science*, new series, 63 (April 23, 1926). The continuing fascinated bafflement of laymen is typified in a brief Editor's Easy Chair essay, "Einstein Gets Us Guessing," *Harper's*, 158 (April 1929).

Albert Einstein's own insistence that the results of scientific investigation, no matter how abstruse, must be made available to the general public is contained in a 1948 Foreword to Lincoln Barnett, *The Universe and Dr. Einstein*, of which I used the 1957 revised edition. The problem of science popularization and science education is discussed in Sir Richard Gregory, "The Message of Science," *Science*, n.s., 54 (November 11, 1921) and in James Harvey Robinson, *The Humanizing of Knowledge* (New York: Doran, 1923). H. L. Mencken's blast at the inaccuracy of science news reporting was quoted in *Science News Letter*, 12 (July 1927). A study by Otis Caldwell and Charles W. Finley, who concluded that science reporting in the newspapers was not so bad after all, was summarized in *Scientific Monthly*, 16 (May 1923).

Biographical data on Edwin Slosson, the first director of Science Service, may be found in the *Dictionary of American Biography* (New York: Scribner, 1935), XVII. The guidelines for writers of news stories for Science Service are quoted in *Science*, n.s., 58 (October 5, 1923). The A.A.A.S. symposium on science and the press was fully reported in *ibid.*, 67 (March 16, 1928) and 68 (August 3, August 10, 1928). Slosson's suggestion that the more "impractical" sciences might have greater intrinsic popular appeal was quoted in *ibid.*, 67 (May 4, 1928). J. O. Perrine's insightful short essay, "The Fun of Being a Scientist," appeared in *Scientific Monthly*, 27 (July 1928).

Representative comment in the more popular media included Robert L. Duffus, "Can We Plan Our Future?", *Collier's Weekly*, 73 (January 12, 1924), and the editorial "Pure and Applied," *Saturday Evening Post*, 198 (June 5, 1926). The establishment of the National Research Endowment in order to balance the "pure" side of that equation was announced in *Science*, n.s., 63 (January 1, 1926) and further described in *ibid.*, February 5; see also George Ellery Hale, "Science and the Wealth of Nations," *Harper's*, 156 (June 1928). A fuller discussion of the National Research Endowment, which (for both legal and economic reasons) was re-christened the National Research Fund, may be found in Lance E. Davis and Daniel J. Kevles, "The National Research Fund: A Case Study in the Industrial Support of Academic Science," *Minerva*, 12 (April 1974).

There is considerable disagreement as to the exact degree of Albert Einstein's responsibility for the famous letter to FDR proposing development of an atomic bomb. For the conflicting views of

Leo Szilard, Edward Teller, and Einstein's own executor, see chapter 6 in Robert Jungk, *Brighter Than a Thousand Suns: a Personal History of the Atomic Scientists* (New York: Harcourt, 1958).

The charge of elitist dogmatism in science—what we would nowadays perhaps term "scientism"—was aired in an editorial, "Science Says," printed in *The Nation*, 127 (October 17, 1928), and in an article by James Truslow Adams, "Is Science a Blind Alley?", *Harper's*, 156 (February, 1928). Many other examples could have been cited; both scientific positivism and humanistic or religious rebuttals to it were staple fare in the upper-middlebrow magazines of the twenties. That this charge of elitism had some substance may be inferred, at times inadvertently, from Edwin Slosson's own writings. See in particular Slosson, "Action and Reaction in Spreading Science," *School and Society*, 23 (February 20, 1926), and his series "Science Remaking the World," *World's Work*, 45 (November, December, 1922; January, February, March, 1923). The "scientific" racist slander of mulattoes is quoted from Marjorie Mac-Dill, "Will Blending of Races Produce Super-Men?", *Science News Letter*, 12 (November 26, 1927). Again, many other examples could have been cited; see Thomas F. Gossett, *Race: the History of an Idea in America* (Dallas: SMU Press, 1963), ch. 15. The Bishop of Ripon's proposal for a ten-year moratorium on scientific investigation, and the rebuttals he generated, were reported under the title "Is Scientific Advance Impeding Human Welfare?", *Literary Digest*, 95 (October 1, 1927).

V. Prohibition

This chapter began as a paper read before the Western Historical Association, October 14, 1972. With the title "Prohibition and Democracy: The Noble Experiment Reassessed," it was published in the *Wisconsin Magazine of History*, 56 (Spring 1973), where it was adorned—as is that journal's admirable custom—with appropriate contemporary photographs and cartoons. One of the latter, "The Real 'Repealer,' " was originally drawn by my father for the parish paper of a local church further described in chapter 3. I have quoted also from his unpublished sermon manuscript "The Tide of Prohibition," duplicate of a copy in the Manfred A. Carter

Collection housed in the George Arents Research Library, Syracuse University.

Prohibition has drawn considerable attention in recent years from historians, both as a national phenomenon, as in James H. Timberlake, *Prohibition and the Progressive Movement* (Cambridge, Mass.: Harvard University Press, 1963), and at the state level, as in the studies by Norman H. Clark, *The Dry Years: Prohibition and Social Change in Washington* (Seattle: University of Washington Press, 1965) and Gilman Ostrander, *The Prohibition Movement in California, 1848–1933* (Berkeley and Los Angeles: University of California Press, 1957). It has been discussed from the standpoint of sociology, for example in Joseph Gusfield, *Symbolic Crusade: Status Politics and the American Temperance Movement* (Urbana: University of Illinois Press, 1963), and it has received the scholarly attention of a chastened, post-Prohibition Protestantism, most notably in Paul C. Conley and Andrew A. Sorensen, *The Staggering Steeple: The Story of Alcoholism and the Churches* (Philadelphia: Pilgrim Press, 1971). From Conley's and Sorensen's study was quoted the surprisingly un-Catholic statement "The state only can save us," made in 1884 by Archbishop John Ireland.

A typical liberal historian's interpretation of the 1932 Democratic convention song "Happy Days Are Here Again" is a harbinger of the New Deal, rather than of beer, as Arthur M. Schlesinger, Jr., *The Crisis of the Old Order, 1919–1932* (Boston: Houghton Mifflin, 1957), 314. Articles on Al Smith by David Burner, "The Brown Derby Campaign," *New York History,* 46 (October 1965), and Jordan A. Schwarz, "Al Smith in the Thirties," *ibid.*, 45 (October 1964), were useful for this chapter, as was George Wolfskill, *The Revolt of the Conservatives: A History of the American Liberty League, 1934–1940* (Boston: Houghton Mifflin, 1962), especially chapter 2, "The Constitution in a Bottle." Biographical details on Tom Lewis of the United Mine Workers may be found in David J. McDonald and Edward Lynch, *Coal and Unionism: a History of the American Coal Miners' Unions* (Silver Spring, Md.: Lynald Books, 1939). A biography of Frances E. Willard by Mary Earhart, *Frances Willard: From Prayers to Politics* (Chicago: University of

Chicago Press, 1944) threw much light on the early social structure of the Woman's Christian Temperance Union, as did the Appendix to a study of that organization in Rockford, Illinois, by one of my students (Dona J. Helmer, "The Rockford Central WCTU," unpublished seminar paper, Northern Illinois University, 1972). The defense of the WCTU by its president during the twenties, Ella A. Boole, *Give Prohibition Its Chance* (Evanston, Illinois: Revell, 1929), is indispensable.

From Andrew Sinclair, *Prohibition: The Era of Excess* (Boston: Atlantic Monthly Press, 1962) I derived the idea that the wet–dry struggle could be studied in part as a *literary* controversy; hence the quotations from Jack London, *John Barleycorn* (New York: Century, 1913) and from Ring Lardner, Sr., *The Big Town* (New York: Scribner, 1925). However, such material has certain limits as historical evidence; witness Sinclair's far-fetched enlistment of Emily Dickinson as a "wet," on the ground that she once wrote with approval of an "intoxicated bee"! That quotation is of a piece with the Sinclair book as a whole, which abounds in exaggeration, distortion, and a simplistic Freudianism. See my review of it for the *American Scholar*, 31 (Spring 1962), 328.

The chapter's opening questions and answers on Prohibition, between Albert Einstein and his American interviewer, are from Don Arnald, "Einstein on Irrelevancies," *New York Times*, May 1, 1921, Section III, p. 22. From the *Times* also came stories on the founding of the Women's Organization for National Prohibition Reform, April 4, 1929, pp. 1 and 12. That organization's further history is traced in Grace N. Root, *Women and Repeal: The Story of the Women's Organization for National Prohibition Reform* (New York: Harper, 1934). Herbert Agar's essay "Prohibition and Democracy: A Plea for Limiting the Suffrage" appeared in the *English Review*, 52 (May 1931). H. L. Mencken's philippic against the "democratic pestilence" which found fruition in measures like the Eighteenth Amendment is in Mencken, *Treatise on the Gods* (New York: Knopf, 1930). The quotation from William Randolph Hearst is in Francis J. Tietsort, ed., *Temperance—or Prohibition?* (New York: Hearst Temperance Contest Committee, 1929), which contains the prize-winning essays in the contest sponsored by Hearst's *New*

York American. Walter Lippman, *Public Opinion* (New York: Macmillan, 1922), especially the chapters on "the making of a common will" and "the image of democracy," and his *The Phantom Public* (New York: Macmillan, 1925), are cautions against any hasty conclusion as to what "the will of the people" in the twenties really was, about Prohibition or anything else.

The editorial "Soft Morals," which defined the Prohibition controversy as "an inevitable class issue," appeared in the *Ladies' Home Journal,* 40 (March 1923); it is reprinted in my anthology *The Uncertain World of Normalcy: the 1920s* (New York: Pitman, 1971). The quotations from Bernard Shaw and Lord Bryce are in Harry S. Warner, *Prohibition, An Adventure in Freedom* (Westerville, Ohio: World League Against Alcoholism, 1928). The dry polemic which received endorsement from the bibulous Warren Harding was that of Roy A. Haynes, *Prohibition Inside Out* (Garden City, New York: Doubleday, 1923). A post-Repeal dry appraisal is Deets Pickett, *Temperance and the Changing Liquor Situation* (New York: Methodist Book Concern, 1934). Two "muckraking" accounts of Repeal are Fletcher Dobyns, *The Amazing Story of Repeal: An Exposé of the Power of Propaganda* (Chicago: Willett, 1940) and Ernest Gordon, *The Wrecking of the Eighteenth Amendment* (Francestown, New Hampshire: Alcohol Information Press, 1943). The letter Dobyns quotes from Pierre du Pont appears also in *Lobby Investigations: Hearings Before a Subcommittee of the Judiciary Committee, United States Senate, 71st Congress, 2nd Session, Pursuant to Senate Resolution 20* (Washington, 1929), IV, 4236.

The comparison between the Eighteenth Amendment and "that other Prohibition Amendment which outlawed slavery" appeared in the *Christian Advocate,* 101 (July 1, 1926). The comment by Herbert Hoover on Prohibition as a violation of the traditional sanctity of private property is in Hoover's oft-mentioned but usually misquoted *American Individualism* (New York: Doubleday, 1921). The entire range of opinion, both concurring and dissenting, in the Supreme Court's decision that the government could legitimately tap bootleggers' phones (*Olmstead* v. *United States,* 277 U.S. 438) deserves study, as an early anticipation of the dangers to civil liberty posed by advancing technology today.

VI. Women

The lack of library references to America's first actual woman governor (in fact as well as in name) is appalling. Nellie Tayloe Ross did not make it into the *Dictionary of American Biography*, nor does she appear in the compendium *Notable American Women*— nor even in *Who Was Who!* A brief sketch of her did appear in a work usually considered less reliable than the *DAB*, the *National Cyclopedia of American Biography*, Volume E (New York, 1938). Reference to Mrs. Ross in the periodical press of the twenties is also sparse, in contrast to Miriam "Maw" Ferguson, whose colorful and corrupt regime received appropriate coverage in the media— and to this day receives a line or so in the textbooks. It was Miriam Ferguson, not Nellie Ross, who was judged at the time as the "test" of whether a woman should or could govern. Imagine the uproar that would properly arise if a similar standard should guide our choice of which black politicians should be singled out for historical remembrance!

By far the most perceptive (and compassionate) contemporary judgment on the Ferguson governorship was that of Duncan Aikman of the *El Paso Times*, who is himself an unduly neglected figure from the twenties; see Aikman, "Politics and Ma Ferguson in Texas," the *Independent*, 115 (December 19, 1925). Except for one article on a limited aspect of the governing process by Cecilia Hendricks, "When a Woman Governor Campaigns," *Scribner's Magazine*, 85 (July 1928), nothing comparable to Duncan Aikman's essay on the Fergusons was published on Mrs. Ross during the twenties. Fortunately for history, Nellie Tayloe Ross was a person having both candor and self-perception, and her three-part autobiography, published in (of course) a women's magazine, was invaluable: Ross, "Governor Lady: An Autobiography," *Good Housekeeping*, 85 (August, September, October 1927). It is augmented to a small degree by a lighter piece she published a year later, "Mine Own People," *ibid.*, 87 (July 1928), which makes clear her keen sense of regional identity.

The general breakthrough of women into national politics in 1924 did receive widespread media notice. See *Current Opinion*, 77 (December 1924) for the rotogravure portrait of Mrs. Ross; *Literary Digest*, 83 (November 22, 1924), whence came the quotation from the *Boston Transcript;* the *Independent,* 115 (December 26, 1925), for brief accounts of the women then or recently members of Congress; *World's Work,* 50 (September 1925), which carried the photos of Mrs. Ferguson peeling potatoes and feeding the chickens. Additional data on Representatives Mary Norton and Edith Nourse Rogers are in the *Congressional Directory,* 81st Congress, second session (Washington, 1950). Joseph Lash, *Eleanor and Franklin* (New York: Norton, 1971) contains considerable information on Eleanor Roosevelt's hard-headed and effective political activities during the twenties.

Betty Friedan's observation that women not so long ago were expected to get total satisfaction out of making peanut butter sandwiches and scrubbing the kitchen floor was quoted in Peggi Flesch, "Friedan Describes Female Role," the *Northern Star* (student newspaper, Northern Illinois University, DeKalb, Illinois), March 15, 1973. The corroboration of that dismal appraisal by Louis E. Bisch, "Are Women Inferior?", was published in *Century Magazine,* 113 [new series, 91] (April 1927). John Macy, "Equality of Woman with Man: a Myth," appeared in *Harper's,* 153 (November 1926); the same author's "Logic and the Ladies, with a Word About Their Other Mental Processes," ran in *ibid.,* 157 (November 1928). James M. Cain's misogynist essay, "Politician: Female," was printed in the *American Mercury,* 3 (November 1924). These citations barely skim the surface of this kind of commentary; like racism, its expression seems inexhaustible. It came out that way sometimes even when the male writers were trying hard to say something nice. A particularly unctuous example is Bruce Barton, "Let Us Talk About Women," *Collier's Weekly,* 76 (August 22, 1925).

The fact that Grace Coolidge learned of Calvin's decision not to run again for President in 1928 only at second hand is detailed in Ishbel Ross, *Grace Coolidge and Her Era: the Story of a President's Wife* (New York: Dodd, Mead, 1962). That book reminds us also that there was much more to Mrs. Coolidge than simply the symbolic First Lady whose pleasant manner before the public took some of the ice out of her spouse's social performances. The comment by Belle Moskowitz tacitly acknowledging the importance of her own role in Al Smith's state administration in Albany is quoted in Matthew and Hannah Josephson, *Al Smith: Hero of the Cities* (Boston: Houghton Mifflin, 1969). Mrs. Moskowitz's subsequent battle with FDR after he had succeeded Smith as governor of New York is described in Frank Freidel, *Franklin D. Roosevelt: the Triumph* (Boston: Little, Brown, 1956). Her public endorsement of the concept of female inferiority was reported in the *New York Times*, April 28, 1926; see also editorial in *ibid.*, April 29.

The glamorized working girl who had "awakened to the fact that the 'superior sex' stuff is all bunk" was described (and pictured) in Samuel Crowther, "Aren't We All Rich Now?", *Collier's Weekly*, 76 (November 7, 1925); but see the cautionary discussion in the second chapter of William Henry Chafe, *The American Woman: Her Changing Social, Economic, and Political Roles, 1920–1970* (New York: Oxford University Press, 1972). My brief discussion of Zelda Fitzgerald in this context owes much to the study by Nancy Milford, *Zelda* (New York: Harper, 1970), of which I used the more recent paper (Avon) edition. I am indebted to Myra Dinnerstein, Director of Women's Studies at the University of Arizona, for a critical reading of this passage. The anonymous "Confessions of an Ex-Feminist" appeared in the *New Republic*, 46 (April 14, 1926); see also Florence Guy Seabury, "Men Who Understand Women," *The Nation*, 119 (November 12, 1924).

The heretical notion that growing girls should have other identity models in addition to that of future wife and mother was proposed in the unlikely pages of *Good Housekeeping*, 81 (December 1925), in an article by the head of a girls' private school, Jessica G. Cosgrove, titled "Romantic Love: a Keen Analysis of the Part the Mother Plays in her Daughter's Choice of a Husband." Margaret Mead's departure for Samoa was duly noted in the all-seeing *New York Times*, November 8, 1925; her observation that in those days unescorted field-tripping "out there" was considered no life for a lady is recorded in Mead, *Blackberry Winter: My Earlier Years* (New York: Morrow, 1972).

Glenna Collett's remark that the tomboy ideal was healthier than the old image of the shrinking violet was quoted in "Best Sports For Women," *Literary Digest*, 82 (September 13, 1924). Helen

Wills's comment that to improve their game women athletes should compete against opponents better than themselves, especially men, appeared in a news feature "Feminine Laurel Bearers," *Review of Reviews*, 74 (September 1926). Elizabeth Halsey's comments on "The New Sportswoman" appeared in *Hygeia*, 5 (September 1927). Continuing resistance to women's athletics was expressed in Henry Curtis, "Should Girls Play Interschool Basketball?", *ibid.*, 6 (November 1928) and in William T. Tilden, II, "Can Women Compete with Men in Sport?", *Country Life*, 42 (August 1922).

Gertrude Ederle's Channel-crossing feat was thoroughly covered by the media. See especially the article, "How a Girl Beat Leander at the Hero Game," *Literary Digest*, 90 (August 21, 1926), which included the quotations from swimming coach Tom Robinson, from the *New York Herald Tribune*'s W. O. McGeehan, from the *Boston Globe*'s "Uncle Dudley," and from Carrie Chapman Catt. The description from the *Brooklyn Eagle* of Gertrude at an earlier age was quoted in *ibid.*, 80 (March 8, 1924). See also Sol Metzger, "The Great Year in Sport," *Country Life*, 43 (December 1922), which includes a charming picture of Ederle at fifteen, and Walter Camp's Sport Page, *Collier's Weekly*, 73 (March 8, 1924). Biographical details on Miss Ederle appear in Norman E. White, "At the Age of 17 This Girl is a World Champion Swimmer," *American Magazine*, 98 (November 1924), and in an Associated Press story on the retired champion at the age of sixty-six by John T. McGowan, "Swimming First Love Despite Age," which I read in the (Tucson) *Arizona Daily Star*, September 16, 1973. That item ran alongside another AP story, "American Girl New Queen of Channel," describing a girl swimmer of the new generation, Lynn Cox, who had just set a new Channel record at the age of sixteen. A still more recent essay, prompted by the fiftieth anniversary of Ederle's crossing, is Tony Kornheiser, "Gertrude Ederle All Aglow In Sports Spotlight Again," *New York Times*, April 28, 1976.

Helen Wainwright, "Swim and Grow Beautiful," was published in *Collier's Weekly*, 78 (August 14, 1926). The swimsuit ads cited in this chapter appeared in *ibid.*, 76 (July 4, 1925), 24–25, and in the *Saturday Evening Post*, 199 (July 3, 1926), 86–87.

VII. Advertising

All standard accounts of the twenties, beginning with Wesley C. Mitchell's excellent essay in *Recent Economic Changes* (New York: McGraw-Hill, 1929), contain some discussion of advertising as a social force, but few discuss in any detail the advertisements themselves. One recent exception is a short passage in the chapter by Stanley Coben included in Richard Abrams et al., *The Unfinished Century* (Boston: Little, Brown, 1973). Professor Coben quotes, from Gerard Lambert's personal account *All Out of Step* (New York: Doubleday, 1956), the inside story of how the word *halitosis* was inflicted upon our language. But that is a rather minor example. Obviously there is a vast reservoir here waiting to be tapped, by students both of popular and of elite culture. One acute critique of advertising in the twenties has appeared since my manuscript was completed, namely Stuart Ewen, *Captains of Consciousness* (New York: McGraw-Hill, 1976); its conclusions differ quite sharply from my own.

To give some idea of the extent of this reservoir, no fewer than eight of the examples cited in this chapter came from a *single* issue of the *Saturday Evening Post*, 198 (July 3, 1926). They represent Aqua Velva ("Here's after shaving comfort on the hottest day"), Buick ("It's the new and better thing that stirs the people's heart"), Coca-Cola ("It had to be good to get where it is"), Graybar Electric Fans ("Two ways to keep cool"), Gruen ("How the jeweled toy of princes became an accurate timekeeper"), Post's Bran Flakes ("Survival of the fittest"), the Society for Electrical Development ("One day of life"), and Swift's Premium Bacon ("Just to taste it makes you long for the woods"). From another issue of the *Post*, of March 26, 1927, whose Index to Advertisers is cited at the beginning of this chapter, came three more: Elgin ("Were your watch and your sweetheart both young together?"), Curtiss Candy Bars (for "rugged grown-ups with hearty appetites"), and Campbell ("Soup and the prettiest girl in the office").

Next to the *Saturday Evening Post*, the *American Magazine* was the most copious source for these ads—a fact which may reflect the high advertising linage for both magazines. Taking them in chronological order, from vol. 102 (1926): July, "Health has few allies, disease few enemies more powerful than the paint brush"; September, Singer's "Who has the oldest sewing machine?", Coca-Cola's 'Through all the years since 1886," and a Metropolitan Life ad which warned that "one-eighth of the people of the United States are overweight to such an extent that their health is menaced"; October, the advertisement for Dr. Eliot's Five-Foot Shelf; and November, "Don't talk to Eric about wide-open spaces." From vol. 103 (1927) came, in January, RCA's "Great music—*at home* as you never could get it before"; in February, "Music: you love it! Why don't you learn to play?"; in March, Crane Piping's "Carved in stone above the Gothic doorway . . ."; and in April, Luco-Lac Brushing Lacquer's "If you enjoy colorful things, you may now have them with slight effort." In the Depression year 1930 (vol. 109, February), with what were probably quite unintended political overtones, appeared Eleanor Roosevelt's testimonial for Cream of Wheat: "John Aspinwall Roosevelt is fortified for the 'strenuous life' by a care all boys can have."

Collier's Weekly, 76 (December 5, 1925), furnished the somber Listerine advertisement "They say it behind your back"; other *Collier's* ads are cited in chapter 6. In the *Ladies' Home Journal,* 42 (1925) were published, in August and December, the Victrola ads cited in this chapter; in September, the advertisement for Edison Mazda illustrated by Norman Rockwell, "Remember the lamps you used to have to trim . . . ?"; and, in December, "Don't let your great-great grandmother tell you what to eat!" From the *Literary Digest,* 80 (March 8, 1924) came "Do Your Words Hit the Bull's Eye?"; and in *ibid.,* 82 (September 13, 1924), were published both the Yellow Strand Wire Rope advertisement ("Where pull counts") and the Borden condensed milk ad. In *Scientific American,* 124 (March 1921), appeared—perhaps most appropriately in that magazine!—the "confident, precise, powerful" Frankensteinian giant who "rears his head above the incompetence of Man"; and in *ibid.,* 139 (November 1928) was published G.E.'s more benign little essay "Crowds—and the Street Car's Answer."

Calvin Coolidge's speech before the American Association of Advertising Agencies on October 27, 1926, was reported in the *Literary Digest,* 91 (November 13, 1926); from that account was quoted also the editorial in the *New York Sun*. A pioneering, but from a scholarly point of view unsatisfactory, study of a previously neglected subject is Gerald Carson, *Cornflake .Crusade* (New York: Rinehart, 1957). Bruce Bliven's horrid word-portrait of the flapper, originally in the *New Republic,* September 9, 1925, was quoted in Elizabeth Stevenson, *Babbitts and Bohemians: the American 1920s* (New York: Macmillan, 1967); incidentally, Stevenson's discussion "The Evolution of the Flapper" (pp. 139–141) is a model of what imaginative and thoughtful study of magazine art can yield. John Howe's interview with the organ and piano manufacturer Rudolph Wurlitzer appeared in the *American Magazine,* 98 (November 1924). Assistant Secretary of Commerce Julius Klein's rhapsodic "It's Great to be a Young Man Today" appeared in *ibid.,* 109 (February 1930)—in retrospect a most inopportune time for such sentiment to be expressed.

The argument that advertising got more shrill, misleading, and vulgar under the stimulus of the Depression is made by E. S. Turner in *The Shocking History of Advertising* (New York: Dutton, 1953), of which I used a later paper edition. The cartoon portraying the Depression as a gym instructor working the fat off Middle America while an undernourished "forgotten man" looks on is in the Manfred A. Carter Collection housed in the George Arents Research Library, Syracuse University. The passing of "Charles Atlas" (Angelo Siciliano), who launched his own nationally popular muscle-building course in the very year of the Crash, was duly noted in *Time,* January 8, 1973; *Newsweek,* same date; and the *Britannica Book of the Year* (Chicago, 1973).

In this chapter, as elsewhere in the book, the Lynds' *Middletown* (New York: Harcourt, 1929) was invaluable. Alvin Toffler, *Future Shock* (New York: Random House, 1970) was also helpful, as was the taped address by Frederik Pohl at the 1968 MLA, a transcript from which was edited by Thomas Clareson and published in *Extrapolation,* 10:2 (May 1969). Mr. Pohl's satire of a future civilization literally governed by advertising agencies, written in collaboration with the. late C. M. Kornbluth, was serialized in *Galaxy Science Fiction,* 4 (June, July, August, 1952), with the title "Gravy Planet"; it was published in book form in 1953 as *The Space Mer-*

chants. Depending on the peculiar mechanics of mass paperback printing and distribution, it is usually readily available in paper.

VIII. Business

Andrew Carnegie's inspirational remarks in Pittsburgh, "The Road to Business Success: A Talk to Young Men," were preserved for posterity in Carnegie, *The Empire of Business* (New York: Doubleday, Page, 1902). Henry Ford's observation that unlike Model T's no two men are exactly alike was quoted by Andrew's unrelated namesake, Dale Carnegie, in *Public Speaking, a Practical Course for Business Men* (New York: Associaion Press, 1928). Meat packer Philip Armour's remark that if he had had it all to do over again he would rather have been a great speaker than a great capitalist is reported in *ibid.* Pierre du Pont's activities during the twenties are described in a detailed and definitive monograph by Alfred Chandler and Stephen Salsbury, *Pierre S. Du Pont and the Making of the Modern Corporation* (New York: Harper, 1971). I am indebted to Professor Boyd Shafer, recently retired from the University of Arizona, for having directed my attention to this study of du Pont. Alfred P. Sloan's judgment that General Motors "had become too big to be a one-man show" is in Sloan, *Adventures of a White Collar Man* (New York: Doubleday, 1941), as cited by Gilman M. Ostrander in a stimulating and controversial work, *American Civilization in the First Machine Age, 1890–1940* (New York: Harper, 1970). Gus Dyer's dictum that the only way to produce a man "is to pitch him out . . . and let him make himself" is quoted in a valuable study by James W. Prothro, *The Dollar Decade: Business Ideas in the 1920s* (Baton Rouge: Louisianna State University Press, 1954).

Prothro drew on the *American Magazine* as an important source for this subject, as I have; several of the articles referred to in this chapter are cited also in that book. However, more often than not my inferences from these magazine articles differ markedly from the interpretation which appears in *Dollar Decade;* this is the case not only for the present chapter but elsewhere, even when we quote the same passages from the original. Compare for example my discussion of Shailer Mathews's experimental laboratory in religion, in chapter 3, with the account of the Mathews interview that appears in Prothro. The reader is invited to go back to the pages of the *American Magazine* and assess these differing historical judgments for himself. The quotation from Sumner Blossom, editor of the *American Magazine* from 1929 until its demise in the ruthless, no-quarter circulation wars of the fifties, is in Theodore Bernard Peterson, *Magazines in the Twentieth Century*, 2nd rev. ed. (Urbana: University of Illinois Press, 1964). Further information on the *American Magazine* may be found in Frank Luther Mott, *A History of American Magazines*, IV (Cambridge, Mass.: Harvard University Press, 1957).

I list here the *American*'s parade of successful men in chronological order as they wrote or were interviewed: George W. Goethals, as interviewed by Samuel Crowther, "Don't Fear to Attempt a Thing Just Because It Looks Big," *American Magazine*, 93 (January 1922); anon., "Man Who Was Made by Being Fired," *ibid.*, 94 (December 1923); A. E. Lefcourt, as interviewed by H. A. Stewart, "Don't Keep Half your Brain Busy Trying to Hide Something," *ibid.*, 97 (April 1924); Charles W. Brown, as interviewed by William S. Dutton, "Brown Got His Business Training on Board a Sailing Ship," *ibid.*, 102 (July 1926); Charles F. Stern, as interviewed by David Chalmers, "It took the Fear of Blindness to open Stern's Eyes," *ibid.*, 102 (August 1926); E. D. Stair, as interviewed by William S. Dutton, "It's the Last Push that Breaks the Back of Failure," *ibid.*, 102 (September 1926); Arthur L. Humphrey, as interviewed by William S. Dutton, "It's Your 'Emergency Behavior' that Proves your Mettle," *ibid.*, 102 (October 1926); Bruce Barton, "Do You Believe in Luck? I Do," *ibid.*, 105 (April 1928); William W. Atterbury, as interviewed by William S. Dutton, "Do Young Men Have the Chances Their Fathers Had?", *ibid.*, 105 (May 1928); Walter S. Gifford, as interviewed by Sherman Gwinn, "Days of Drudgery Will Soon Be Over," *ibid.*, 106 (November 1928); and J. G. Lonsdale, as interviewed by Neil M. Clark, "Right Now is the Time to Begin to Get Rich!", *ibid.*, 110 (October 1930).

The little saga of the young man who quit his job in advertising to become a garage mechanic, and thereby prospered, can be found in the *Literary Digest*, 92 (March 5, 1927). The essay by the prudently anonymous person who explained "What I Do When I Get Fired" was printed in *Collier's Weekly*, 72 (July 7, 1927). *Collier's* also published the article against inherited wealth by William G. Shepherd, "How Much Money Should a Man Leave to His Sons?", *ibid.*, 70 (December 9, 1922). An editorial on the same subject in *ibid.*, 72 (September 29, 1923), "Born Wealth Stops the Progress by which Earned Wealth is Made," was illustrated by the well-known political caroonist J. N. "Ding" Darling. The sarcastic remark "Men get up about eight o'clock and go down to New York to Business. They don't never go to work" appears in Ring Lardner's jaunty novel *The Big Town* (New York: Scribner's, 1925).

For the managerial transformation of the twenties, the Report of the Committee on Recent Economic Changes of the President's Conference on Unemployment (Herbert Hoover, Chairman), *Recent Economic Changes in the United States* (New York, 1929), is invaluable, particularly the chapters by Willard L. Thorp, on "The Changing Structure of Industry," by Melvin T. Copeland, on "Marketing," and by Henry S. Dennison, on "Management." The article "Man and the Job," by G. M. Eaton, appeared in *Industrial Management*, 65 (March 1923). David A. Shannon's comment that banking concentration in the twenties "made the old 'money trust' seem juvenile" appears in Shannon, *Twentieth Century America: the Twenties and Thirties*, 3rd ed. (Chicago: Rand McNally, 1974). For a devastating criticism of Dale Carnegie's *Public Speaking*, and also of the entire organizational ethic it reflects, see Donald Meyer, *The Positive Thinkers* (New York: Doubleday, 1965).

Stuart McKenzie's essay on the way to wealth through common stocks, "Me and Rockefeller," appeared in the *American Magazine*, 102 (October, 1926), as also did the cautionary advertisement by Adair Realty & Trust, "The Ticker Says *Nothing* about To-Morrow!", *ibid.*, 102 (August 1926). On the stock market mystique of the twenties, Frederick Lewis Allen, *Only Yesterday* (New York: Harper, 1931) and John Kenneth Galbraith, *The Great Crash* (Boston: Houghton Mifflin, rev. ed. 1961), are unsurpassed. Scott Fitzgerald's remark about the twenties, "Even when you were broke you didn't worry about money," is quoted in Donald R. McCoy, *Coming of Age: the United States during the 1920's and*

1930's (Harmondsworth, Middx.: Penguin, 1973). Internal Revenue Board figures indicating that "Wealth in America is Undergoing a Wide Distribution" appeared in *Current Opinion*, 72 (April 1922); see also "Yes, We Have No Billionaires," *Literary Digest*, 82 (September 13, 1924). More sobering IRB statistics were cited in "America's Expanding Incomes," *ibid.*, 96 (February 4, 1928).

The question of the standard of living, as distinguished from dollar income, was extensively but at times superficially discussed in the media of the twenties. The provocative article on consumer purchasing power by Eunice Fuller Barnard, "What Our Parents Didn't Pay For," appeared in *Survey*, 61 (November 1, 1928). See also Stuart Chase, "New Standards of Living," *The Nation*, 129 (October 30, 1929), and a more recent appraisal by the labor historian Irving Bernstein, *The Lean Years* (Boston: Houghton Mifflin, 1960). The folksy General Electric advertisement entitled "Dad" appeared in the *American Magazine*, 102 (September, 1926). The essay on the plight of the shabby-genteel, "How the American Middle Class Lives," "by one of them," appeared in *Scribner's Magazine*, 86 (December 1929). Not quoted in my text, but highly relevant to it, is an editorial "Prosperity as a Habit," *Saturday Evening Post*, 200 (March 10, 1928), to which the editorial I quoted from the *New Republic*, 55 (August 8, 1928) might be read as a rejoinder.

IX. Politics

Arthur M. Schlesinger, Jr., *The Imperial Presidency* (Boston: Houghton Mifflin, 1973), is not quite such a recantation from its author's previous political views as some of that book's earliest reviewers have supposed. But Robert K. Murray, *The Harding Era* (Minneapolis: University of Minnesota Press, 1969), the first full-scale study on that subject to have been researched and written since the Harding Papers were opened to scholars in 1964, is a massive reinterpretation of the man from Marion, Ohio—whose reputation admittedly had no place to go but up. In particular, Professor Murray chides his fellow historians for having neglected the content of the addresses compiled by James W. Murphy, official reporter for the United States Senate, under the title *Last*

Speeches of President Warren G. Harding, June 20 to August 2, 1923 (Washington: n.p., 1923); they are a major source for this chapter. Some areas of the Harding Administration, however, have been relatively unaffected by Murray's revisionism. On Teapot Dome, for example, the studies by Burl Noggle, "The Origins of the Teapot Dome Investigation," *Mississippi Valley Historical Review*, 44 (September 1957), and J. Leonard Bates, "The Teapot Dome Scandal and the Election of 1924," *American Historical Review*, 60 (January 1955), remain standard.

Information on the revolutionary situation abroad in the month Harding was inaugurated was taken from the *New York Times* for March 1921. A lively account of the interwar years in Europe is Sigmund Neumann, *The Future in Perspective* (New York: Putnam, 1946); I found particularly helpful the chapter entitled "The War After the War." Mark Sullivan's political appraisals, "One Year of President Harding" and "Two Years of President Harding," appeared in *World's Work*, 43 (November 1921) and 45 (November 1922). The article "The Impending Republican Split" was published in *ibid.*, 46 (August 1923). Lowell Mellett, "What Every President Knows," was printed in *Collier's Weekly*, 67 (March 5, 1921). The article Florence Kling Harding was reading to her husband at the moment of his death was Samuel G. Blythe, "A Calm Review of a Calm Man," *Saturday Evening Post*, 196 (January 28, 1923).

Although I have used William Allen White, *A Puritan in Babylon: the Story of Calvin Coolidge* (New York: Macmillan, 1938), corrected at certain points by more recent studies, I have found Coolidge his own best (and worst) advocate. Calvin Coolidge, *Foundations of the Republic: Speeches and Addresses* (New York: Scribner's, 1926) was especially enlightening. See also Edward Elwell Whiting, *Calvin Coolidge: His Ideals of Citizenship as Revealed Through his Speeches and Writings* (Boston: W. A. Wilde, 1924) and Coolidge, *Have Faith in Massachusetts* (Boston: Houghton Mifflin, 1919). "Coolidge's Fighting Message for Prosperity" was the description given the President's 1927 Annual Message to Congress as it was reported in the *Literary Digest*, 95 (December 17, 1927). But according to the news columnist Frank

R. Kent in a witty essay, "The Press and Mr. Coolidge," *American Mercury*, 6 (August 1924), a caution is in order here: colorful adjectives such as "fighting," when attached to Calvin Coolidge's own mild words by the over-friendly media of his day, should be taken with a grain of salt.

The skillful creation of a heroic "image" for a man constitutionally unable to put his own best foot forward has been described in Craig Lloyd, *Aggressive Introvert: a Study of Herbert Hoover and Public Relations Management, 1912–1932* (Columbus: Ohio State University Press, 1972). On the expansion of the Commerce Department's foreign policy function under Hoover, see Joseph Brandes, *Herbert Hoover and Economic Diplomacy* (Pittsburgh: University of Pittsburgh Press, 1962). The encounter between Will Irwin and Belle Moskowitz during the 1928 campaign is described in Irwin, *The Making of a Reporter* (New York: Putnam, 1942). The edition of Will Irwin's *Herbert Hoover: A Reminiscent Biography* (New York: Century, 1928) which I used was an inherited personal copy; on the final page my father had scribbled in soft pencil his own appraisal of Hoover: "A good tinkerer—not enough of a philosopher." Others, such as Paul Conkin, Edgar Robinson, and William Appleman Williams, have argued on the contrary that Herbert Hoover was the one major political figure on the scene who *did* have a philosophy. Williams's gloss upon that political philosophy he attributes to Hoover, to the effect that one lets the system come apart at the seams rather than violate its principles, is in an essay "What This Country Needs . . . ," which may be read in the wise, witty, and provocative little book, William Appleman Williams, *Some Presidents from Wilson to Nixon* (New York: Vintage, 1972). The well-crafted study by Joan Hoff Wilson, *Herbert Hoover, Forgotten Progressive* (Boston: Little, Brown, 1975), is now the best biography of Hoover.

I have discussed the 1928 campaign on the Democratic side in two articles: "The Campaign of 1928 Re-Examined: A Study in Political Folklore," *Wisconsin Magazine of History*, 46 (Summer 1963), most recently reprinted in Frank Otto Gatell et al., eds., *The Growth of American Politics*, II (New York and London: Oxford University Press, 1972); and "The Other Catholic Candidate:

the 1928 Presidential Bid of Thomas J. Walsh," *Pacific Northwest Quarterly*, 55 (January 1964). Detailed essays on the three national elections held during the twenties have been written by Donald R. McCoy (on 1920), David Burner (on 1924), and Lawrence H. Fuchs (on 1928), as chapters in Arthur M. Schlesinger, Jr., ed., *History of American Presidential Elections*, III (New York: Mc-Graw-Hill, 1971).

The campaign biography of Al Smith by Norman Hapgood and Henry Moskowitz, *Up from the City Streets: A Life of Alfred E. Smith* (New York: Grosset and Dunlap, 1927), remains one of the most informative books we have on the background of the New York governor. An interesting contemporary apologia for the socio-political institution that nurtured Smith is Charles Willis Thompson, "The Tammany Monster," *Catholic World*, 128 (October 1928), which is reprinted in my anthology *The Uncertain World of Normalcy: the 1920s* (New York: Pitman, 1971).

Seemingly remote from the issues debated by Hoover and Smith, but germane to the politics of the twenties nonetheless, is the topic in the history of ideas discussed in Edward A. Purcell, Jr., *The Crisis of Democratic Theory: Scientific Naturalism and the Problem of Value* (Lexington: University Press of Kentucky, 1973). One possible alternative to "Coolidge prosperity" and to Hoover voluntarism was described—evidently with no awareness that a later generation of Americans might find it shocking—in Isaac Marcosson, "The Reborn Italy," *Saturday Evening Post*, 199 (July 3, 1926). Not touched upon in this chapter, but basic for under-standing its international context, are the lectures delivered at the New School during 1926–27 by Nathaniel Peffer, *The White Man's Dilemma: Climax of the Age of Imperialism* (New York: Arno Press, 1972; first copyright 1927).

Index